The Mystery Box

**SCREENPLAY
BY
JOEL BROWN**

**Producer
Joel Brown**

**DIRECTOR
GOD (JESUS)**

Associate Producer

CreateSpace

June 12, 2016

Flixrapeutic Productions
for
A Book in Screenplay Format

~ A Journey for Transformation with Cinema ~

ISBN-13: 978-1534653870
ISBN-10: 1534653872

Printed in USA by CreateSpace (www.createspace.com/)

DEDICATION

Honorable Mention:
Rafael Barreiro
Courtneay Sanders
Dafne Basave
Judith Mayton
Even Culp
Norah Swiney
Mark Labash
Roger Bush
Laura Holland
Eric Hudgens
Jonathan Cyprowski
Charles Zwick
Frank Ashby

'You're a Teacher'
*"SOME of the people I admire most in my life are teachers!
Every day they greeted me with a smile. Their patience
allowed them to go over the lesson, again and again if I
didn't understand. When they were faced with rebellion,
disrespect or temptation, their character made them stand
firm. They worked so hard. Remembering them still
encourages me. Today I am a teacher, and I try to be the
inspiration to my students that my teachers were to me.
Every morning I pray for strength, courage and knowledge.
I want my students to learn, but I also want them to have
character. Have you thought about who is watching you
today? Who might notice your kindness, patience and joy?
Who might be motivated to work hard or to be honest
because they know that you are?"*
- Kim Markus-Jones, Burns, Tennessee (Friday, October 19)

*"Whether you turn to the right or to the left,
Your ears will hear a voice behind you, saying,
"This is the way; walk in it.""* - Isaiah 30:21

INTRODUCTION

This book had first originated as a senior paper for school, asking the question. Can films transform a life? As it seeks to answer it through film analysis and cinema therapy, using the discipline of scripture meditation to help in this research experimentation.

In fact, so far I found that every movie has the ability to affect its viewer differently. Some films evoke wonder and excitement, while others revoke fear and sorrow. But a commonality among all films is a prevailing message or theme. Moreover, some films can call people to attention in such profound questions that it changes the way we perceive life, as we once knew it.

For example, Dr. Birgit Woltz, author with a Ph.D and psychotherapist has said. "You can learn how to take advantage of a movie's impact to change unwanted emotions, attitudes, and behaviors. More importantly, she shows how favorite films can make and evoke self-esteem, courage, and true authenticity."

She adds. "Using films for self-improvement allows a shift in perspective when viewed with conscious awareness."

With this, my learning objective and benefits that I have gained through this senior paper and up until now would be not only how to use the power of film to find healing and growth for myself, but to for others and discovering an uncommon way in solving problems.

While the idea for this paper turned book was birth at a University that was built on the belief of healing with all it's founder Oral Roberts stood for, as the class that inspired it the most was my acting and media analysis.

For the reason, that I didn't know watching films could actually be an art and it taught me how to critique films, as my acting classes were therapeutic for me.

While my plan of execution for this paper was picking great actors of mine, study how they made themselves great from their films that were dissected and break it all down by answering questions in a 'Media Analysis: Art of Watching Films' textbook with a template of questions for the cinema therapy portions as I also interpreted an actor's character study. In attempt to find out how films can be therapeutic, and ended up discovering more about cinema therapy, social work and see my top favorite actors in a new light as either movie-fathers or brothers.

Furthermore, this paper turned book has become a testimony, as not only will you find scholarly research on the chronology of films in between watching the films for my analysis on them, but also there are self-cinema therapy sessions as part of my documentation of my findings with Biblical scriptures that were brought to my attention during the films I watched.

Lastly, how I have benefited from this paper turned book then-and-now would have been. It allowed me to have a stronger foundation on film analysis, more of a passion for the art of watching films, a knowledge of how cinema therapy works and how social work can interpret the use of films into a practice to help people creatively solve problems.

Summing it all up, this has been such a unique opportunity to learn about transformational effects of films through positive psychology, cinema therapy, as it has brought me now to pursuing studying it more to receive a comprehensive education in Cinema Therapy to get certified in the field for the use in helping the general public find healing and growth.

Yet, I thought I might extend the answering of that question into a book on how God has used cinema to help bring healing, growth and transform my life.

This book will take you on a cinematic journey, as I hope it does for you what it did for me.

Lastly, along the journey of this book you will find QR codes. For example, these...

 Scan here with a QR code reader for more information on how to use them.

...in the film analysis and cinema therapy section, displayed under the title of the movie for access to the movie's trailer to enhance your experience.

INT. PRELUDE – DAY

In our society cinema is huge, but what can get over-looked is the power a movie has to transform a life. Which makes movies just as educational, as they are as entertaining. In order for a person to understand the power a movie has to transform a life, as we'll look into the chronology of films, cinema therapy, media analysis, the art of watching films, how having a favorite actor contributes to it, my own experimental sessions, and testimonies to help in using the power of film for healing and growth.

But first, have you ever been to a movie and didn't think to look at your watch or forgot what time it was, until after the movie you realized the time wasn't what you had thought it would be? Have you ever been in a therapist's office and noticed there's no physical object of anything that keeps track of the time, in the room?

Similarly, therapist or counselors don't have clocks in theirs sessions, nor won't tell or even show the time for a reason, as I think the same goes with movies. They don't want your mind to be occupied by the time, and keep it away from an object that might provoke stress or anxiety. This would explain why the atmosphere is so important, because it will determine the mood.

With this, I truly believe that God gives everyone a green pastures and still waters for a place they can find rest, mines is the theater. In which inspired me to rewrite my own version of Psalm 23, based on it. "The Lord is my director; I have no objective or no need to use the Stanislavsky method or Meisner technique. He makes me to recline back in cozy theaters; He shows me pleasant motion pictures. He blows my mind; He sends me on a journey of adventure for all His glory. Yaaas, though I'm blocked through scenes of horrible darkness, I'll fear no evil; for You make a cameo with me and steal the show; Your props and Your set, they comfort me. You provide a crafts service for me 25/7 in front of my critics; You capture my best headshot with grace and no Photoshop; my thirst is quenched, because there is unlimited refills. Expecting popcorn, raisin nets, sprite (goodness), discounts and bonuses (mercy) to follow me. Throughout the calendar of my life; and I will rest with my eyes open in the theater of my director for all eternity."

INT.   STORY OF FILM – DAY

In order to know where something going we must first know where it has been, so let's explore the chronology of films to better understand cinema.

The Paramount Theater – the movie theatre has been a much-needed refuge during times of trouble. During the Depression, viewers were swept away by the sunny-natured Shirley Temple, making them forget about their troubles for a while. It was farewell to all the worries and cares of the day. When the PARAMOUNT THEATER opened its doors, we forgot about names like Hitler and Mussolini. It was time instead to unwind and dream a little. The PARAMOUNT introduced new young singers like Frank Sinatra, and showed films with big stars like Clark Gable and Betty Hutton. These were the times that tried men's souls, but the glitz and glamour of Hollywood kept us distracted and entertained. We retained our perspective, and most importantly, allowed ourselves to hold on, to our national sense of humor. While we can see how cinema was birth through visionaries to revolutionize the world with new ways of perspective and vision, bringing great things out of film stripes that give us ideas for new innovations. For example, Yasujirō Ozu was the greatest film director from japan that ever lived. For the technical style and innovation of his films for the narrative content, as he did not conform to Hollywood conventions.

Now, let's go back through the movie timeline of key moments in history and evolution of the cinema. Specifically, through the chronology of film, by watching a documentary film that was directed and narrated by Mark Cousins.

A Northern Ireland film critic that's bases it on his 2004 book, 'The Story of Film.' Moreover, this documentary is titled, 'The Story of Film: An Odyssey.' Which explores the emerging of cinema, the evolution of cinema therapy and the occurring themes in movies that show throughout the time-line of cinema, to establish a foundation for my research. While the themes I looked for when watching, 'The Story of Film' documentary were: Abandonment, abuse, adoption, alcohol, drugs, codependency, boys, brothers and sisters, cheating, denial, divorce, family, food, friends, gambling, men's stories, death, dying, suicide, dreams, fantasies, esteem, jealousy, family, fathers/mothers, fear, friends, girls, goals, hate/dislike, love, caring, nurturing, lying, money, moving, physical illness, emotional illness, relationships, sexuality, women's stories, special issues, prejudice/racism, school, sex, stealing, teasing, violence.

First, in episode one of 'The Story of Film: An Odyssey.' We see the Birth of the Cinema, "this first chapter shows the birth of a new art form – the movies – the passion that has always driven film, more than money and marketing." From

A Journey for Transformation with Cinema

1895-1918, the world discovers a new art form.
As, the themes were: men stories, women stories,
everyday life, industrialization, experimentation,
magic, discovery, western, and boxing. While
from 1903-1918, we see how thrill becomes story.
As, the themes during this time period were:
industrialization, family, dreaming, fantasies,
nurturing, caring, love, relationship, mystery,
fear, death/dying, inventive, men stories, women
stories, fathers and mothers, prejudice and
racism, violence, spirituality.

Second, in episode two of 'The Story of Film: An
Odyssey'. We see the Hollywood Dream, this is the
fascinating story of the movies in the roaring '20s
as Hollywood became a glittering entertainment
industry. Whereas, from 1918- 1928. The themes
that followed were: dreams, fantasies, dying,
industrialization, esteem, stealing, love,
relationships, money, men stories, innovative,
comedy, fathers, caring, boys, politics, moving,
athletics, non-fiction, psychology, gambling,
alcohol, greed, abuse, violence, death, realism,
mothers, romance, friends, dying, grief/loss,

spiritual, women stories.

Third, in episode three of 'The Story of Film: An Odyssey.' We see the Golden Age of World Cinema, visiting Paris, Berlin, Moscow, Shanghai and Tokyo in the 1920s to discover the places where moviemakers were pushing the boundaries of the medium. Whereas, from 1918 – 1932, the themes were: love, sex, prejudice, romance, surreal, sexuality, comedy, impressionism, psychology, death, violence, men stories, boys, fear, industrialization, expressionism, grief, greed, paintings, poetics, conventional, abstract animations, experimental, dream, fantasy, haunting, boys, mothers, dying, humanism, brothers, fathers, caring, mothers, girls, suicide, moving, school, women stories, Japanese films, Chinese films, deaf cinema.

Fourth, in episode four of 'The Story of Film: An Odyssey.' The Great American movie genres and the brilliance of European film can be seem. With this, the arrival of sound, in the 1930s upended everything allowing us to witness the birth of new types of film. Including horror movies, Westerns, musicals and more. Moreover, in the 1930s, the themes that had occurred were: horror, westerns, musicals, industrialization, romance, expressionism, fear, violence, alcohol, men stories, friends, love, money, drugs, gang family, relationships, feminized comedy, women stories, cartoon fantasies, boys, love, stealing, lying, moving, political, sports, dreams, realistic fantasy worlds, escapism.

Fifth, in episode five of 'The Story of Film: An Odyssey.' The devastation of war and a new movie language can be seen as part of Post-War Cinema, as this chapter shows how the trauma of war made cinema more daring. Start in Italy, then going to Hollywood to chart the darkening of American film." While from 1939 – 1952, the themes that had occurred were: war, devastation, daring, trauma, grief, losses, friends, neo-realism, men stories, violence, death, dying, relationships, westerns, power, alcohol, stealing, fathers, boys, musicals, women stories, money, love, dark worlds, film noirs, romance, design, dance, sexuality, joy of being alive, esteem, moving, marry couples, and feel good movies.

Sixth, in episode six of 'The Story of Film: An Odyssey.' The swollen story can be found in world cinema bursting at the seams as this involved sex & melodramas. As, this chapter explores sex and melodrama in the movies of the 1950s. Whereas, from 1953 – 1957, the themes that has occurred were: violence, emotional illness, rebel, men stories, special issues, sex, sexuality, obsession, abandonment, relationships, social justice, mythological, spiritual, realism, family, fathers, mothers, boys, girls, industrialization, caring, economics, marriage, stepping into the world, physical illness, death, rich, women suffering, jealousy, idealism, socialism, love, alcohol, hate and dislike, abuse, anger, punk/rock, brothers, rage, racism, society, gothic, and erotic.

Seventh, in episode seven of 'The Story of Film: An Odyssey' was when the shock of the new modern filmmaking in Western Europe took place in. As it was a European New Wave, where we discover how French filmmakers in the late '50s and '60s had planted a bomb under the movies and see how this new wave had caused it to sweep across Europe. Whereas, from 1957 – 1964, the themes that had occurred were: sexuality, spirituality, immorality, death (god then people), relationships, love, violence, pain, mortality, despair, loneliness, stealing, inner chaos, abuse, men stories, crimes, people are imprisoned in their own bodies that they must escape from to find grace, women stories, society, modern life, puzzles, comic cinema, husbands, wife, esteem, fantasies, memories, myth, sex, rapture, physical illness, questioning, boys, fleeting moments, mental state, emotional illness, real life, comedy, western, brothers, beauty, moving, special issues, hate, dislike, family and mothers. Thus, it was where a revolution of films became more personal and self-aware.

Eighth, in episode eight of 'The Story of Film: An Odyssey'. New directors and a new form had emerged, as the new wave in cinema sweeps around the world in the 1960s. As we discover

the films of Roman Polanski, Andrei Tarkovsky
and Nagisa Oshima. Also from 1965 – 1969, the
themes that occurred during this time period
were: modern, personal, political, relationships,
violence, friends, family, animation, puppetry,
haunting, men stories, death, suffering, girls,
special issues, spiritual, imagery, boys, fathers
and mothers, love, dreams, searching, comic,
self-aware, trauma, humiliation, greed, cynicism,
women stories, teasing/bullying, hate, dislike,
struggles, emotions of history, brothers and
sisters, moving, physical illness, poetics,
industrialization, suicide, grief, youth rebellion,
realism/documentaries, stealing, horror,
nudity/sex/sexuality, spirituality, care-free,
fantasies, self-lost and space travel.

Ninth, in episode nine of 'The Story of Film: An
Odyssey' was a period of new American cinema of
the 70s. Paul Schrader discusses his screenplay
for Taxi Driver, Robert Towne talks about
Chinatown, and Charles Burnett explores Black
American cinema. While from 1967 – 1979, the
occurring themes were: esteem, money,

industrialization, upside-down (in order to be happy you must be sad first), friends, men stories, violence, light-hearted, mocking, alcohol, emotional illness, lying, uncertainty, special issues, codependency, love, sex, Catharism, spirituality, drugs, black/Jewish, relationships, women stories, idealism, nature, life, romance, sexuality, Broadway musicals, gangster family, death, and tragedy.

Tenth, in episode ten of 'The Story of Film: An Odyssey' as this was a period where some radical directors in the 70s had made state of the nation movies. For instance, movies to change the world as this is the story of the movies that tried to change the world in the '70s. While we start in Germany, then head to Britain, Italy, Australia and Japan. Now from 1969 – 1979, the themes we see are: search for meaning, identity, history, nudity, sex, fear, prejudice, love, darkness of human identity, women stories, alcohol, family, sexuality/sexual identity, men stories, relationships, friends, stealing, violence, gender, diversity, intimacies, death, special issues, abuse,

Japanese identities, African identities, modernism, liberation, betrayal, self-hood and political.

Eleventh, in episode eleven of 'The Story of Film: An Odyssey,' we see innovation in popular culture from around the world.   In which, the Arrival of Multiplexes and Asian Mainstream had arrived. While this chapter explains how films such as Star Wars and Jaws were innovative, then travels to the 1970s India to show how Bollywood was doing new things. Whereas, from the 1970s and onwards, we also can see the following themes: girls, women stories, violence, fantasies, myths, fathers/brothers, social, transcendental, spirituality, racism, fighting, rage, anger, kung-fu, sex, men stories, immoral gangsters, rivalry, relationships, love, fear, realization, heroes, Bollywood musicals, friends, esteem, special issues, horror, realism, romance, sci-fi, good vs. evil, sensation, and contemplation.

Twelfth, in episode twelve of 'The Story of Film: An Odyssey,' moviemaking and protest around the world is seen as Fight the Power: Protest in Film. Moreover, this is a period about that tells the story of how brave filmmakers spoke truth to power. While director John Sayles discusses these years, as we discover the growth of Chinese cinema. Also, from the 1980s, occurred the following themes: speaking truth to power, moving, special issues, spiritualism, stealing, mystic, men stories, good and bad, relationships, political, economics, nudity, sensation, death/dying, girls/boys, war, violence, mothers, fathers, family, social, psychological, love, hate and dislike, fear, music videos influenced film, impressionism, dreams, physical illness, friends, advocating, self-defense, protest, alcohol, sexuality, sex, poverty, abuse, suicide, beauty, pain, and sensuality with machines.

Thirteenth, in episode thirteen of 'The Story of Film: An Odyssey,' where the last days of celluloid before the coming of digital. Meaning, new boundaries: world cinema in Africa, Asia & Latin America. While cinema around the world in the '90s entered a golden age as the story starts in

Iran, where we meet Abbas Kiarostami, who rethought moviemaking." Whereas, from 1990 – 1998, the themes that had occurred were: emotions, passionate, special issues, family, girls, reenactment, therapeutic, moving, reality, love, relationships, innocence, friends, boys, mothers, tragedy, goals, search for meaning, society, loneliness of life, J-horror, terror, violence, horror, fear, haunting, spirituality, suffering, industrialization, women stories, men stories, suicide, death, and dreams.

Fourteenth, in episode fourteen of 'The Story of Film: An Odyssey,' were the first days of digital reality losing its realness in America and Australia. With this, New American Independents & the Digital Revolution as this is the story of the movies in the English-speaking world in the '90s. Whereas, from the 1990s, the themes that had occurred were: violence, heroes/villains, good and evil, hate and dislike, men stories, family, mothers/fathers, boys/girls, love, relationships, admiration, ethics, courage, imagination, fantasies, friends, fear, women stories, post-modern, irony, stealing, death/dying, lawlessness, esteem, drugs, sex, school, disaster/tragedy, nudity, industrialization, science fiction/political, war, denial, emotional illness, special issues, nurturing, goals, alcohol, sexuality, romantic, remixed reality (musicals), better and bigger than life.

Eventually, during this period was introduced both cinema and psychology that were based on a common historical, social and cultural background created by the power called modernity. However, it was only in the 1960s when the theory of cinema was established by applying psychoanalysis and psychology whilst cinema therapy being established in the 1990s with the application of cinema into psychology. The two areas which began in 1895 only crossed roads after 60 years and it took another 100 years until they were reunited in the field of art therapy. The reasons why cinema therapy started too late were in cinema therapy, there are technological issues (such as video machines, camera, editors, lights) whether view a movie or product of a movie. However, only in the 1990 did we get issues related to the technology resolved. In Korea, in 1988 after the 88 Olympics, almost all homes had video machines; almost all neighborhoods had video stores which established easy access to video clips/movies by becoming somewhat of a cinema library. Projectors, speakers and electronic black boards in public facilities (such as school and libraries) became available in late 2000's, as it is also evidence about the historical fact that the establishment of media environment has close relations with cinema therapy.

Another difficulty in cinema therapy was the cost pressure in making movies such as cast of films and production costs. There were also procedural difficulties to apply to personal therapy since it required a lot of staff in the areas of lighting, design, costume, and actors. However, with the recent spread of digital cameras and the development of internet, issues related to editing and shooting a movie has great been resolved. This provided us with simplification and increased effectiveness in the process of making a movie, leading to high potential for various developments regarding future cinema therapy.

Thus, the point to note is that the late development of cinema therapy, even though cinema therapy started only after the 1970s, was not because cinema itself was less of a healing, but it's the technological constraints related to the media environment.

Briefly, cinema therapy according to Wikipedia's definition "is a form of supplemental therapy for medical and health issues. It is also used as a form of self-help and aids in inmate rehabilitation. Cinema therapy was fathered, defined, trademarked, and popularized by Dr. Gary Solomon, the first to write on using movies as therapy." In fact, in the book, 'Movie Therapy: Using Movies for Mental Health.' It mentions, "There are several types of cinema therapy, with varying degrees of entertainment and therapeutic value. Popcorn therapy is primarily cinema entertainment that may result in an emotional release. Evocation cinema therapy, helps individuals connect with story lines and the movie characters. In the process they learn about themselves in more profound ways. Cathartic cinema therapy helps a person access their emotions, for instance. If they are in a depression, and may be used in the early stage in psychotherapy."

Thus, cinema therapy has been said by its proponents to change individual's thoughts, feelings and ability to manage life events. In fact, movies are used in some prisons to help individuals understand what led them to commit and be convicted of crimes.

Continuing on, the fifteenth episode of 'The Story of Film: An Odyssey' learning how film moves full circle and about the future of the movies. For instance, cinema today and the future was the main topic in this series that concludes by examining current-day cinema. Yet, goes beyond the present to look at what the future holds for moviemaking.

INT. CHRONOLOGY OF FILM = DAY

Moving on, to the chronology of film, let's go back through the movie timeline of key moments in history and evolution of the cinema.

In 1889, William Kennedy Laurie Dickson, commissioned by Thomas Alva Edison, builds the first motion-picture camera and names it the Kinetograph.

In 1894, The Edison Corporation establishes the first motion-picture studio, a Kinetograph production center nicknamed the Black Maria (slang for a police van). The first Kinetoscope parlor opens at 1155 Broadway in New York City. Spectators can watch films for 25 cents.

In 1895, In France, Auguste and Louis Lumière hold the first private screening. The brothers invent the Cinématograph, a combination camera and projector. The image of an oncoming train is said to have caused a stampede.

In 1903, Edison Corporation mechanic Edwin S. Porter turns cameraman, director and producer to make The Great Train Robbery. With 14 shots cutting between simultaneous events, this 12-minute short establishes the shot as film's basic element and editing as a central narrative device. It is also the first Western.

In 1905, the first movie theater opens in Pittsburgh.

In 1909, the New York Times publishes the first movie review, a report on D. W. Griffith's Pippa Passes.

In 1910, Thomas Edison introduces his kinetophone, which makes talkies a reality.

In 1911, the first feature film is released when the two reels of D. W. Griffith's Enoch Arden are screened together.

In 1912, Photoplay debuts as the first magazine for movie fans.

In 1914, in his second big-screen appearance, Charlie Chaplin plays the Little Tramp, his most famous character. Winsor McCay unleashes Gertie the Dinosaur, the first animated cartoon.

In 1915, D. W. Griffith's technically brilliant Civil War epic, The Birth of a Nation, introduces the narrative close-up, the flashback and other elements that endure today as the structural principles of narrative filmmaking.

In 1916, Charlie Chaplin signs on with Mutual Studios and earns an unprecedented $10,000 a week.

In 1919, Charlie Chaplin, D. W. Griffith, Douglas Fairbanks, and Mary Pickford establish United Artists in an attempt to control their own work.

In 1920s Film History, was the Early Cinematic Origins, and The Infancy of Film.

In 1920s Film History, the Pre-Talkies and the

Silent Era.

In 1921, the Sheik, directed by George Melford, debuts and establishes star Rudolph Valentino as cinema's best-known lover.

In 1923, German Shepherd Rin Tin Tin becomes film's first canine star.

In 1924, Walt Disney creates his first cartoon, "Alice's Wonderland."

In 1925, Sergei Eisenstein makes Potemkin, a revolutionary portrait of mutiny aboard a battleship. In the hands of Eisenstein, montage is raised to the highest structural role in filmmaking, serving as the unifying element of the medium. Ben-Hur, costing a record-setting $3.95 million to produce, is released.

In 1927, popular vaudevillian Al Jolson astounds audiences with his nightclub act in The Jazz Singer, the first feature-length talkie.

In 1928, Walt Disney introduces Galloping Gaucho and Steamboat Willie, the first cartoons with sound. The Academy Awards are handed out for the first time. Wings wins Best Picture.

In 1930, as head of the Motion Picture Producers and Distributors of America, William Hays establishes a code of decency that outlines what is acceptable in films.

In 1930s Film History, the Talkies, the Growth of the Studios and 'The Golden Age of Hollywood'.

In 1931, double features emerge as a way for the unemployed to occupy time.

In 1934, it Happened, One Night sweeps the Academy Awards, winning Best Picture, Director, Actor, and Actress.

In 1935, although a primitive, two-color process was first used in 1922, audiences weren't impressed by Technicolor, until a three-color system appeared in Becky Sharp.

In 1937, Walt Disney's first full-length animated feature, Snow White and the Seven Dwarfs, hits theaters and becomes an instant classic.

In 1939, the big-screen adaptation of Gone with the Wind premieres, and will go on to gross $192 million, making it one of the most profitable films of all time. It's also one of the longest films, clocking in at 231 minutes. Spencer Tracy wins his second consecutive Best Actor Oscar. He won the 1937 Oscar for his role in Captains Courageous and the 1938 award for Boys Town.

In 1940s Film History was the War and Post-War Years, the Beginnings of Film Noir.

In 1941, in Citizen Kane, Orson Welles subordinates all previous technological and cinematic accomplishments to his own essentially cinematic vision. Using newly developed film stocks and a wider, faster lens, Welles pushes the boundaries of montage and mise-en-scène, as well as sound, redefining the medium. Actress Greta

Garbo retires at age 36.

In 1942, Casablanca premieres in theaters.

In 1946, the Cannes Film Festival debuts in France. The Best Years of Our Lives debuts, and is immediately recognized as a classic post-War film that accurately—and poignantly—portrays the readjustment families face when loved ones return from battle. The film won Oscars for Best Picture, Best Director, and Best Supporting Actor. Roberto Rossellini's Neorealist ode to the Italian Resistance, Rome, Open City, presents an alternative to Hollywood with its use of street cinematography, grainy black-and-white stocks and untrained actors, lyrically capturing the despair and confusion of post-World War II Europe.

In 1948, the Hollywood Ten, a group of writers, producers and directors called as witnesses in the House Committee's Investigation of Un-American Activities, are jailed for contempt of Congress when they refuse to disclose if they were or were not Communists.

In 1950s Film History was the Cold War and Post-Classical Era, the Era of Epic Films and the Threat of Television.

In 1953, to counteract the threat of television, Hollywood thinks big and develops wide-screen processes such as Cinema Scope, first seen in The Robe.

In 1955, on the Waterfront nearly sweeps the 1954 Academy Awards, winning Best Picture, Best Actor (Marlon Brando), Best Supporting Actress (Eva Maria Saint), and Best Director (Elia Kazan). 70mm film is introduced with Oklahoma! James Dean dies in a car accident at age 26.

In 1959, Jean-Luc Godard's Breathless, typical of the French New Wave use of the jump cut, the hand-held camera and loose, improvised direction, is made for $90,000 in just four weeks. The jump cut's assault on seamless editing and the presumption of time continuity opens new possibilities for filmmakers.

In 1960s Film History, the End of the Hollywood Studio System, and the Era of Independent, Underground Cinema.

In 1960, Alfred Hitchcock's Psycho terrifies audiences and becomes one of the year's most successful films, as well as one of the most memorable psychological thrillers.

In 1961, West Side Story is adapted for the big screen, and will go on to win Oscars for Best Picture, Supporting Actor (George Chakiris), Supporting Actress (Rita Moreno), and Directing (Robert Wise and Jerome Robbins). Audrey Hepburn delights as Holly Golightly in Breakfast at Tiffany's, but Henry Mancini emerges as the real star. He won two Oscars and four Grammy Awards for the score, which included the hit "Moon River."

In 1962, Marilyn Monroe dies of a drug overdose

at age 36. Government regulations force studios out of the talent agency business.

In 1964, Red Desert makes spectacular use of the recently perfected zoom lens, which increases the optical mobility of a shot and its expressive capacities.

In 1965, The Sound of Music premieres. An instant hit, the film was one of the top-grossing films of 1965 and remains one of film's most popular musicals.

In 1968, the motion picture rating system debuts with G, PG, R and X.

In 1969, Midnight Cowboy wins the Best Picture Oscar, the first and only time an X-rated movie received the honor.

In 1970s Film History was the Last Golden Age of American Cinema (the American "New Wave"), and the Advent of the Block-buster Film.

In 1970, George C. Scott gives one of film's most memorable performances in Patton. He won the Best Actor Oscar for his turn as the title character, but refused the gold statuette.

In 1973, at the 1972 Academy Awards, Sacheen Littlefeather stands in for Marlon Brando and refuses his Best Actor Oscar for his role in The Godfather, to protest the U.S. government's treatment of Native Americans.

In 1974, one Flew Over the Cuckoo's Nest sweeps the top Oscars, winning Best Picture, Director, Actor, and Actress.

In 1976, the Steadicam is used for the first time in Rocky.

In 1977, Star Wars hits theaters—for the first time—and will go on to be the second highest-grossing film of all time. Saturday Night Fever sparks the disco inferno and the popularity of movie soundtracks.

In 1980s Film History was Teen-Oriented Angst Films, and the Dawn of the Sequel, with More Blockbusters.

In 1990s Film History was the Era of Mainstream Films and Alternative or Independent ("Indie") Cinema; and the Rise of Computer-Generated Imagery; also the Decade of Remakes, Re-releases, and More Sequels.

In 1990, the X rating is replaced by NC-17 (no children under 17).

In 1993, lost in Yonkers is edited on an Avid Media Composer system, the first non-linear editing system to allow viewing at film's required "real-time"-viewing rate of 24 frames per second. By converting film into digital bits, film can now be cut on a computer.

In 1994, Steven Spielberg wins his first directing Oscar for Schindler's List.

In 1995, Tom Hanks wins his second consecutive

Best Actor Oscar. He won in 1994 for his role in Philadelphia and in 1995 for Forrest Gump.

In 1997, Titanic crashes into theaters. It is the most expensive film of all time, costing between $250 and $300 million to produce and market.

In 1998, Titanic becomes the highest-grossing film of all time, raking in more than $580 million domestically. Titanic captures a record-tying 11 Academy Awards, including those for Best Picture and Best Director (James Cameron). The American Film Institute announces its list of the top 100 films of all time. Citizen Kane tops the list.

In 1999, Star Wars Episode I—The Phantom Menace opens and breaks a string of box office records. The film grosses $102.7 million in its debut five-day weekend. The Blair Witch Project hits theaters and becomes an instant cult classic. It grosses more than $125 million at the box office and cost only $30,000 to make.

In 2000s Film History was the New Millennium, an Age of Advanced Special Effects (3-D and Performance Capture), and the Era of Franchise Films.

In 2000, Warner Bros. announces that 11-year-old British actor Daniel Radcliffe will play the titular wizard in Harry Potter and the Sorceror's Stone, the first film to be adapted from the wildly popular series of young adult books by J. K. Rowling. The film is due out Thanksgiving 2001.

In 2001, the Academy of Motion Picture Arts and Sciences creates as new category for the Oscars: Best Animated Feature. Shrek wins the trophy. A potential strike by the Writers Guild of America threatens to cripple Hollywood as the WGA and Alliance of Motion Picture and Television Producers grapple over several sticking points in their contract, including payments to writers when films and TV shows go to video or are broadcast as reruns. The first installments of both the Harry Potter and Lord of the Rings movies premiere. Both go on to gross more than $300 million at the box office.

In 2002, my Big Fat Greek Wedding becomes the most profitable movie of all time. It earns more than $200 million at the box office, while costing only about $5 million to make.

In 2003, Finding Nemo replaces The Lion King as the highest-grossing animated film of all time. Finding Nemo doesn't hold the honor for long. Shrek 2 shoots to the top of the list in 2004.

In 2005, with the release of Stars Wars Episode III: The Revenge of the Sith, George Lucas completes his six-film series.

In 2006, the Walt Disney Co. pays $7.4 billion for Pixar Animation Studios, the powerhouse that created the Toy Story films, Monsters, Inc., Finding Nemo, and The Incredibles.

In 2009, fewer tickets were sold (1.3 billion vs. 1.4 billion tickets), although slightly higher revenue (over $10 billion) was due to steeper ticket prices for 3D.

In the 2010s Film History, Film Trends and Oscar Reflections For 2010: Attendance was down at movie complexes in 2010 - it was almost 6% lower (the lowest in 15 years) than in. Fantasy Films Mostly Nixed in Favor of Real-Life Non-Fiction Stories. Filmgoers (and Academy members) preferred a heavy dose of non-fiction stories that reflected life's struggles and challenges, character conflicts, or stories about real-life disabilities where one could care about a character. Poor Response to High-Profile Sequels. If it wasn't the critics, then it was poor audience response to sequel films such as the superfluous comedy Sex and the City 2 (2010) with its extravagant stars not in the Big Apple but in the Middle East, or the third episode of The Chronicles of Narnia: The Voyage of the Dawn Treader (2010) that was received only lukewarmly as another fantasy film with nothing special in it. Even though Iron Man 2 (2010) made over $300 million domestically, few liked it and it was the sole comic book film of the year to receive an Oscar nomination (Best Visual Effects) - proving there was an overall decline (and exhaustion) with superhero action films. A Decline in the Cult of Major Film Celebrities and Stars. The best film openings were for a well-directed solid story, rather than for a big-name major Hollywood star or celebrity. The Hype of 3-D. The phenomenon of 3-D didn't entirely live up to its promise, repeating its 1950s status as a short-lived fad. The prediction that 3-D films following the record-breaking Avatar 3-D (2009) would be the wave of the future fizzled in early 2010. It proved to be an unnecessary, gimmicky enhancement of the special effects, in most cases, and had nothing to do with the plot, character development, or acting quality. Backlash came from users who complained about eye strain, the silly glasses, dark images, shoddy transfers, etc. The Strength of Feature-Length Documentaries. Movie audiences had a more positive attitude toward screen entertainment of all kinds, thanks to growing familiarity with reality TV and YouTube. There were a number of film distributors who

took chances on self-produced, low-budget
projects independent of the studios (and financed
through a phenomenon known as
"crowdfunding"), during a time when the number
of studio films declined. Documentaries could be
made cheaply, with widely-available and
affordable, low-cost digital film equipment. Many
docs of feature-length made a strong showing as
unexpected hits during the summer months of
2010. The New Revolutionary Business Model for
Hollywood. According to the LA Times in late
September 2011, Hollywood's business model was
poised to make a revolutionary shift. Due to a
rapid 40% decline in home entertainment
revenue (from the once-profitable sale of DVDs,
the previous revenue model), the newest switch
would be to on-demand services and the
acceleration of the delivery of movies over the
Internet. Many options would be developed to
accommodate consumers' Internet-connected
digital devices (smartphones, tablets, and TVs),
in order to facilitate digital movie consumption
(and collection) via downloads. The article ("The
Revolution Will Be Downloaded") predicted: "It

may be the biggest shift in Hollywood's business model since the explosion of the DVD in the late 1990s." However, the complexity of downloading a film on one device for viewing it on another device (in the bedroom, minivan, or portable DVD player) wasn't yet clearly delineated. Various options were being considered to increase home entertainment media sales: Storing and Watching Movies in the "Cloud". Digitizing DVD Collections. Different Price Points. Social Networking. Multiple Screens. Distribution Rights Partner Up Hollywood Studios with Subscription Internet Video. Hollywood studios were now selling distribution rights for their films and TV programs to Internet companies, as opposed to traditional TV channels, in a move to make more revenue. Major Hollywood studio DreamWorks Animation SKG, Inc, a large supplier of media content (films and TV specials), ended its long-running pay-TV deal with cable station HBO in 2011. It signed a new deal to pump its content through Netflix. This was the first time a major Hollywood supplier chose Web streaming over pay television. Netflix planned to begin exclusively streaming DreamWorks films starting with movies released in 2013 and running through 2016. At the same time, Amazon was competing by bulking up its streaming video service (dubbed Amazon Prime) with movies and TV shows from 20th Century Fox (including 2,000 older films and TV shows).

INT. CINEPHILLA - DAY

Furthermore, throughout history and in the present we are seeing a passionate interest in cinema as this can also be referred to in the term, Cinephilla. Author Christian Keathley, explains. "Cinephilia is a system of cultural organization that engenders rituals around the gaze, speech, and the written word. De Baecque and Frémaux define cinephilia first and foremost as "a way of watching films," and only secondarily as a way "of speaking about them and then of diffusing this discourse." It follows that their proposal places special emphasis on practices of spectatorship and reception. They offer a description of the ways in which the lives of cinephiles become organized around rituals." (6). For example, film clubs and publications where started by people throughout the beginning of the silent era by those who felt passionately cinema could discuss their interest and see rare and old works.

Yet, there are two anecdotes that I have discovered about the cinephiliac. First, "the cinephiliac anecdote— a form that is designed to produce unexpected and useful knowledge about the movies, the starting point being what our proprietary discipline might regard as an excessive or inappropriately zealous cinephiliac pleasure" (150). Author Christian Keathley said. Second, "with the cinephiliac anecdote, the cinephile tells a story about— or a story that embodies— his or her relationship with the cinema, a story that has the effect of knowledge in the generalizable sense about its object, as well as in some personal sense." Added the author, Christian Keathley.

To summarize, in the book by the author Christian Keathley, 'Cinephilia and History or the Wind in the Trees' Michael Arnzen has explained.

One "new and strange" way of experiencing life in the 20th century has been through that relatively young medium, the "motion picture." Literally embodying the uncanny in the manner in which its technology animates a series of inanimate still pictures, the cinematic eye has become a metaphor for subjectivity— from "mindscreens" to the "male gaze"—and we haven't "looked" at the world in the same way since its emergence" (150). Thus, with social media having evolved we can see this cinephile take another form in cyber space, making it much more easier to connect with a community of people who are passionate about cinema and share your story that you have experienced with cinema.

INT. ON-DEMAND CULTURE – DAY

Currently, the future of cinema and digital distribution is becoming fast, cheap and hypermobile. In the 'On-Demand Culture' book it "addresses the continued changes that are taking place within the realm of media distribution and consumption, especially as we seek to make sense of an emerging "on-demand culture," one that provides viewers new forms of immediate access to movies and television shows, even while introducing a number of potential constraints" (1-2).

To demonstrate, author Chuck Tryon says. "Although a number of Hollywood marketing experts have emphasized that moviegoers are much more likely to see movies based on friends' recommendations than on critical reviews, the relationship between social media and movie attendance remains unclear." Moreover, Chuck Tryon adds. "Twitter, perhaps more than Facebook, came to be associated with an energetic, empowered, and responsive movie-going audience. In fact, Twitter's initial utility came from the fact that users could link the service to their text messaging service on their cell phones, allowing them to send and receive tweets via their cell phones as text messages in an era before smart phones became more commonplace."

In the book, 'On-Demand Culture: Digital Delivery

and the Future of Movies,' by Chuck Tryon. So, in
attempt to see where cinema if going I found some
important quotes to help break the book down.

In chapter one, 'Coming Soon to a Computer near
you the Digital Delivery and Ubiquitous
Entertainment.'

Author Chuck Tryon points out, "In an interview
discussing the closure of all of the Blockbuster
Video stores in Canada, Kaan Yigit, president of
Solutions Research Group, commented that "this
is the Netflix decade for movies. Kids growing up
will hardly ever know there was a time you
actually went to a store to get a movie." Yigit's
comments underscored the perceived mobility of
movies and television shows across a variety of
platforms and devices, a shift that seemed to
make trips to the video store unnecessary. These
changes in film distribution—formerly associated
with physical copies of DVDs sold at big-box
retailers or rented from local video stores—have
altered not only the economics of the movie
industry but also the perceived value of movies

themselves, creating even deeper interconnections between the movie industry and digital hubs such as Apple, Amazon, Netflix, and Facebook" says Chuck Tryon.

In this we can see how the digital delivery of movies is replacing the physical copies, to be everywhere and anywhere the people are at.

Chuck Tryon also adds. "Although a number of key narratives about digital delivery began to emerge in 2011, there was some uncertainty about how audiences were using it. Still, the enduring perception was that digital delivery provided users with more choices and more flexibility in consuming media content. But in fact, a number of real restrictions and limitations determined when and where users could access movies. To address these concerns, look at the tensions between what I call restricting and resistant mobilities. On the one hand, digital delivery, I suggest, is shaped by the methods through which access is limited, whether this involves temporal restrictions, such as a "window" that provides exclusive distribution rights, or spatial restrictions, such as limitations on where a viewer can watch. On the other hand, audiences have cultivated a wide variety of legal and illegal, or authorized and unauthorized, strategies to work around these limitations.

In this we can see how digital deliver provides more choices and flexibility for the consumer, while at the same time comes with restrictions and limitations that determine where and when films can be consumed. As, wifi could be one of the causes with access being allowed in certain countries. However, even though having a mobile device with an internet connection and Netflix seems like we're holding a movie theater in the palm of our hands "to-go," it's not the same. For instance, the price we will pay for this is authenticity that only the brick and mortar movie theaters can give us.

In chapter two, 'Restrictive and Resistant Mobilities - Negotiating Digital Delivery.'

Chuck Tryon says, "a more extended exploration of the issues related to the practices and the business of digital delivery. It starts with the observation that, despite the promises of digital utopians, on-demand culture is characterized not by universal access but by the process of limiting and restricting when and where content is available. Thus, although a number of film critics and cultural observers have fantasized about the possibility of a "celestial multiplex," most online collections are incomplete, providing users with only partial catalogs that are subject to frequent change." He adds, for instance. "The networks and methods through which movies and television shows will be distributed are far from settled. Although Netflix appeared to be a dominant player in early 2011, with its vast streaming catalog and its expansion throughout much of North and South America and Europe, there is little guarantee that it will be able to maintain this position. The studios themselves hope to create models that will allow direct distribution to consumers, and UltraViolet seemed to offer an alternative that would provide the industry with greater control over how media content circulates, although the studios were forced to retool their UltraViolet offerings just a few months after its initial public launch."

In this we can see the issue that come with the practices and business of digital delivery, while we are not exactly at having universal access (probably meaning whenever and wherever we want to see a film on our device there it is), but rather in a waiting stage that limits and restricts us to when and where see can see content. This would probably explain why online catalogs are only providing a partial catalog for their consumer, for the reason of the movie not being available while it is in theaters and them having to wait to add those new movies in with their collections. Yet, we see a plan for the future of cinema in a creation of a model to allow direct distribution to the consumer and greater control on how media content is circulated throughout the public.

In chapter three, 'Make any Room your TV Room.

Digital Delivery and Media Mobility.'

Chuck Tryon says, "In March 2011, Time Warner Cable launched an iPad application that would allow subscribers to stream some of their television content to their iPad, a total of approximately thirty cable channels, as long as they were connected to a Time Warner wireless router associated with a cable account. Like other digital delivery platforms, the app was announced as a transformative way of watching television and movies. The advertisement promoting the launch, "Make Any Room Your TV Room," consists of a series of quick cuts between various tablet computer users holding or watching the tablet at arm's length in various rooms and spaces throughout a range of middle-class, presumably suburban houses. A businessman holds it in front of his entertainment center, another man watches baseball on an iPad propped on his exercise machine, and a third follows a cooking show as he prepares a meal in the kitchen. An African-American woman watches in a clothes closet, presumably while doing housework, and another woman watches with the device propped on her bathtub, her polished toenails resting just above the water's surface. In all cases, the tablet is placed in the center of the frame, suggesting the continued presence of the screen anywhere inside or near the family home, quite literally placing the iPad at the center of our media world. At the same time, most of the scenes are shot from the user's point of view, promoting the perspective that platform mobility encourages personalized viewing, given that all of the subjects in the ad appear to be alone. The individualized viewer is in control, the advertisement suggests, able to choose when, where, and what he or she watches."

First off, I think the campaign 'Make any Room Your TV Room' commercial is a fascinating and genius idea, as platform mobility encourages personalized viewing. But on the other hand, it's I see this as the consumer having a form of universal access under the control of a media conglomerate. In fact, the company may make it look like the viewer is in control, but are we really being controlled for the motive of money and power? A definition of freedom is "the power or right to act, speak, or think as one wants without hindrance or restraint; the state of not being imprisoned or enslaved." Thus, it's like were are giving access to watch media content when and where ever we want from a mobile device that can become like a jail cell, isolating each consumer from watching movies in community at a movie theater. As this doesn't seem like freedom, but more of like slavery, if it's under the control of having to connected to a companies wireless router associated with a cable account. For a biblical example, Moses and Egypt's slaves under Pharaoh's ruling.

Also, Chuck Tryon adds. "As Francesco Cassetti points out, these new devices can, in some cases, become embedded in a socially networked and engaged film culture, one in which users share, blog, tweet, and even remix films, a potential made possible by the logic of platform mobility. Further, micro-ethnographic examinations of local uses of media technologies often reveal how

users resist and reshape these media discourses
to their own purposes in their everyday practices
of movie and television viewing. We must, as
Shaun Moores suggests, remain attentive to
media users' "practical consciousness of media
environments," even as those platforms evolve
and become imbued with new meanings and uses.
Thus, even while we recognize the role of industry
discourse—in all of its different and sometimes
contradictory forms—on media consumption, we
must also attend to the ways in which platform
mobility offers a powerful expression of the
cultural desire for a greater autonomy over when,
where, how, and what we watch. Although the
theatrical experience may seem to be distinct
from the practices associated with platform
mobility, I argue that its changing nature
illustrates the ongoing reinterpretations that
shape how we perceive movies and the activity of
moviegoing. Though initially marketed as a
special event, 3D has become a relatively
standard practice for major studio films. More
crucially, the technology reinforces the
perception that films have become files, capable

57

of circulating easily among devices and available for periodic upgrades (from DVD to Blu-Ray; from 3D to IMAX 3D). Again, as we will see, consumers are depicted as having new choices and new viewing experiences."

In this I can see how these new devices are creating face to screen community by surrounding the engaged film culture with the social network to share our media experiences, as I think there needs to be a balance between face to screen and face to face with engaging in media content to be healthy. While one this I noticed from the start of the history of cinema was movies brought people together and built community, not just isolate us with our experience being shared looking in to the world from the outside. Therefore, if moviegoing is marketed as a special event and with that meaning to built community amongst people. We shouldn't allow technology to reinforce the perception that films have become files, because files can be thought of as being for personal use and that will generate more ideas for isolating us with new choices and viewing experiences. Instead, of discovering new way to bring the consumer together as a community like our forefathers of cinema did in the past and cinema seems to be founded upon community since it takes more then one person to really make a professional movie.

In chapter four, 'Breaking through the Screen. 3D, Avatar, and the Future of Moviegoing.'

Chuck Tryon says, "At Showest 2005, one of the pre-eminent trade conventions for the motion picture industry, Avatar and Titanic director James Cameron, in cooperation with Texas Instruments, sought to promote the emerging format of digital projection in theaters. At the time, theater owners were reluctant to change over, given that conversion costs were estimated at $100,000 per screen. However, Cameron argued that digital projection could help to launch a transformation in film spectacle through the use of digital 3D, which would, in turn, bring audiences back to movie theaters by providing them with an unprecedented visual experience. In his typical visionary language, Cameron promised that with digital 3D projection, we will be entering a new age of cinema. Audiences will be seeing something, which was never technically possible before the age of digital cinema—a stunning visual experience which "turbocharges" the viewing of the biggest, must-see movies. The biggest action, visual effects and fantasy movies will soon be shot in 3D. And all-CG animated films can easily be converted to 3D, without additional cost if it is done as they are made. Soon audiences will associate 3D with the highest level of visual content in the market, and seek out that premium experience."

In this we can see how 3D is beg used to break the consumers from the screen to bring audiences back to movie theaters by providing them with an unprecedented visual experience, while I like the idea of this to built community and at the same time keep cinema advancing forward with digital 3D projection to take the experience of seeing visual content in the market to a higher level.

Chuck Tryon says, "By the middle of 2012, it seemed clear that digital delivery would fully supplant film projection. At CinemaCon in April 2012, John Fithian, president and CEO of the National Association of Theater Owners, announced that Twentieth Century Fox would stop producing film prints within the next couple of years. The announcement was greeted with little surprise, given that the studio had already stopped distributing film prints in China on January 1. Fithian speculated that the use of "the format of celluloid film could cease by the end of 2013." Thus, despite the mixed reception of 3D, the format had successfully served to usher in the transition to digital delivery." Chuck Tryon also adds, "Despite the numerous attempts to market 3D technology both in theaters and in homes, many consumers opted instead for the cheapest alternative possible, leading to the popularization of low-budget formats such as the Redbox kiosk service. Thus, while theaters faced a future of perpetual upgrades, watching movies at home, an activity typically associated with informality and convenience, often involved seeking out the best possible value."

You can kind of see this change coming with 3D technology both in theaters and at home for this digital delivery transition, because there is a 'monkey see-monkey do' type of pattern that we can see throughout history where what we see the technology that is introduced at the theaters become adapted for the consumer to have at home. So, the audience won't have to go to the theater for an activity of informality and convenience.

In chapter five, 'Redbox vs. Red Envelope, or Closing the Window on the Bricks-and-Mortar Video Store.'

Chuck Tryon says, "The digital delivery of movies seems to democratize access to a wide array of movies, but it also threatens to disrupt some of the traditional ways in which studios have been able to produce revenue, especially after a film leaves movie theaters. Specifically, the persistent

availability of movies in streaming catalogs
lessens consumers' need to buy a copy of a film
and, in turn, decreases the value of that title. The
popularity of Netflix—U.S. subscribers watched an
average of eighty minutes per night, far more
than even the most popular cable
network—showed that users had embraced the
convenience of video on demand (VOD)."

Chuck Tryon says, "the place of Redbox within the
business of movie rentals can tell us quite a bit
about everyday film culture. Although Netflix,
Mubi, and other long tail distributors continue to
promote themselves in terms of their deep
catalogs and their ability to give customers more
meaningful engagement with film culture, rental
kiosks have become a crucial site through which
home audiences rent and watch movies. The
popularity of Redbox's kiosks unsettled
traditional DVD distribution patterns. As a result,
studios worked to negotiate a retail window of
twenty-eight days between the "street" date when
new DVDs would be available for purchase and
the date when they would be available for rental

via Netflix and Redbox. Moreover, rental kiosks help to challenge the idea that consumers are necessarily interested in access to the deeper catalogs celebrated by digital utopians such as Chris Anderson. Instead, kiosks might be productively read as a "disruptive innovation," one that meets the unrecognized needs of a group of consumers, especially parents seeking to use a DVD as an "electronic babysitter." Finally, Redbox reminds us that, as media scholars, we must engage not only with the textual artifacts of a media-saturated culture but also with the distribution cultures in which these texts circulate."

I can see how Redbox vs Red Envelope can give an audience a free will of choice to watch more movies on an affordable budget from the privacy of our homes, and it making it easier for the consumer to get a movie rather than having to make a commute to the Brick-and-Mortar Video Stores with transportation being a factor if they don't have it. But if the consumer would rather stay at home to have a movie sent to them, instead of making the trip (for those who have cars) to support the Bricks-and-Mortar Video Stores we will see mostly all of them closing shop for not be able to produce revenue. But is the Bricks-and-Mortar Video Stores offered digital distribution to their consumers this could preserve them, and offer two choices for them. Moreover, these Bricks-and-Mortar Video Stores could come up with new ways to get the consumer into the physical store. The way I view a physical copy of a DVD is it's a souvenir that holds a memory of not just an experience of a movie, but also of the store that you bought it from and the emotion you was reflecting when you bought it as you can't get that with a digital copy of a movie as the kiosks eliminate having to stand in line and the offer of self-service. While I can see how the kiosks can be a "disruptive innovation," for any parent to use a DVD as an "electronic babysitter." Who would leave a child to watch a digital copy of a movie on a computer? Which would be the reason why there needs to be DVDs and digital movies, because a DVD can be preserved and is nice to have as a back-up copy while digital can be lost if not saved in a crash.

In chapter six, 'The Twitter Effect - Social Media and Digital Delivery.'

Chuck Tryon says, "movie and television watching continue to be defined as social activities to be shared with friends and family or, in the case of movie theaters, a wider public. As Charles Acland has noted, discourses on moviegoing have long emphasized "the material and sensory experience of commune," and opening weekends are particularly identified with the pleasurable opportunity "to be with strangers and to be part of the crowd."   Similarly, television watching has long been identified with a wide range of social activities, such as watching with family or friends and discussing the shows afterward. In this regard, social media tools have begun to play a vital role in promoting collective viewing activities that allow viewers to identify movies and television shows they might want to see and to discuss those texts with others. At the same time, social media can be used to promote movies and even to structure the cultures of anticipation associated with films and television shows." For an example, Chuck Tryon adds. "For the most part, social media have been promoted as a means of providing users with a more interactive and collective media experience. Audiences could cultivate collective, simultaneous viewing experiences through practices such as live-tweeting and social check-in services. In turn, these tools could provide users with richer media experiences, allowing them to identify the content they want to see and to demonstrate their knowledge of popular culture. In the best cases, filmmakers and theater owners could use social media tools to build a community that could help them to promote interest in specific movies or even in special screenings."

I love what social media is doing for cinema by providing a rich experience for the consumer to identify movies they might want to see and to discuss those texts with others, as I can see how this builds community and draws the audience back into the physical theaters. Simply, it can be seen as distribution of sending out and receiving new information for a studio to consumer relationship. While I see more moviegoing connect groups starting up from this, viewing movies together and discussing them afterwards.

In chapter seven, 'Indie 2.0 - Digital Delivery, Crowdsourcing, and Social Media.'

Chuck Tryon says, "Social media tools became a powerful component of what independent filmmaker Kevin Smith referred to as "Indie 2.0," a new model of distribution based upon leveraging the participation and, in some cases, the financial contributions of audiences who might be interested in supporting a film. In both cases, social media and digital delivery technologies contribute to a transformation in the value of a media property." While Chuck Tryon, gives an example. "At the 2011 Sundance Film Festival, prolific indie filmmaker Kevin Smith announced that he would be holding an "auction" for his latest movie, Red State , a low-budget horror film that satirized the homophobic and

publicity-hungry Westboro Baptist Church,
survivalist groups, and media sensationalism,
among other targets. Eager for a scoop, members
of the entertainment press packed into the
theater, awaiting the kind of bidding war that had
been commonplace at past festivals. However,
rather than holding the promised auction, Smith
immediately "sold" the film to himself for $20
before proceeding to offer an elaborate lecture on
the ways in which expensive distribution and
marketing plans made it difficult for indie films to
make a profit. Smith's auction served as a
commentary on the distribution cultures that had
formed around Sundance during the 1990s, when
his 1994 film Clerks, which he had financed using
credit cards and filmed in the convenience store
where he worked, became an unexpected hit after
it were purchased at the festival by Miramax.
Thus, the auction of Red State allowed Smith to
underscore the ways in which the
Miramax-Sundance model was broken beyond
repair. Smith's performance helped to illustrate
the role of festivals in generating hype for new
and innovative filmmakers, or at least those who

can easily be marketed to art-house audiences."

In this we can see how Kevin Smith became a pioneer to filmmakers to create a new and innovative way to distribution of film, based on the leveraging the participation and financial contribution of audiences who might be interested in supporting it that caused other filmmakers to duplicate the "Indie 2.0" model.

Furthermore, Chuck Tryon says. "Although a number of DIY projects attracted attention from both the social media and the mainstream media, it is important to note that many similar projects went unnoticed. To some extent, successful films benefited from the involvement of figures who already had some celebrity, such as Kevin Smith, Louis C.K., or even Pete Postlethwaite. In this sense, DIY culture not only placed emphasis on finding alternative distribution models but also served a larger pedagogical purpose, one that called for a more transparent relationship between producers and consumers of media content. This line was further blurred through references to the techniques of crowdsourcing and crowdfunding, by which filmmakers sought to tap the creative potential and financial support of movie audiences. Thus, although digital delivery practices have offered new avenues for media conglomerates to market directly to the consumer, these tools—and the discussions they have provoked—have also opened up new ways of thinking about the interactions between producers and consumers." Chuck Tryon adds, "collaborative projects—and the culture of self-distribution in general—promote what might be called a "pedagogy of self-distribution," in which media makers teach others how to use digital delivery and social media tools to promote and distribute their films, allowing filmmakers and audiences to develop new categories for distinguishing their films from both independent and mainstream movies. These pedagogical and productive activities fall into two commonly cited practices: crowdfunding and crowdsourcing. Crowdfunding is the process of soliciting financial contributions from supporters of a project, while crowdsourcing involves the use of collective

71

labor—from fans, supporters, and other participants—to produce and distribute a text."

Through this we can see the effects of the power of one can do, as Kevin Smith inspired a movement of DIY projects that attracted attention from both social and mainstream media. In which, was the start of crowdfunding and crowsourcing for the promotion and distribution of films as this also developed new categories for distinguishing them from both independent and mainstream movies. As, digital delivery and social media tools is changing the way filmmakers distribute and finance films.

In chapter eight, 'Reinventing Festivales. Curation, Distriution, and the Creationg of Global Cinephilia.'

Chuck Tryon says, "In July 2010 stalwart directors Ridley Scott and Kevin Macdonald engaged in what was billed as "a historic cinematic experiment" when they invited YouTube users to submit video footage for a

planned two-hour documentary entitled Life in a
Day. The filmmakers stipulated only that the
footage had to be recorded on July 24 (which,
when delivered in shorthand, appeared as 24/7)
and submitted to the Life in a Day YouTube page
no later than July 31. Scott and Macdonald would
then select footage to be compiled into a
feature-length film, one that would draw on
YouTube's worldwide reach to capture a snapshot
of a global community linked by video sharing.
The invitation included several enticements
beyond the opportunity to be associated with a
film produced by the directors of Blade Runner
and Last King of Scotland, respectively. Life in a
Day was guaranteed a slot at the 2011 Sundance
Film Festival, and twenty contributors to the film
would be invited to attend the film's premiere
there and immerse themselves in the celebrity
culture associated with Sundance. Participants
whose footage was included in the final film would
also receive a credit as co-directors, a recognition
that seemingly confirmed the fantasy that cheap
digital production tools would democratize
cinema. This model of democratized filmmaking

has long been aligned with new technologies, and in the case of Life in a Day it proved especially alluring. Macdonald and Scott received well over 80,000 submissions, demonstrating how easy it had become to produce and share content." To demonstrate, Chuck Tryon wrote. "Rather than using a successful festival screening to launch a theatrical run, independent film distribution has been redefined to entail a wide variety of digital delivery platforms, including streaming services such as Netflix and video-on-demand services such as IFC Festival Direct. Furthermore, distributing films during a festival—creating what might be called a "festival window"—profoundly alters the traditional window system that has guided distribution since the popularization of VHS during the 1980s. Finally, festivals have deepened their use of social media tools in order to expand the festival experience, allowing people not attending the festival to gain admission to events that were once considered exclusive and providing those who attend the festival with a more interactive experience."

With the forward movement of technology and
cinema, comes the reinventing of the festivals,
curation, distribution and the creation of Global
Cinephilia. While we see that this came through
an experiment of inviting Youtube users to
submit video footage for a planned two-hour
documentary entitled, 'Life in a Day' to capture a
snapshot of a global community linked by video
sharing and showing how you can make a movie
with less to gain more views using social media.
In the end, one cinematic experiment created a
way for filmmakers and audiences to collaborate
with each other on the making of a film. Thus,
changing the way how an audience interacts with
filmmakers in cinema.

INT. DIGITAL FUTURE - DAY

Lastly, in chapter nine, 'Digital Future.'   Chuck
Tryon tells us, "Digital delivery not only affects
the economic models of the movie industry but
also promotes an on-demand culture, in which the
practices of moviegoing and the perceptions of
media culture are transformed. Movie viewers
are now re-imagined as individualized and mobile,

able to watch practically anywhere or anytime they wish, while having access to aspects of film culture—such as film festivals and art-house movies—that have in the past been available only in specific locations." In fact, Chuck Tryon adds. "David Bordwell argues, now that cinema has become digital, it follows the logic of the "platform," one that is subject, like all information technologies, to "innovation, development, and obsolescence." Furthermore, movies, like the technologies themselves, are produced under the idea of the upgrade, with blockbuster franchises available to be rebooted when the technology improves. All of these changes point to a transformation in movie and television culture as users attempt to navigate the new delivery formats. At the same time, the social role of movies maintains some continuity with the past, as moviegoers worldwide continue to attend theatrical premieres in vast, if not record-breaking, numbers. These events remind us that for millions of people movies still hold a significant place in our cultural imagination, even if the accelerated velocity with which they pass through theaters and into other formats has altered their social role. Audiences still hold out hope that a movie will excite, challenge, engage, or entertain them."

Briefly, what I have learned from this chapter was when cinema upgrades it transforms how the movie culture as users navigates the new delivery format, and can still stay true to the continuity we have seen in the past. So, no matter what form we see cinema take in the future, there will still be a significant need for the hope a movie brings to an audience whose hearts seems to be forever beating for change.

To sum up, "it began in the 20th century with silent films. But in 1927, mouths were opened and lines were spun, eventually to form a worldwide web." Said Carey Lewis, an author who has associations with the Actors Models and Talent for Christ organization, as she couldn't have put it any better.

So, from 2000 onwards, the themes that I have

found to occur during this decade were: reality, power, indecision, moving, lawlessness, school, esteem, impressionism, love, violence, boys/girls, fathers/mothers, special issues, marriage, sex, dying/death, physical illness, women stories, apathetic, haunting, nudity, men stories, anger, fighting, dream-like and realistic, sexuality, hate and dislike, friends, relationships, drugs, alcohol, fear, emotional illness, abuse, social, reality/fantasies, spirituality, search for meaning, guilt, denial, human feeling, caring, family, nurturing, abandonment, psychological, and social upheavals.

Overall, the best way to sum up the chronology of film in a brief way that couldn't be said any better. Is how Carey Lewis, an author who has associations with the Actors Models and Talent for Christ organization saying. "It began in the 20th century with silent films. But in 1927, mouths were opened and lines were spun, eventually to form a worldwide web." While concerning the future, filmmakers suggest that cinema is in provocative hands. Lastly, 'The Story of Film: An Odyssey,' ended with an epilogue about what cinema holds for the year 2046. Whereas; the predicted themes that I am foretelling with this show are: innovative, sci-fi, dreams, fantasies, friends, industrialization, psychological, special issues, goals, playing a game of living and dying together, love, men stories, codependency, emotional illness, physical illness, abandonment, social, moving, family boys/girls, friends, fathers/mothers, and money.

INT. CINEMA'S TRANSFORMATION - DAY

Now that we've established a firm footing on the chronology of film to know where we've been and going, let's embark on the transformation of the spirit, mind and body through cinema.

Cinema is by far the coolest, weirdest, and outstanding medium. For the reason, you go to a movie theater to wait for a photoplay that appears like a phantom. You look in to a disfigured body and the mind of a person who had the dream for a movie to write the story, and it has a spirit behind it that can influence transformation for the good or bad. After it is explained further below, you will probably see things differently.

INT. THE MIND - DAY

First, let's explore the mind realm, and how movies can affect it.

In the book, 'The Power of Movies: how screen and mind interact. Colin McGinn, a professor of philosophy at Rutgers University said. "Old Movie Theater buff Rene Descartes brought this in discussion, "Descartes split the human being into two – the body and the mind, respectively. The body is a substance with mass and bulk, a three-dimensional occupant of space, a physical organism. The mind, by contrast, lacks these attributes, being constituted by thought: it is a weightless, intangible being, existing alongside the material body" (64). In an essay, entitled "why we go to the movies," Munsterberg writes that "the photoplay expresses the action of the body ... the inner mind which the camera exhibits must lie in those actions of the camera itself by

which space and time are overcome and
attention, memory, imagination, and emotion are
impressed on the bodily world" For example of
the mind in movies "Munsterberg's idea, simply
put, is that the movie mimics the mind's process
by containing analogues of key psychological
functions: the close-up mirrors attention, the
flashback is memory, the flash forward is
imagination or expectation – all this combined
with that "light flitting immateriality." All films
are mentally presentational, "thus when the mind
and movie come into contact, it is like one mind
finding another; we see ourselves in film – our
very consciousness stretched out before us.
Moreover, cinema provides this kind of mentally
analogy" Colin McGinn mentions in the book, 'The
Power of Movies: how screen and mind interact'
(68). "The power that movies have over the
viewer, their psychological impact. In effect, by
linking movies to some of our most basic natural
traits: First, films engage our perceptual faculties
in fundamental ways, particularly through the
visual stance of looking into. Second, they answer
to our metaphysical status as psychophysical

beings, the mind-body nexus that constitutes our nature; in particular, they play upon our ambivalent relationship to our own body. Thirdly, movies delve into our dreaming self, that submerged and seething alter ego that emerges when the sun goes down. In the cinema we relive the life of the dreaming self. Movies thus tap into the dreaming aspect of human nature" (Colin McGinn 192). In the book, 'Psychology at the movies.' Author, Skip Dine Young, a Professor of Psychology at Hanover College in Indiana and licensed clinical psychologist says. "Like all art, movies are saturated with the human mind – they are created by humans, they depict human action, and they are viewed by a human audience." Author, Skip Dine Young, a Professor of Psychology at Hanover College in Indiana and licensed clinical psychologist. "Films are windows or mirrors into the world of human behavior, the workings of the mind, and human nature itself. Contained in movies, we can see individual development taking place – the operation of unconscious defense mechanisms, social psychological processes, and so on. Here, film is a

landscape on which psychological entities are
projected... it is possible to gain greater insight
into individuals and society" (20). However,
psychology in movies simply reflect reality.
Which brings us to, the cinematic moment, when
emotions and the comprehension of movies meet.
"The cinematic moment is when cognitive and
emotion process occur as viewers sit in their
seats, gaze at the screen, and try to make sense
out of their immediate experience. Then there is
cognitive psychology and the movies, as "our
minds are very active when we watch movies.
The interrelated mental activities of perception
and comprehension are represented as follows:
film is to perception, perception is to images and
sound, images and sound is to comprehension and
emotion, comprehension and emotion is to story.
Perception and comprehension are important
topics in the domains of cognitive psychology
cognitive science and neuroscience. These fields
study various processes that constitute human
thinking including sensation, perception,
attention, memory, organization, problem
solving, and so on. The confluence of film studies

and cognitive science is part of an exciting intellectual trend combining scientific methods (experimental and laboratory observations) with the humanities (textual analysis) to help understand not only the perception and comprehension of film, but the human mind itself. " (Colin McGinn 96-97). The narrative comprehension of movies, "movies tells stories. The perceptual detail of a film combine to create an overall structure, and in most films, that structure is narrative.

Thus, when viewers try to understand a film, they must look at how the piece of the story fit together. Story and plot have often been distinguished in narrative analysis. Story represents the casual, temporal, and spatial relationships between narrative events the plot refers to what information is presented to the audience in what way (how the story is told). The story is imaginary (mental or cognitive) in the sense that it emerges internally as the result of how the viewer processes the plot. Thus, we can say that the plot belongs to the film, while the story belongs to the viewer. While many Hollywood movies are plotted in sequential order, there are exceptions. All of these spatial relationships apply to watching a movie, with one exception: we are spatially limited by the camera, not by the movement of our bodies. The emotional comprehension of movies, "there is a tendency to think of feelings and thoughts as separate – the heart is hot and impulsive, while the head is cold and rational.

The emotional arousal, "when they watch a movie, people experience a range of emotion. For example, laughter, tears, expressions of terror, and jolts of surprise can all be witnesses in the audience's physical reactions. Films are so effective at evoking emotion that they have become a crucial element in emotion research" (Colin McGinn 100-102). Whereby, there are emotional themes, "there has been a close connection between emotion and story.

Also, stories provoke feelings, an observation that intertwines emotional theory with narrative theory. The cognitive schemas (mental structures) people use to comprehend their actions and those of others are called "scripts". We have scripts for all of the actions we perform or witness, from trips to the store to weddings. Since scripted events are important for helping us get through the day, achieving success, and ultimately survive, they have an emotional resonance that lets us make intuitive decisions about what is valuable and what is dangerous. Scripts not only apply to understanding people and events but to comprehending fictional events in movies; with in a literary or cinematic context, these scripts are called themes. As we watch a movie and witness variations of events we have seen before, certain scripts are triggered, bringing on automatic emotional response.

Then, there are emotions, character motivation and empathy. "The use of provocative themes is not the only way in which films connect comprehension with feelings. Another is figuring out why characters do what they do. But to maintain cognitive and emotional involvement, we have to "get inside" the characters. As the character onscreen is developed, further characteristics are introduced that lead viewers to better understand his or her motivations.

Thus, when viewers recognize the motivational structure, they identify with that character. This identification need not to be intense or lasting, but it has to occur long enough for the character's actions to make sense and serve the development of the story" (Colin McGinn 104-106). Moving on to brain functioning and the movies, "the application of brain science to film viewing is in its infancy, but the early findings are intriguing. While direct laboratory research is sparse, we can reasonably speculate that the viewer's emotional experience while watching cinematic stories is related to brain functioning. The autonomic nervous system, the system regulating automatic bodily functioning (such as the breathing and heart) and the subcortical areas of the brain seem particularly involved. These areas deal beneath the cortex with the primitive functions necessary for immediate survival – hunger, wakening, breathing, and so on. Strong emotional reactions, particularly negative reactions, are partially located in this primitive zone. Even though filmed objects are not "real," our perceptual and cognitive systems often treat them as though they were real, thereby enhancing our emotional reactions" (Colin McGinn 107-108). Psychiatric disturbances, "movies often provoke powerful emotional reactions, but occasionally people will respond to a movie so strongly that they develop symptoms of trauma, depression, or psychosis. While movies do not have the power to make secure individuals into nervous wrecks, these examples exemplify the interaction between symbolic images presented in cinema and the psychological make-up of a particular individual. The combination of symbols in the film ignited their existing personal issues" (Skip Dine Young 140). Effects on fear and imagination, "fear and anxiety are common emotions when viewing films and they are central to the enjoyment of horror films and thrillers. However, sometimes fear is an effect that lives on when the movie is over. Vision images from the media leave a strong impression and take on lives of their own. This process, which can be both good and bad, has received considerable research attention" (Skip Dine Young 140-141). Effects on attitudes, beliefs and stereotypes in movies. "Media affects how viewers' categorize, understand, and evaluate their world. These critical cognitive processes touch nearly every aspect of life. Movies appear to be part of a cultural web of influences which reveal themselves not so much as patterns, but as the shadow of such patterns. A variation on the concern that media causes particular thoughts and emotions is that media also has the power to diminish emotional response" (Skip Dine Young 142-143). For example, if people are exposed to excessive violence, they may become numb and stop feeling distress.

INT. THE BODY - DAY

Second, now that we know the power of film on the mind, let's how cinema can be seen as having a body and also how movies can affect the things we do.

In the book, 'The Power of Movies: how screen

and mind interact. Colin McGinn, a professor of philosophy at Rutgers University said. "It is the idea of the spiritual body, "conceived entirely nonbodily, but the idea of the dematerialized body. This can be seen (though not touched) and it has a kind of spatial presence" (69). As, the kind of body associated with the idea of phantom, spectral presences in human form. For instance, we go to a movie to wait in front of a white screen for a light to project a body of images with sound. Briefly, "this is the idea of the human body with the material stuffing taken out of it, transformed into something impalpable" (70). Thus, "the film image of a person is analogous to this notion of the spiritual or dematerialized body. Making it a creature of light and radiance, as there are representations of such spiritual entities like angels and demons followed by a soundtrack to accompany the spiritual sights. So, "the movie image can be seen as transforming the human body into a dematerialized medium – flat patches of light – and of the meaning of this transformation" (91). As, "the movie image toys with the duality of human beings by dematerializing the body just like a sculpture underlines our materiality to indicate its essential irrelevance. To further demonstrate, "all the resources of cinema – lighting, make up, camera placement, music, voice, background, the actor's physiognomy – can work to reveal the inner being of the character, and the medium itself intensifies the effect of mentality on the screen. The mind is foregrounded related to the body, which is present to the viewer only as a wispy trace. With the body ontologically reduced, etiolated, the soul comes to the viewer in its primal form, asserting its reality in the presence of the dematerialized body" (96). Thus, the movies made me do it – the effects of films: effects on behavior and effects on thoughts and emotions. With this, Skip Dine Young said. "The psychological processes we have considered – perception, comprehension, and interpretation – are the mental means by which viewing films impacts people's lives. Occasionally the meanings viewers form about a film will be so powerful and relevant that they will have an influence on people's lives" (132-133). Effects on behaviors, "subliminal seduction (subconscious

91

media messages that influence our behavior) was a term popularized in the 1970s. Frequently referenced examples included "buy popcorn" messages secretly flashes on the screen to prompt concession sales. Moreover, subliminal effects are sensory stimuli undetectable to conscious awareness which are nevertheless dutifully processed by the brain and subsequently influence behavior ... In real life, many factors affect any given behavior, leading some researchers to make a distinction between the media contributing to certain behaviors (along with other many factors) versus media single-handedly causing behaviors. One of the ways that researchers explain how media can contribute to behavior but not directly cause specific behaviors is priming theory" (Skip Dine Young 134-138). To put it simply, monkey see, monkey do, as we can see so far that movies has the power to transform a life for good or bad, depending on our knowledge to model them out through cinematic identifications that may come across as guidance to a familiar real life situation. Propaganda and effects on culture, Skip Dine

Young has said that "propaganda is designed to cause large numbers of people to think in a particular war. These films are usually created under dire circumstances, in which the emphasis is on action, not analysis ... Our thinking adjusts to new forms of technology as they are introduced and when we watch movies, we are more affected by the fact that it is a movie than by its genre or its overall quality. The more movies we see, the more we begin to see the world like a movie. Along the way, the message can be altered, beautified, or even fabricated in order to give it the right visual appearance. The medium is determining what the message will be as the standards of entertainment, including those refined by Hollywood over many decades, are now applied to news or political rhetoric" (143-145). In the book, 'The Power of Movies: how screen and mind interact. Colin McGinn, a professor of philosophy at Rutgers University said. "The movies present us with such transformation. The idea of bodily transformation is rife in movies: people into monsters (vampires, werewolves), flesh replaced by metal (Robocop), children into adults and vice versa, men into women, ordinary men into superman, people into ghost, and so on. And then there is the general transformation of the solid substantial body into the spiritual body – a kind of analogue for the process of immortalization of these kind of magical or quasimagical transformations. They implement what we can only imagine. They out do the transformations of mere nature (caterpillar into butterfly, rock into lava, life into death, etc...) a part of us still yearns for that primitive prescientific worldview in which anything can happen if the supernatural forces are aligned just right" (81).

INT. THE SPIRIT - DAY

Third, we seen that cinema has a mind and a body. But what about the spirit? Now, let's look into how the spirit of good and evil can influence transformation.

Also,). In the book, 'The Power of Movies: how screen and mind interact. Colin McGinn makes this point. "Watching a movie is like a religious experience, in fact, the similarities of church and cinema are. "Psychologically there is an emotional stirring, a sense of great themes, and moral focusing, and sometimes a state bordering on trance ... There is even something analogous to the conversion experience that can affect the movie viewer: people often speak of the profound impact of a particularly film on their worldview. Movies can be ethically and politically powerful, as much as any harangue from the pulpit. The intensity of the cinema and the church experience is not to be denied. And both places seem alive with spirit, the body taking second place" (79). Overall; the whole person of the spirit, mind and body can be seen in cinema. To explain, cinema is a vehicle that has a mind, represented by the photoplay. The body, representing the movie as it transforms the human body into a dematerialized medium. And there's the spirit, representing itself as spiritual entities, spiritual sights, analogue, attentive faculties and substance.

In fact, Oral Roberts, who is an author, founder of

Oral Roberts University and one of the most well-known and controversial American religious leaders of the 20th century. Believed that *"both natural and supernatural healing powers work together for the healing of people, thus demonstrating that ALL HEALING IS DIVINE."* In fact, Dallin H. Oaks, author, graduate of Brigham Young University, law practitioner and a preacher once said. *"We use nutrition, exercise, and other practices to preserve health, and we enlist the help of healing practitioners, such as physicians and surgeons, to restore health. The use of medical science is not at odds with our prayers of faith."* With this, brings me to science (psychotherapy) and having faith for healing in the use of movies with God's help. As Skip Dine Young tells us that "cinema therapy is the use of movies as tools in psychotherapy. Since movies allow viewers to make metaphorical connections between the content of the film and the real world, a skilled therapist can help clients make these connections to solve problems and facilitate therapeutic progress. In which, movies offer important therapeutic qualities: they are both emotionally engaging and highly metaphorical. Because of this, psychologists and other writers assume value in movie-inspired self-reflection even when it is not led or shared with a therapist; their self-help books assert that reflecting on movies can lead to richer, healthier or more virtuous lives" (157-158).

INT. HANDLING MEDIA INFLUENCES - DAY

In a 21 day Bible reading plan on 'Handling Media Influences.' LifeChurch.tv tells us that the Bible really does have something to say about media, even though it wasn't invented in Bible times as they said. "What we see and hear affects our hearts and minds, and shapes our attitudes and actions. As we can challenge ourselves to make the most of technology and media while guarding ourselves from its potential negative influence."

Day one, some short takeaways on what I learn from this devotional was, to be an influencer through media before it influences you to be something that you're not. "The images we see, the music we hear, and all other varieties of media change our hearts and minds which in turn, shape our attitudes and actions." We can use media to focus our and others relationship on Jesus Christ. "Tell kids who they are. Show them what relationships are for. Challenge them to make the most of the technology and media in our lives to point others to Christ, then share God's love, and to ultimately draw us closer to Him." In addition; loving something to the point it drives you to chase after it and conform to its ways until it becomes apart of your life and you become something you're not, is what I think it mean to crave the things of this world. As you can still use the things of this world, without craving them to reach out and help people. The sorts of things we should crave are things that are eternal, would draw us closer to a growing relationship to Jesus Christ and point others to Him. For example; the Bible, church, outreach, prayer and worship. The ideas that I have for how families can redirect cravings from the things of this world toward the things of God is go on a short-term missions trip, movie devotionals that give an alternative scenario to everyday life situation based on

Biblical principles and media making projects
that allows us to use media instead of it using us.
Another thing is media can be a mirror in a way it
exposes how we may be using it and how it uses
us, making us step back to make changes for
personal growth. While this day's reading was
based out of 1 John 2:15-17 as what this taught
me is not to the world or the things in it, because
it can turn you away from who you are and
having a relationship with Jesus Christ.

Day two, my plan didn't have any scheduled
scripture readings for this day. But what I have
learned from the devotional was this key thought,
garbage in-garbage out. In other words, what's in
my heart is what comes out. Moreover, to keep
these four points in mind when going about media
choices: First, media DOES affect our ATTITUDE
and ACTIONS. Music, books, TV shows, games,
apps, and movies are all media. Second, anything
that goes in our eyes or ears affects our hearts
and minds and comes out in our attitude and
actions. Third, our bodies digest media kind of
like we digest food. Our eyes and ears are
entrance doors to our heart and mind. What we

let in shapes how we think and feel. Then that affects what we do and say. So it goes in your eyes and ears, shapes your brain and heart, and comes out your mouth and actions. Fourth, we know that music does impact your attitude, mind, and heart. That's why movies have soundtracks. That's why people have exercise playlists. The music you listen to DOES shape your heart and mind."

Day three of handling media influences as the scripture was based out of Matthew 7:16-20, and what I learn out of this devotion was the fruit has to match the kind of tree its growing on. For example, people are like tree, just as you can identify a tree by what comes out of it, so you can identify people by there actions. The way we live is our fruit, which explains why it's important to guard ourselves against the content that we can allow movies to feed us. Even though its not about what goes in you that spoils you, but how it inspires the way you to live as what you take in will eventually have to come out just like drinking tea and having to use the bathroom later. The kinds of fruit growing in my life are: love, sometimes I can get angry, exuberance about life, if I don't watch it I can get jealous or envious as I overcome this my celebrating others, willingness to stick to things, self-control, kindness, goodness, faithfulness, gentleness, joy, peace, sometimes I can have anxiety, a sense of compassion in the heart, loyal commitments and able to marshal and direct my energy wisely into a positive outlet. Lastly, if people followed me around to see my media interaction habits, what would they be able to tell about what's in your heart? I try my best to filter out content that shouldn't be fed on and keep positive influences as I think they would tell me I have the fruits of the spirit growing in my heart with some things I might have not seen that need to be pruned. Overall, the most important thing I can take away from this devotional is the way we live is our fruit.

Day four of handling media influences, I was to spend some time together memorizing this verse. Proverbs 4:23, "Guard your heart above all else, for it determines the course of your life." While to me this means, be careful for what you allow into your life, because it becomes thoughts, thoughts lead to words, words lead to action and action leads to your destiny. As, there is and old saying that says, show me your friends and I'll show you your future. Bad company corrupts good morals, as the Bible also tells us.

Day five of handling media influences as the scripture was based on Philippians 4:8, "And now, dear brothers and sisters, one final thing. Fix your thoughts on what is true, and honorable, and right, and pure, and lovely, and admirable. Think about things that are excellent and worthy of praise." For me this is guidance on where to not only fix your thoughts, and it can also be used to help in our media choices. Like, are the lyrics in the song true? Is this movie honorable to God, others and myself? Would this media choice be right to feed on? Is it pure? Does it sound lovely to listen to and watch, as if it's a horror film then its probably not. Lastly, is this media choice that I'm about to feed on admirable? In other words respectable or good to God, women or men.

Day six of handling media influences devotional plan had no scheduled scripture readings for this day, but what I have learned from its devotional was this key thought, "one thing matters more than stuff from a store" during my interaction with media this week. Moreover, there's four key points I've reflected on which are: First, it doesn't have to be "bad" stuff to keep you from growing closer to Jesus. It just has to use up all your time that you could have used to know Him better. Second, our enemy Satan came to kill, steal, and destroy. He can defeat us by distracting us. If we are so busy clicking on links, watching funny videos, playing games, and goofing off, then he has won our hearts without us even putting up a fight. Third, sometimes just allowing us to get our schedules too busy or not being careful about how much time we waste unintentionally is all it takes to keep us from growing our relationship with Jesus. Fourth, we need to make sure the way we spend our time puts God above all else. All of the other stuff in the world is just fluff compared to knowing God. When we put him first, He will give us everything we need. It's not a trade-off, it's a trade-UP.

Day seven of handling media influences

devotional plan, the scripture was based out on Luke 10:38-42 and what I have learned is that Martha was distracted by the big dinner she was preparing as that seemed like a good thing to her. Martha was worried about serving Jesus, and we can see religion through her. Whereas, Jesus thought Mary's choice was better, because Mary found the time to sit to develop a relationship with Jesus and listen to what He was teaching her. Business, school work, jobs, family, ministry, friends, hobbies, sports, TV, movies, computers, video games, internet, cellphone and shopping are some good things that distract us from getting closer to Jesus. We can make being close to God our number one thing by putting him first above everything else, and seeking to spend time with him in the morning when we first wake up to get out of bed.

Day eight of handling media influences devotional plan, the scripture was based out on Matthew 6:33 as what I learned from spending time meditating on this verse is when you take care of God's business first He will take care of yours. In other words, when you have needs, pursue the creator and His creations.

Day nine of handling media influences devotional plan, the scripture was based out on Romans 8:5 and what I learned from meditating on this verse is you are influenced by the positive (the things of the spirit) and negative (fleshly things) thoughts that will end up leading you into the direction you go. This is why I can see how the content we choice to feed on in the media can play a part like a bit in a horses mouth, because wherever the influence pulls on you is the direction that you will go.

Day ten of handling media influences devotional plan, there was no verse for the day. But what I learned from the devotional is, "ON is not the only choice we've got. Choose OFF!" While keeping this point in mind as I interact with media this week, along with these four key points: First, video games ask us, "Are you sure you want to quit?" YES! Media is designed to keep you engaged. It can even feel like being under a spell or being enchanted. You may have to fight hard to stick to God's best for you. Second, we shouldn't make choices based on what everyone else does. The world's standards are not God's standards. Third, God's standards are not a new set of rules you learn at church, they are the way God shows you through His Word. Fourth, we must seek God for His standards for our life. He may not give every kid in every family the same blueprints, plans, boundaries for media. Follow God's lead and follow your parents' rules.

Day eleven of handling media influences devotional plan, the scripture was based out on Amos 7:1-9 and what I learned is about the plumb line as how you can stay straight in life by God's Word. Moreover, what a plumb line does is measure to see how straight something is, in my own words. So, how does this Bible passage create a picture of measuring our life by God's standards? By showing us how much curves towards the ways of the world, so we can make the right adjustments in our lives to straight our ways to align up with the ways of God or the Word of God. In simpler terms, God gives us His laws to live by His way to protect us from having our hearts crumble and we can stay straight by aligning up our lives by how God says for us to live in His Word.

Day twelve of handling media influences devotional plan, the scripture was based out on Exodus 23:2 and what I learned is pertaining to a call to justice. Basically, what it says to me is do not allow a crowd to influence you to follow in to a wrongdoing as it will eventually sway you into twisting justice. Whether if it's in our daily lives being a living testimony of God and what He has done for us.

Day thirteen of handling media influences devotional plan, the scripture was based out on 1 John 1:5-10 and what I learned through this scripture is, if we say we have no sin we are not living in the truth and calling God a liar by continuing to live in spiritual darkness and saying that we have fellowship with God as this verse teaches us about living in the light. While it shows us a way out, through confessing our sins to Him, as God will be faithful to forgive us of our sins and cleanse us from all wickedness.

Day fourteen of handling media influences devotional plan, although there was no verse scheduled for today. But what I learned through the devotional is this though, "on screen is not the real scene, God is the real thing." So, as I reflect on my interaction with media, I will keep these key points in mind: First, on begin that "The reality presented in media is often a COUNTERFEIT of God's truth. Real people aren't that funny, that pretty, that fast, that tough, that anything. Everything you see has been enhanced and scripted and modified to show the view the maker wants to present." The second one being that the "Most media is designed to sell. Some shows may not seem like they're selling things but their job is to attract an audience of a certain group of people so that advertisers can show commercials to sell that group of people products. The world uses media's influence over you to use you to make money and gain power." The third one being "What we think about certain brands or products is based on what that company wants you to think. Whichever message you're exposed to most sways your opinion about which product you want. This also happens with messages that are against what the Bible says—often without us being aware of it." And the last one being that "Almost all of the things media is trying to sell you is stuff that most people in the world will live their whole life without. You do not need what they're selling. If you needed it, you would buy it without them spending millions of dollars trying to sell it to you. Stuff can never satisfy you like the amazing adventure of knowing Jesus will."

Day fifteen of handling media influences devotional plan, the scripture was based out on Matthew 6:19-34 and what I learned is don't spend your money on things that won't last, but spend your money on the thing that will last for eternity (like feeding the poor, building a friendship and such). As, we can put God's needs before ours, and he will provide all the other stuff that we may need. Furthermore, this devotional asked three questions, based around this topic as they were: First, what are some ways the images in media change what we think is the truth? They Photoshop images to make a product look better than it really is, as this gives the audience a desire to want to go out and spend the money for it. Other ways are they add sound effects and visual effect that would please our senses, as this can create an experience that makes us want to go back for more. Second, in what ways do we often try to live for both God and stuff? When we are trying to please both people and God. The last question, how can we keep our focus on God's truth when media with other messages surrounds us? Simple, by not following the crowd, seeking God above all the other stuff, trusting God and making Him our boss to make money serve us.

Day sixteen of handling media influences devotional plan, the scripture was based out on Colossians 3:2, as what this verse means to me is think about the things or moments that you have or want to create that will last forever, instead of on the things that fades in and out of trend. When you wake up each morning to go about your interactions with media to avoid their marketing strategy from planting those thoughts that may give someone a desire to go after something that they probably can do without, as here's a good piece of advice to keep in mind. If it can't be used to advance my calling or help someone through, I can do without.

Day seventeen of handling media influences devotional plan, the scripture was based out of 1 Samuel 16:7 as there was no devotional. While what I learned from this verse of the day is it's not what is on the outside that counts, but it's what on the inside that count, as what's on the inside will manifest on the outward appearance. For example, you can have the most beautiful outward appearance and at the same time your insides look spiritually horrible. So, guard your heart by what you will allow you eyes to take into it.

Day eighteen of handling media influences devotional plan, there was no scheduled scripture readings for this day. As for the devotional, this was the key thought. "Play has its place, but we want to win this race." While what I learned from five of key points in this devotional was: First, "Technology and media aren't bad. We can choose to use it wisely or we're letting it use us. Second, "We should approach every relationship with the intention of showing that person Jesus and sharing God's love with them. Media can be a great tool to share Jesus." Third, "How we spend our time matters to God. God has given each of us exactly the same amount of time in a day. We should spend our time in a way that honors God." Fourth, "Media can be something we use to have conversations with others, to spend time with others, and to build healthy relationships. We will need to lead that to happen on purpose because it rarely happens on accident. We can make our time matter when we stay in control of it." Fifth, "The internet is a way of connecting people anonymously from all over the world. God can use that technology for His glory and our good. But like all other kinds of media, it can easily lead us away from living for Him. It can connect us to people and places we would never visit in real life and into danger." Overall, what this means to me is we don't have to allow technology and media to be use for bad, because it wasn't created to be bad as we can use it for good by using it wisely in a way that honors God, reaching out to people and staying in control of it.

Day nineteen of handling media influences
devotional plan, and the scripture was based out
on 1 Corinthians 9:24-27. What I learned is to be
disciplined like an athlete, so you can stay focus
on obtaining the goal. Training you're your body
to do what it should, so you can run with purpose
in ever step to win the eternal prize. Play by the
rules, so you won't be disqualified in the race by
pushing aside the distractions to put it on your
relationship with Jesus. Moreover, of what I
learned from three questions that the devotional
asked were: First, how does an Olympic champion
live differently from regular people? An Olympic
champion is set apart by his/her disciplines,
training and focus. Second, what are some ways
we should live differently as Christians because
we want to live for Christ? Spending time with
Jesus, as mentioned in the devotional video.
Going on missions trips, involving yourself with
outreaches, getting connected in a connect group,
volunteering in a local church, choosing good
media choices that will influence your
relationship with Jesus and inspire other to want
to have a relationship with Jesus. Third, what

does winning this spiritual race mean? To run with purpose in every step for the eternal prize that will never fade away, fighting the good fight of faith.

Day twenty of handling media influences devotional plan, the scripture was based out on 1 Corinthians 10:23. Now what this verse means to me is that even though we have free-will of choice, there are things that may look good, but they are neither good for us or beneficial for growth (whether its spiritual, mental or physical). For example, we don't have to say "anything goes" when it comes to our media choices and just let them feed us anything. But rather, we can make wise media choices that will help use to live well and to help others to live well also.

Day twenty-one of handling media influences devotional plan, the scripture was based out of Colossians 3:23-24 and what this means to me is to always do your best and put out good work no matter what's in your hand, being paid for it or not. Moreover, a servant is responsible to work what he's been given and to do his best with it.

Keeping in mind that you are working for Jesus through your master's work and we can expect a reward for our work done, as promotion comes from God not man.

Overall, in this Devotional on 'Handling Media Influences, Life Church TV wrote. "Media has influenced people since the beginning, not just in the technology age. The images we see, the music we hear, and all other varieties of media change our hearts and minds, which in turn, shape our attitudes and actions. This plan isn't a set of a new stricter rules or boundaries for us to follow. That would become just one more arbitrary moral code for kids to reject later in life. The goal is to reset our hearts and minds and focus them on our relationship in Christ." As Matthew 15:11, "It's not what goes into your mouth that defiles you; you are defiled by the words that come out of your mouth." In other words, in movie terms, it's not what you see that defiles you, but how it will use you to defile yourself. Don't be someone that sees, hears and does something bad from the content in a movie. As it all comes down to the standard that you want to set for yourself and others, while if you want to set a high standard for yourself you would make wise choices concerning your media content. Whereas, setting a low standard would conform to the world, not using common sense in the content fed on in a film, as religion has nothing to do with it. It's just that you want to protect yourself and keep yourself pure. So, one thing I can take away from this whole devotional is you can use your media choices to influence your relationship with God and to influence others to grow in their relationship with God or have a relationship with God.

Dr. Birgit Woltz said, "like dream work, cinema therapy allows us to gain awareness of our deeper layers of consciousness to help us move toward new perspectives or behavior as well as healing and integration of the total self." Later, she adds. "As observing helps us to "step back," the bigger picture becomes more obvious. This way, watching screen movies helps us learn to understand ourselves and others more deeply in the "big movie" of our habitual rigid, judgemental, or emotional filtering."

INT. MOVIE MENTORS - DAY

With this, having a favorite actor for watching movies can become like a movie-mentor to enhance the transformation process through cinema.

What makes an actor truly great? In a guide to acting performing, on the subject of character building and what makes a truly great actor. Lyn Guardian, a Guardian theatre critic and Dee Cannon who teaches at RADA. Wrote an article that answered that question, as here is what they said. "Great acting, like great writing, is often in the eye of the beholder, but audiences almost always know when they are in the presence of something special. Talent may be enough to get by on screen and TV, but with a few notable exceptions such as Kelly Reilly, the untrained actor often fares badly on stage. The performances that most often thrill us are those where instinct and technique are both in perfect balance but also opposition, and flamboyance and inner life collide head on, transforming feeling into thought and words. When this mixture of abandon and control ignites, what happens is as mysterious as alchemy; the theatre crackles; it leaves the spectator reeling. It makes you believe Eric Bentley's thesis that "the purpose of theatre is to produce great performances."

Lyn Guardian, a Guardian theatre critic and Dee Cannon who teaches at RADA wrote. "What makes an actor truly great? The actor's job is to bring a scripted character to life. RADA's Dee Cannon outlines 10 questions that must be addressed in order to create a fully-realised three-dimensional person."

Lyn Guardian and Dee Cannon writes. "The technique, however, will help you find a character, which in turn informs how you approach the text/script/written word. How do you bring the dialogue alive? How do you know what choices to make? The goal of a trained actor is to become a fully realised three-dimensional character, with a rich backstory. I must believe the character you play is truthful and not a cliche, a caricature, a thin external representation of someone who barely resembles a human being. I must believe what you say is real and that you're not reciting, spouting or commenting."

Through I love and would prefer the Meisner technique, with one reason being that it creates the actor externally and since the focus is for the actor to "get out of his head." I will attempt to ask the same questions , based around Stanislavski's acting technique and his seven questions that Lyn Guardian and Dee Cannon has adapted into ten key acting questions that every actor should answer to be a fully rounded and connected actor. As, the questions I will ask in each media analysis therapeutic session are the following: First, who is the (actor)'s character? Second, where is the (actor)'s character? Third, when is it? Fourth, where have the (actor)'s character just come from? Fifth, what does the (actor)'s character want? Sixth, why does the (actor)'s character want it? Seventh, why does the (actor)'s character want it now? Eighth, what will happen if the (actor)'s character doesn't get it now? Ninth, how will the (actor)'s character get what he wants by doing what? Tenth, what must the (actor)'s character overcome? Eleventh, does this actor fully transform into their character? Twelfth, does the actor show hard work, technique and good direction? Thirteenth, is the actor truthfully and emotionally connected? Lastly; fourteenth, is the audience, do I see none of this, but the fully realized three-dimensional character right in the truth of the moment? What I realized is this, if an actor makes you forget that they are acting and makes their character believable like its real life happening before your eyes then that actor succeed at doing their job as a great actor.

What I have done here is rephrased the question that I would have asked myself going into a role, and asked them in the study of another actor having gone into their row. Breaking down the process of being a fully rounded and connected actor, so I can take my response and the audience's response to the actor's character in the movie to see what makes this actor truly great. In other words, putting the question in to works.

Which asks, what makes an actor truly great?
Lyn Guardian and Dee Cannon, writes. "To fully
transform into a character, to be truthfully and
emotionally connected needs hard work,
technique, good direction. But the audience
should see none of this. They should see nothing
other than the fully realised three-dimensional
character right in the truth of the moment."

In which, in my journey to discovering how
cinema can help transform a life, it helps to have
a favorite actor to study to become a product of
their greatness. So, who is this great actor and
what are at least ten of their greatest films to
study in this?

So, who is this great actor and what are at least
ten of their greatest films to study in this? For me
its: Denzel Washington, Doug Jones, Jamie Foxx,
Leonardo DiCaprio, David Andrew Roy White, Will
Smith, James Cromwell, Johnny Depp, Andrew
Garfield, Ben Davies, Brad Pitt, Dane DeHaan,
Orlando Bloom, and Shia LaBeouf. Thus, while
embarking on this therapeutic film analysis, and

look back at the most memorable roles from
David Andrew Roy White, Will Smith, James
Cromwell and Johnny Depp's career as to be great
find a great actor I will study what and how they
became great then take what I have learned to
apply it to myself to make myself great.

Now, before studying an actor's greatness to
become great. You must learn where they come
from, and where they've been in their acting
journey. While I have researched the mini
biographies of David Andrew Roy White, Will
Smith, James Cromwell and Johnny Depp to
know them as a person over then just as an actor.

INT. DAVID A.R. WHITE - DAY

Starting off with David A.R. White, who suddenly
has inspired me to go back and add him to my list
of great actors. While "David A.R. White has been
a working actor, director and producer in Los
Angeles for twenty years. He was raised in a
small Mennonite farming community outside of
Dodge City, Kansas.At the age of 19, without
knowing anyone, David moved to LA, and only six

122

months after moving, landed a recurring role on the hit top 10, TV CBS sitcom, Evening Shade for four years. He played the best friend of Burt Reynolds's son. David then went on to guest appearances on such shows as: Coach, Saved by the Bell, Sisters, Melrose Place, Martial Law and many others.In 1999, produced and starred in his first feature length film The Moment After. The following year, he produced and starred in the groundbreaking Theatrical film, Mercy Streets opposite Eric Roberts, Stacy Keach and Cynthia Watros. David was nominated for a movie guide's "best actor" award for his dual roles in the film. Sony picked up both films for distribution. David kept producing and starring in films throughout the next several years.Early in 2006, David became a founding partner in the film distribution/production entity Pure Flix.Today, Pure Flix maintains its position as the number one Faith based studio, producing and distributing more films in this genre than any other studio. David also maintains his position as one of the most prolific actors/filmmakers in the faith based arena, as he writes, directs, produces and stars in many of the films.David has starred in close to 20 films. These films have sold millions of units all over the world. Some of his film credits include: SIX...the Mark Unleashed, The Moment After 1,2, In the Blink of an Eye, Hidden Secrets, Holyman Undercover, Run On, Marriage Retreat, Me Again and Jerusalem Countdown (based on the best selling book that sold over 2 million units.In 2012, David created, produced and starred in the UP original film, Brother White. He co-starred with Reginald Vel Johnson, Jackee, Victoria Jackson, academy award nominee Bruce Davison, Ray Wise and his lovely real life wife, Andrea Logan White. At the TCA's that year, David got rave reviews and became a darling, charming the critics with his real life Mennonite stories, (how he grew up just like the Amish, but WITH electricity.)For his performance in Brother White, David was named a finalist in 5th Annual Cable FAX Program Awards in the category of Best Actor/Actress - Family Friendly In September 2012, David starred in Encounter...Paradise Lost, the sequel to sleeper hit The Encounter, which David directed.In early

2013, David starred in the End times thriller
Revelation Road. In September, 2013, David's
sequel, Revelation Road 2 hit's stores
everywhere. He starred again with his wife, Brian
Bosworth, Ray Wise, Steve "Sting" Borden, and
Eric Roberts.In 2014, David produced and Co
Starred in the #1 independent movie of the year,
God's Not Dead. He star with Kevin Sorbo and
Dean Cain in Pure Flix's largest film to date, God's
Not Dead.The film co-starred Kevin Sorbo, Dean
Cain and Willie and Kory Robertson from Duck
Dynasty. Also in 2014, David helped produced a
new Sony Film, which he helped create with his
wife, Mom's Night Out. This movie starred
Patricia Heaton, Trace Atkins, Sean Astin and his
wife, Andrea Logan White.In 2014, David
released the third installment of his Revelation
Road Series...The Black Rider. In this installment,
he Starred opposite James Denton and Kevin
Sorbo. In 2015, David stars in the new
action/comedy dog movie Dancer and the Dame.
He stars opposite Billy Gardell. (Mike on Mike &
Molly)Also in 2015 David just released the follow
up to the God's Not Dead movie, Do You Believe.

In theaters now.David begins production on God's Not Dead 2 in May.David's passion has always been to further the Christian faith based genre with excellence in every way. His love for the Lord has governed the projects he attaches himself to. David and his wife live in Los Angeles with their three children." As posted on IMDb Mini Biography By, Pure Flix Entertainment.

INT. WILL SMITH - DAY

Reading Will Smith's Biography on IMDb.com, Tony Fontana writes. "Willard Carroll Smith, Jr. was born in West Philadelphia, Pennsylvania, the second of four children of Caroline (Bright), a school board employee, and Willard Carroll Smith, Sr., who owned a refrigeration company. He grew up in a middle class area in West Philadelphia called Wynnefield. Will attended the Overbrook High School located in the Overbrook section of Philadelphia, Pennsylvania. He got the nickname "Prince" because of the way he could charm his way out of trouble. Bright student Will also signed up with the high-status Julia Reynolds Masterman Laboratory and Demonstration

School in Philadelphia.Pursuing music, he met
Jeffrey A. Townes at a party and they soon began
performing together as "D.J. Jazzy Jeff and the
Fresh Prince". When the duo took off in
popularity, Smith made and spent a lot of money
on a house, cars and jewelry, leading to his
near-bankruptcy in his early twenties.Luckily, in
1989, he met Benny Medina, who had an idea for
a sitcom based on his life in Beverly Hills. Smith
loved the idea as did N.B.C. which put on the The
Fresh Prince of Bel-Air (1990). The plot was
simple - Will basically played himself; a
street-smart West Philly kid transplanted to
Beverly Hills. The series lasted six years. During
that time, he ventured into movies where the
critics took note of him in Six Degrees of
Separation (1993). With the success that came
with the action picture Bad Boys (1995), Will's
movie career was set. He had a huge Blockbuster
hit with Independence Day (1996), where he
plays the alien-battling Marine Corps Captain
Steven Hiller."

INT. JOHNNY DEPP - DAY

A mini biography of Johnny Depp from Hollywood Prayer Network as an author tells us. "John Christopher Depp II was born in Owensboro, Kentucky, the youngest of four children. His parents are Betty Sue Palmer, a waitress, and John Christopher Depp, a civil engineer. Depp moved frequently during his childhood. He and his siblings lived in more than 20 different places, eventually settling in Miramar, Florida in 1970. Depp began to play in various garage bands with he was 12. In 1978, Depp's parents divorced when he was 15. His mother remarried to Robert Palmer (died 2000), whom Depp has called "an inspiration to me". He dropped out of school when he was 15, and fronted a series of music-garage bands, including one named 'The Kids'. However, it was when he married Lori Anne Allison that he took up the job of being a ballpoint-pen salesman to support himself and his wife. A visit to Los Angeles, California, with his wife, however, happened to be a blessing in disguise, when he met up with actor Nicolas Cage, who advised him to turn to acting, which culminated in Depp's film

debut in the low-budget horror film, A Nightmare
on Elm Street (1984), where he played a teenager
who falls prey to dream-stalking demon Freddy
Krueger. In 1987 he shot to stardom when he
replaced Jeff Yagher in the role of undercover cop
Tommy Hanson in the popular TV series 21 Jump
Street (1987). In 1990, after numerous roles in
teen-oriented films, his first of a handful of great
collaborations with director Tim Burton came
about when Depp played the title role in Edward
Scissorhands (1990). Following the film's
success, Depp carved a niche for himself as a
serious, somewhat dark, idiosyncratic performer,
consistently selecting roles that surprised critics
and audiences alike. His movie roles include:
What's Eating Gilbert Grape (1993), Ed Wood
(1994), Don Juan DeMarco (1995), Donnie
Brasco (1997), Fear and Loathing in Las Vegas
(1998), Sleepy Hollow (1999), Pirates of the
Caribbean: The Curse of the Black Pearl (2003),
Secret Window (2004), Finding Neverland
(2004), Charlie and the Chocolate Factory
(2005), Sweeney Todd: The Demon Barber of
Fleet Street (2007), Public Enemies (2009), Alice

in Wonderland (2010), The Rum Diary (2011), Dark Shadows (2012), The Lone Ranger (2013), Into the Woods (2014) and Mortdecai (2015)." Michelle Regalado, who is currently an Entertainment Writer at Wall St. Cheat Sheet and graduate from NYU with a degree in Journalism. Wrote this about Johnny depp, and his ten greatest movies of all time. She says, "Johnny Depp has long since been a staple on the big screen, proving his versatility and fearlessness by taking on some of the most eccentric characters in film history.

INT. DENZEL WASHINGTON - DAY

Denzel Hayes Washington, Jr. was born on December 28, 1954 in Mount Vernon, New York. He is the middle of three children of a beautician mother, Lennis (Lowe), from Georgia, and a Pentecostal minister father, Denzel Washington, Sr., from Virginia. After graduating from high school, Denzel enrolled at Fordham University, intent on a career in journalism. However, he caught the acting bug while appearing in student drama productions and, upon graduation, he moved to San Francisco and enrolled at the American Conservatory Theater. He left A.C.T. after only one year to seek work as an actor. His first paid acting role was in a summer stock theater stage production in St. Mary's City, Maryland. For more information, go to http://www.imdb.com/name/nm0000243/bio?ref _=nm_ov_bio_sm

INT. DOUG JONES - DAY

Doug Jones is the youngest of four brothers, Doug Jones was born on the 24th May, 1960, in Indianapolis, Indiana, and grew up in the city's Northeastside. After attending Bishop Chatard High School, he headed off to Ball State University, where he graduated in 1982 with a Bachelor's degree in Telecommunications, with a minor in Theatre. He learned mime at school, joining a troupe and doing the whole white-face thing, and has also worked as a contortionist. After a hitch in theater in Indiana, he moved to Los Angeles in 1985, and has not been out of work since - he's acted in over 25 films, many television series. For more information, go to

http://www.imdb.com/name/nm0427964/bio?ref
_=nm_ov_bio_sm

INT. JAMIE FOXX - DAY

Jamie Foxx was born Eric Marlon Bishop in
Terrell, Texas, to Louise Annette Talley and
Darrell Bishop, who worked as a stockbroker and
had later changed his name to Shahid Abdula. His
mother was an adopted child. When her marriage
to his father failed, his maternal grandparents,
Mark and Estelle Talley, stepped in and, at age 7
months, adopted Jamie too. He has said that he
had a very rigid upbringing that placed him in the
Boy Scouts and the church choir. During high
school, he played quarterback for his high school
team and was good enough that he got press in
Dallas newspapers. He studied music in college.
He released a music album in 1994, "Peep This",
and sings the theme song for his 1999 movie, Any
Given Sunday (1999). However, in 1989, his life
changed when a girl friend challenged him to get
up onstage at the Comedy Club. In fact, he says he
took his androgynous stage name because he
learned that women got preference for mike time

on open stage nights. That led to his being cast in Roc (1991) and In Living Color (1990) and ultimately to his own WB network TV series. He has a daughter, Corinne Foxx, born in 1995, who lives with her mother. Jamie Foxx is an American actor, singer, and comedian. He won an Academy Award for Best Actor, BAFTA Award for Best Actor in a Leading Role, and Golden Globe Award for Best Actor in a Musical or Comedy, for his work in the 2004 biographical film Ray. The same year, he was nominated for the Academy Award for Best Supporting Actor for his role in the action film Collateral. Other prominent acting roles include the title role in the film Django Unchained (2012), the super villain Electro in The Amazing Spider-Man 2 (2014) and William Stacks in the 2014 version of Annie. Foxx also starred in the 1990-1994 sketch comedy show In Living Color and his own television show from 1996 to 2001, the sitcom The Jamie Foxx Show, in which he played Jamie King Jr. For more information go to http://www.imdb.com/name/nm0004937/bio?ref _=nm_ov_bio_sm

INT. LEONARDO DICAPRIO - DAY

Leonardo DiCaprio, Few actors in the world have had a career quite as diverse as Leonardo DiCaprio's. DiCaprio has gone from relatively humble beginnings, as a supporting cast member of the sitcom Growing Pains (1985) and low budget horror movies, such as Critters 3 (1991), to a major teenage heartthrob in the 1990s, as the hunky lead actor in movies such as Romeo + Juliet (1996) and Titanic (1997), to then become a leading man in Hollywood blockbusters, made by internationally renowned directors such as Martin Scorsese and Christopher Nolan.

Leonardo Wilhelm DiCaprio was born November 11, 1974 in Los Angeles, California, the only child of Irmelin DiCaprio (née Indenbirken) and former comic book artist George DiCaprio. His father is of Italian and German descent, and his mother, who is German-born, is of German and Russian ancestry. His middle name, "Wilhelm", was his maternal grandfather's first name. Leonardo's father had achieved minor status as an artist and distributor of cult comic book titles, and was even depicted in several issues of American Splendor, the cult semiautobiographical comic book series by the late 'Harvey Pekar', a friend of George's. Leonardo's performance skills became obvious to his parents early on, and after signing him up with a talent agent who wanted Leonardo to perform under the stage name "Lenny Williams", DiCaprio began appearing on a number of television commercials and educational programs. DiCaprio began attracting the attention of producers, who cast him in bit part roles in a number of television series. For more information go to http://www.imdb.com/name/nm0000138/bio?ref _=nm_ov_bio_sm

INT. JAMES CROMWELL - DAY

James Cromwell was born in Los Angeles but raised in Manhattan and educated at Middlebury College and Carnegie-Mellon University, James Cromwell, the son of famous film director John Cromwell, studied acting at Carnegie-Mellon. He went into the theater (like both his parents) doing everything from Shakespeare to experimental plays. He started doing television in 1974, gaining some notice in a recurring role as Archie Bunker's friend Stretch Cunningham on All in the Family (1971), made his film debut in 1976, and goes back to the stage periodically. Some of his more noted film roles have been in Revenge of the Nerds (1984), Star Trek: First Contact (1996) and the surprise classic about a charming pig, Babe (1995). He garnered some of the best reviews of his career (many of which said he should have received an Oscar) for his role as a corrupt, conniving police captain in L.A. Confidential (1997). For more information go to http://www.imdb.com/name/nm0000342/bio?ref _=nm_ov_bio_sm

INT. ANDREW GARFIELD - DAY

Andrew Russell Garfield was born in Los Angeles, California, to a British-born mother, Lynn (Hillman), and an American-born father, Richard Garfield. When he was three, he moved to Surrey, U.K., with his parents and older brother. Andrew was raised Jewish. He went to a private school, the City of London Freemen's School. He began acting in youth theatre productions while he was

still at school. At age 19, he went to the Central
School of Speech and Drama. His first
professional roles were on the stage and in 2005
he made his TV debut in the Channel 4 teen series
Sugar Rush (2005) in the UK. More TV work
followed (reaching a wider UK audience in a
two-part story in the third season of Doctor Who
(2005)), as well as a number of movie
appearances. Garfield played Eduardo in The
Social Network (2010) and Tommy in Never Let
Me Go (2010), two films that brought him to full
international attention. That same year, he was
cast as the title character in the reboot of the
Spider-Man film franchise, The Amazing
Spider-Man (2012). He reprised the role in the
sequel, The Amazing Spider-Man 2 (2014).
Garfield's upcoming roles include Ramin
Bahrani's 99 Homes (2014), with Michael
Shannon, and Martin Scorsese's Silence (2016),
opposite Adam Driver. For more information go to
http://www.imdb.com/name/nm1940449/bio?ref
_=nm_ov_bio_sm

INT. BEN DAVIES - DAY

Ben Davies has been acting since before he could walk. In fact, he was still in diapers when he appeared in his first national TV and print ad campaign. The scion of a successful model and an All American athlete, Ben was blessed with both striking physical features and a strong physical body. He was ranked the No. 1 high school decathlete in the nation by Track & Field News and went on to join the University of Florida Collegiate Track and Field team in his quest for Olympic gold. Multiple injuries, and a complex and risky surgery to repair a torn labrum in his shoulder, left Ben frustrated on the sidelines, wondering whether he would ever compete again; wondering if his athletic scholarship would even be renewed. It was at that low point that Ben got the call to audition for Sherwood Pictures' highly anticipated new film, Courageous. Ben booked the co-starring role of David Thomson and won the "Light In Hollywood Award" for that performance. Transitioning from athletics to full time acting, Ben has landed the lead role in ten feature films earning awards and nominations for 'Best Male

Actor" in three film festivals. Action roles requiring great athletic ability were always Ben's favorite until he was offered the male lead in I'm Not Ashamed, the true story of Rachel Scott at Columbine High School. "I spent over a year doing research on Rachel Joy Scott before playing Rachel's special friend Nathan Ballard including spending time with her mother, and even living homeless. Rachel was fearless, compassionate and loved people. I wanted my character and performance to highlight just how special and amazing Rachel was," Davies said. In addition to acting and athletics, Ben is also an award winning writer -winning inspirational screen play in the Nashville Film Festival 2014,. is a popular public speaker, and TV host. Ben enjoys sharing his faith and strives to be a role model. For more information go to http://www.imdb.com/name/nm3910031/bio?ref _=nm_ov_bio_sm

INT. BRAD PITT - DAY

Brad Pitt is an actor and producer known as much for his versatility as he is for his handsome

face, Golden Globe-winner Brad Pitt's most widely
recognized role may be Tyler Durden in Fight
Club (1999). But his portrayals of Billy Beane in
Moneyball (2011), and Rusty Ryan in the remake
of Ocean's Eleven (2001) and its sequels, also
loom large in his filmography. Pitt was born
William Bradley Pitt on December 18th, 1963, in
Shawnee, Oklahoma, and was raised in
Springfield, Missouri. He is the son of Jane Etta
(Hillhouse), a school counselor, and William Alvin
Pitt, a truck company manager. He has a younger
brother, Douglas (Doug) Pitt, and a younger
sister, Julie Neal Pitt. At Kickapoo High School,
Pitt was involved in sports, debating, student
government and school musicals. Pitt attended
the University of Missouri, where he majored in
journalism with a focus on advertising. He
occasionally acted in fraternity shows. He left
college two credits short of graduating to move to
California. Before he became successful at acting,
Pitt supported himself by driving strippers in
limos, moving refrigerators and dressing as a
giant chicken while working for "el Pollo Loco".
Pitt's earliest credited roles were in television,

starting on the daytime soap opera Another World (1964) before appearing in the recurring role of Randy on the legendary prime time soap opera Dallas (1978). Following a string of guest appearances on various television series through the 1980s, Pitt gained widespread attention with a small part in Thelma & Louise (1991), in which he played a sexy criminal who romanced and conned Geena Davis. This lead to starring roles in badly received films such as Johnny Suede (1991) and Cool World (1992). But Pitt's career hit an upswing with his casting in A River Runs Through It (1992), which cemented his status as an multi-layered actor as opposed to just a pretty face. For more information go to http://www.imdb.com/name/nm0000093/bio?ref _=nm_ov_bio_sm

INT. DANE DEHAAN - DAY

Dane DeHaan has made a formidable impression on film and television audiences and is one of the industry's most sought after actors of his generation. Dane is shooting Gore Verbinski's A Cure for Wellness and will soon begin production

starring in Luc Besson's Valerian. DeHaan has
recently finished shooting the indie, Two Lovers
and a Bear, directed by Kim Nguyen and starring
opposite Tatiana Maslany. Dane can soon be seen
in Weinstein Co's Tulip Fever, directed by Justin
Chadwick opposite Alicia Vikander, Christoph
Waltz, Zach Galifianakis and Jack O'Connell.
DeHaan can also most recently be seen in the
independent film Life, opposite Robert Pattinson
and directed by photographer and film director
Anton Corbijn. Based on a true story of James
Dean (DeHaan). DeHaan was also recently seen in
Sony Pictures' The Amazing Spider-Man 2 in the
role of Harry Osbourne opposite Andrew Garfield,
Emma Stone and Jamie Foxx. Directed by Marc
Webb, the action-adventure film was released on
May 2, 2014 and has grossed $694 million
worldwide to-date. In 2013, DeHaan was
nominated for a Gotham Award in the
"Breakthrough actor" category and at the
Hamptons International Film Festival in the
"Breakthrough Performer" category for his
leading role in Sony Picture Classics' critically
acclaimed beat generation film Kill Your Darlings.

Directed by John Krokidas, the film is loosely based on the life of poet Allen Ginsberg (Daniel Radcliffe). For more information go to http://www.imdb.com/name/nm2851530/bio?ref _=nm_ov_bio_sm

INT. ORLANDO BLOOM - DAY

Orlando Jonathan Blanchard Bloom was born in Canterbury, Kent, England on January 13, 1977. His mother, Sonia Constance Josephine (Copeland), was born in Kolkata, India, to an English family then-resident there. The man he briefly knew as his father, Harry Bloom, was a legendary political activist who fought for civil rights in South Africa. But Harry died of a stroke when Orlando was only four years old. After that, Orlando and his older sister, Samantha Bloom, were raised by their mother and family friend, Colin Stone. When Orlando was thirteen, Sonia revealed to him that Colin is actually the biological father of Orlando and his sister; the two were conceived after an agreement by his parents, since Harry was then-unable to have children. Orlando attended St. Edmunds School in

Canterbury but struggled in many courses because of dyslexia. He did embrace the arts, however, and enjoyed pottery, photography and sculpturing. He also participated in school plays and was active at his local theater. As a teen, Orlando landed his first job: he was a clay trapper at a pigeon shooting range. Encouraged by his mother, he and his sister began studying poetry and prose, eventually giving readings at Kent Festival. Orlando and Samantha won many poetry and Bible reciting competitions. Then Orlando, who always idolized larger-than-life characters, gravitated towards serious acting. At the age of 16, he moved to London and joined the National Youth Theatre, spending two seasons there and gaining a scholarship to train with the British American Drama Academy. Like many young actors, he also auditioned for a number of television roles to further his career, landing bit parts in British television shows Casualty (1986), Midsomer Murders (1997) and Smack the Pony (1999). He also appeared in the critically acclaimed movie Wilde (1997). He then attended the Guildhall School of Music and Drama. It was

there, in 1998, that Orlando fell three stories
from a rooftop terrace and broke his back. Despite
fears that he would be permanently paralyzed, he
quickly recovered and returned to the stage. As
fate would have it, seated in the audience one
night in 1999 was a director named Peter
Jackson. After the show, he met with Orlando and
asked him to audition for his new set of movies.
After graduating from Guildhall, Orlando began
work on the "Lord of the Rings" trilogy, spending
18 months in New Zealand bringing to life
"Legolas", a part which made him a household
name. Today, he is one of the busiest and most
sought-after actors in the industry. For more
information go to
http://www.imdb.com/name/nm0089217/bio?ref
_=nm_ov_bio_sm

INT. SHIA LABEOUF - DAY

Shia Saide LaBeouf was born in Los Angeles,
California, to Shayna (Saide) and Jeffrey Craig
LaBeouf, and is an only child. His mother is from
an Ashkenazi Jewish family, while his father has
Cajun (French) ancestry. His parents are

divorced. He started his career by doing stand-up comedy around places in his neighborhood, such as coffee clubs. One day, he saw a friend of his acting on Dr. Quinn, Medicine Woman (1993), and wanted to become an actor. Shia and his mother talked it over, and the next day, he started looking for an agent. He searched in the yellow pages, called one up, and did a stand-up routine in front of him. They liked him and signed him, and then he started auditioning. He is well known for playing Louis Stevens on the popular Disney Channel series Even Stevens (1999) and has won a Daytime Emmy Award for his performance. His best known role is as Sam Witwicky, the main protagonist of the first three installments of the Transformers series: Transformers (2007), Transformers: Revenge of the Fallen (2009) and Transformers: Dark of the Moon (2011). For more information go to http://www.imdb.com/name/nm0479471/bio?ref _=nm_ov_bio_sm

INT. FILM THERAPY & ANALYSIS - DAY

To demonstrate, allow me to put this knowledge

into practice by combining a movie analysis with cinema therapy and questions based on the Stanislavski's acting technique to relate to my favorite actor/movie-mentor, in an experimentation of my own.

Before I enter into the experimental portion of this senior paper, I want to sign an agreement between God and me.

Dialectical Behaviour Therapist's Agreement
Private & Confidential

I, Joel brown, agree to make every reasonable effort to conduct the Flixrapuetic Senior Paper as competently as possible. This includes my working within the yielding to the Holy Spirit (my counselor) and also abiding by the principles of the Bible. Beyond this, I can expect my counselor, God-the Holy Spirit to make His best effort to be helpful, comforting, to help me gain insight, and wisdom, and learn new skills and to teach me behavioural tools I need to deal more effectively with my current living situation. I will renew my mind, according to Romans 12:2 by the Word of God and gaining a new perspective. I also make it clear and understand that only God can "save," and can I solve the problems or change negative behaviors as the God-The Holy Spirit can solve my own problems. Also, it is God-the Holy Spirit who can help me to develop and practice new behaviors that may help me build a life worth living that aligns up with the Word of God, He can in the final analysis build my life for me and continue on with the process after, because I know He who started a good work in me will be faithful to complete it until the day of Jesus Christ. The wisdom of counselor/therapist, the Holy Spirit as guide is helpful and welcomed: to show me the way, as He walks me on the path that I am on. I trust my care is in staying with my counselor God-the Holy Spirit while He does what only He could do best in my walk with Him on the path of this flixrapuetic senior project. Moreover, Father-God, Jesus. You know me better then I, I forgive and release and let go the people who have done me wrong for they know not what they do. I give you total control over this senior paper as I enter in to it, yielding to the Holly spirit to be my counselor, healer, advocator, and comforter from start to finish. As I can't trust men, because they have failed me, but I know I can trust you. I ask that you not only make yourself more real to me through these titles, but to every single person who comes into contact with it, even if its just a glimpse and show every person how real you are as I pray that this will fall into even my enemies hands to fall in love with you so they can be forever transformed by your power that you are willing to use through cinema. While I pray that you will provide for me for the funds to be able to purchase the films, that I have chosen to watch for this paper that aren't supplied by Netflix. So take me, heal me, model me, change me and transform me into the image of Christ to draw men unto You for You to receive the Glory. Jesus name I pray, amen.

INT. STILL MINE/FILM ANALYSIS - DAY

The first media analysis therapeutic session was on analyzing your response to a film. In fact, I discovered, through the media analysis textbook. "The cinema is a work of art when motion conforms to a perceptible rhythm with pause and pace and where all aspects of the continuous image relate to the whole." Said Josef Von Sternberg, Director. Moreover, I also did a brief character study on a great actor as I watched the film.

Scan here to see the trailer of 'Still Mine.'

Now the film that I watched was titled, 'Still Mine (PG-13)' with James Cromwell. Furthermore; some key acting questions that every actor should answer to be a fully rounded and connected great actor, from studying a truly great actor: First, who is James Cromwell's character? Craig Morrison. Second, where is James Cromwell's character? Mainly living on a farm in the country, and visits a small town on occasion with the location being in St. Martins, NB and St. John, NB. Third, when is it? Based on a true story, so I would have to say around November 15, 2010. Fourth, where have James Cromwell's character just come from? In the beginning he started in a courtroom, driving in his pickup truck, farmhouse, chicken's pen, cow stable, he was in the fields some, building his new house, in a lawyer's office, hospital, the beach, church, and at a building permit office in the town. Fifth, what does James Cromwell's character want? He is devoted and determined to build a new house for his wife, as it's hard for him to release her into anyone else's care or not let her go. Sixth, why does James Cromwell's character want it? Out of love for his wife, as he wants to fulfill her dream of having a new home with a beautiful view on the beach. Seventh, why does James Cromwell character want it now? Things have begun to change as Irene has been showing signs of early dementia, and he wants to see a comfortable life with Irene in their final years in the new house rather than in the standard care of a nursing home. Eighth, what will happen if James Cromwell's character doesn't get it now? He would have built the new home regardless, or jail. Ninth, how will James Cromwell's character get what he wants by doing what? Go through the regulatory process of building permits, and win the legal battle for building the new house. Staying focused on his heart's desire, which is his wife Irene and the new house. Also, not letting anyone or anything stand in the way of seeing a comfortable life for the two in their final days. Tenth, what must James Cromwell's character overcome? Sacrifice, risk, not quitting and by being devoted and determined to the needs of his wife, as well as doing what it takes to meet the needs of the new house in the process of building it. Eleventh, does James Cromwell fully transform into his character? Yes, most defiantly as he had a great performance through out the whole film. In fact, another side of an IMDb movie reviewer backs me up on how great James Cromwell did with his character. Victoria said. "James is an ordinary man, and one we can all sympathize with. He's a good man, and you'll be rooting for him all the way. He's a man passionate about his beliefs, and his wife. I give all the credit to James Cromwell's fantastic performance. He's always been a great character actor, but never has he shined like this. He conveyed his emotions perfectly." As I do agree, James Cromwell knocked this ball out of the park and inspired me. Twelfth, does James Cromwell show hard work, technique and good direction? Yes, as he is a versatile method actor. Thirteenth, is James Cromwell truthfully and emotionally connected? Defiantly, as these make a performance believable and he was. Fourteenth, as the audience, I do see none of this, but the fully realized three-dimensional character right in the truth of the moment.

Moving on, to the analyzing my response to a film part and answering Dr. Culp's five movie critique questions.

On description, describing the story in objective terms. According to Netflix is, "When an elderly farmer tries to build a new home for his ailing wife, he faces the wrath of an overzealous government inspector.

On meaning, describing what the story/director is trying to say is still devoted and still determined.

On worldview, describing what rules/principles/values is in use by the characters. First, for rules, you should try to put yourself above the law or think that you are. Second, for principles mercy (Matthew 5:44), Contentment (Matthew 6:25), Hope (2 Corinthians 4:16-18), Christian Fellowship (2 Corinthians 6:14), Faith (Galatians 5:5-6), Perseverance (Philippians 3:13-14), Prayer (Philippians 4:6), Contemplation and reflection (Colossians 3:2-3), Forbearance (Colossians 3:12-13), Industriousness (2 Thessalonians 3:10), Fidelity (Hebrews 13:4), Evangelism (1 Peter 3:15), Loyalty (1 Peter 4:8), Generosity (1 John 3:17), and Love (1 John 4:16-19). Third, for the values were: marriage, family, their farm, neighbors, land and church.

Discussing the characters' behavior based upon biblical principles is Craig Morrison reminded me of Nehemiah and Irene Morrison reminded me of Ruth for her loyalty to her husband.

On interpretation, describing what the movie means to me personally is nothing shouldn't stop you from building what's on your heart to build as courage breeds honor when adversity comes up against you. Whereas; the unforgettable line for me was when Craig Morrison said, "age is just an abstraction, not a straight-jacket." What this means to me is you can't put a limit on age, as the scripture that follows this comes from 1 Timothy 4:12. Moreover, the other scriptures that was brought to my attention either during or after the movie were: Psalms 127:1; Proverbs 15:22; Ecclesiastes 4:9-12; Proverbs 22:3; Matthew 16:18; 1 Chronicles 29:28; Nehemiah 1-7 and Nehemiah 11-13.

Did I have any strong prejudices against this particular type of film? No, not really as the movie 'Still Mine' is a drama. Does this film have any special qualities that set it apart from other films of the same type? Yes, one of them was I liked how Craig Morrison wouldn't allow himself or anyone put a limit on him because of his age as he kept on building the house as you wouldn't normally see this type of drive by an elderly man in a movie. It breaks the stereotype.

How much did my personal subjective responses to the following aspects of the film affect my judgment: actors, treatment of sexual material, and scenes involving violence? My personal subjective responses to the aspects of the actors wasn't really affected that much as there wasn't really any violence in the movie except for a few curse words and the use of God's name in vain, but what I felt concerning the treatment of the brief nudity to provoke sex has just happen afterwards even though they didn't show a degrading scene as it could have had been done without and I started to get uncomfortable when Irene told Craig to take off his clothes. Can I justify the brief nudity in the film aesthetically, or are these scenes included strictly to increase box-office appeal? I can't really justify what I won't stand for in a film for the reason being if someone in the youth age range goes sees the movie, the director causes the minds that are weak to stubble into thinking a lustful thought as I totally believe that scene was included strictly to increase box-office appeal for the reason sex sell for Hollywood.

What were my expectations before seeing the film? How did these expectations influence my reaction to the film? At first, seeing it on Netflix I scrolled passed it as it didn't really look that interested. Then if wasn't till when I discovered James Cromwell was a Shakespearian-type actor and he was in the film is when I got interested enough to add it to my list of movies to watch as I read the brief synopsis to push it to the side. Later, reading the movie reviews on it helps me to form a better expectation around someone else's view on it as I ended up enjoying it.

Was my mood, mental attitude, or physical condition while seeing the movie less than ideal? I would have to say yes, it was less than ideal for my mood. For the reason, being that my reaction to the film affected going into it was some what of anxiety, but that went away as I began to get more calm and at peace the more I got into the film and enjoy the story being told. One thing I notice is that it helps to watch a film with an actor who you can call a favorite, because you have someone you can relate with as they inspire you to see an alternative perspective through their situation in the film. I can see how this can be a type of movie mentor type of relationship, with the actor from the screen.

The physical environment in which I watched the film was not really less than ideal, as using what I had to make the most of the experience of watching a film can make the difference in how this fact influence my perception. While I was still able to get out of the film, the insights and scriptures of need, to help influence a new perception to put to practice in everyday life.

Watched the movie on a laptop computer screen and listening to the sound come from a Altec Lansing multimedia computer speaker system, in which scenes I felt I lacked the intensity of involvement needed to enjoy the film most completely was the emotional scene and the scenes where the musical score was the strongest and the scenes with wide shots that showed beautiful landscapes. Now the scenes that works for the small-screen format would probably have to be the ones that were emotional, because it involved a close-up and that close-up puts the audience more on an intimate level with the character to involve you more into the character's story.

If you read reviews or scholarly essays before your viewing, what observations or opinions caught your interest? Having read reviews before viewing the movie 'Still Mine,' my observation on what caught my interest was seeing how other had rated the film as it had a 5-star rating and reading how the film impacted each person that watched it makes me want to watch it to have my own unique experience to see what I could get out of it. So, what is my own opinion after having seen the movie? The movie 'Still Mine' was based on a true story of the actual Craig Morrison as it has the potential to influence an audience to be devoted and determined at building whatever is on their heart to build in their own lives, while it told a dramatic story. Moreover, the actors did a great job as well as all the cinematic elements in the film. Last note is that I walked away feeling encouraged, and insight that gave me a new perspective on how I can see situations that happen in every day life.

INT. ME AGAIN/CINEMA THERAPY - DAY

My first cinema therapy session on transformation and renewal by watching the film, 'Me Again.'

Scan here to see the trailer of 'Me Again.'

As I prescribed a movie based on an issue and followed some guidelines for watching movies with conscious awareness in this order: First, start with a film that supports your treatment goal. Second, choose a film from film recommendations. Third, making sure to clarify intent when assigning a film in which might mistake the role identification. Fourth, familiarize yourself with Guidelines for watching films and discuss guidelines. Fifth, discuss the positive or negative reactions to film. Sixth, use material according to your theoretical orientation. Seven, afterwards reflect on evocative questions and answer them after watching the selected film as it does help to write down my answers.

First, do you remember whether your breathing changed throughout the movie? Yes, on the scene where an African American family was celebrating a hardworking mother's birthday as there was a burden that she saw was a privilege to carry for her family and I felt the love that the family was giving back to her. It was heart warming, and a bit emotional. Could this be an indication that something threw you off balance? Yes, as the character, Muriel (Della Reese) was a reminder of my mom and what she does for a living to care for our family for the past years out of love. In all likelihood, what affects you in the film is similar to whatever unbalances you in your daily life.

Second, ask yourself: If a part of the film that moved you (positively or negatively) had been one of your dreams, how would you have understood the symbolism in it? By reflecting on the setting, the positive/negative mood, what's happening, the interaction between the people in it, going to a trust-worthy Christian dream interpretation dictionary and the reference Bible scriptures that pertain to it.

Third, notice what you liked and what you didn't like or even hated about the movie. What I liked about the film was the story, the message, insights and the acting. On the other hand, what I disliked is seeing the different that each person carried in the various situations that Rich had a privilege to walk-in and share. Which characters or actions seemed especially attractive or unattractive to you? Rich's character seemed attractive to me, and the action of walking in someone else's shoes for the privilege of sharing their burden and the gift of love with them. Did you identify with one or several characters? Yes, one character and that was Rich.

Fourth, were there one or several characters in the movie that modeled behavior that you would like to emulate? Yes, there were two characters as they were Rich and Tony. Did they develop certain strengths or other capacities that you would like to develop as well? Yes, as I saw other capacities in both the character Rich and Tony that I would like to develop.

Fifth, notice whether any aspect of the film was

especially hard to watch. Could this be related to something that you might have repressed ("shadow")? Yes. The life of the starving fashion model with all the derogatory words of abuse, starving herself to look beautiful in front of the camera to the world, and as a result of her being a starving model she made herself sick to faint after becoming dizzy. Another character was Colin, for the reason that he represented that gets over-looked for his 'bad boy' and 'the kid your parents warned you about' image as he had a whole bunch of problems that no one, except for Rich wanted to take the time to share the gift of love with him just by talking and giving a wake-up call to restore him in the right direction. Uncovering repressed aspects of our psyche can free up positive qualities and uncover our more whole and authentic self.

Sixth, did you experience something that connected you to your inner wisdom or higher self as you watched the film? Yes I did, as I jotted down many insights and a scripture that I was made aware of during the movie. While the scripture and insights are: Proverbs 13:4, "...the desire of the diligent are fully satisfied." For the insights: Either you are something and feeling like nothing, or nothing and feeling like something. Old thing become new. Sometimes God will let you walk through blindness to change your perspective on what He wants you to experience from someone or something's life to not just be in a place where you can say you relate to them, but also so that you can see how much you're loved and be able to share that gift of love with others who are going through a similar situation. Another insight is that no matter where you are, your state of being, or view of life. There is always someone who is going through a situation that is much worse, with a much heavier burden that they are carrying. So, share your burden with others, because it's not a burden, it's a privilege. Another insight is what you feel is your choice as happiness is up to you regardless of the situation is in. Another insight is you have to fight your enemy and defeat him as that enemy is not people, things or situations, but you have always been the enemy. Moreover, it's not about being someone else, but being the best YOU—you could be. A another really good insight that I also took away from the film was your miracle could come in an amazing experience of seeing through the views of other people in their situations, and another way to look at it is that sometimes your miracle could be a wake-up call to show you that the best person to be is you to make you want the people who love you the most. Reflecting on this, I also got out that the most effective ministry is when you can walk in someone else's shoes to know how to relate with someone and have that common ground with to be able to reach out to them to share a gift of love the you once received. As through every person that Rich got to experience life in their shoes was missing love.

Seventh, many of the mentioned guidelines and insights turned out to be useful, as with the help of the Holy Spirit I am considering using them not only in "reel life" but also to adapt them to "real life" because they are intended to make me become a better observer.

Eighth, if the film had a unique message for you, what was it? I believe the message of the movie is it's not about being someone else, but being the best YOU—you could be and you are love wherever you are at in life. But, if there is one insight that was a recurring theme for me that I took away from the film the most would probably have to be to share the burdens of others, because it's not a burden, it's a privilege.

Ninth, what new ideas for new behaviors did you have? What you feel is up to you, happiness is your choice and it's not a burden, it's a privilege as the blessing is in the burden.

And finally the tenth question that I asked myself was, what other films can you identify that might take the discussion a step further? The other films that I can identify with, as I have already taken them to a discussion are: Brother White and Finding Normal.

INT. AFTER EARTH/FILM ANALYSIS - DAY

The second media analysis done as a therapeutic session was on analyzing the thematic elements of the film, 'After Earth' with Will Smith.

Scan here to see the trailer of 'After Earth.'

Concerning the Thematic Elements, I discovered a quote that gives and example of it by director and screenwriter, Paul Schrader. "Movies are about things—even bad movies are about things. Rambo III is about something. It has a theme, even if it doesn't want to have a theme . . . You have to know in some way what you are about to do. Even if that theme gets rerouted or ends up in subtext, somehow there has to be some sense of why you are doing this."

But before I get into analyzing the movie 'After Earth' on the thematic Elements, there are thirteen key acting questions that every actor should answer to be a fully rounded and connected great actor, from studying a truly great actor.

Who is Will Smith's character? General Cypher
Raige.

Where is Will Smith's character? Nova Prime has
become mankind's new home.

When is it? 1,000 years after earth.

Where have Will Smith's character just come
from? He returns from an extended tour of duty
to his estrangled family, and is going on a trip in a
spacecraft.

What does Will Smith's character want? While
Cypher goes on a mission and take his son Kitai
with him, as they encounter an asteroid along the
way. Whereas, their craft crash-lands on an
unfamiliar and dangerous earth as Cypher breaks
both of his legs to make him slowly dying in the
cockpit. This causes Cypher to put his trust in is
son Kitai to retrieve a rescue beacon to save both
of their lives, as Kitai ends up becoming a soldier
through this journey.

Why does Will Smith's character want it? He

wants it and Kitai to retrieve it to save both of their lives, and so they could be rescued.

Why does Will Smith's character want it now? For the reason of being on dangerous earth, and it being a life or death situation.

What will happen if Will Smith's character doesn't get it now? In the condition that Cypher is in, every minute looks like it brings him closer to death from the look of it as he is counting on Kitai to retrieve this rescue beacon and signal for help.

How will Will Smith's character get what he wants by doing what? All his character can do is remain calm from his current location without taking any painkiller to relieve his pains and becoming severely drowsy, as he guides Kitai on the mission to where the tail of the craft is that has to rescue beacon.

What must Will smith's character overcome? First, he must overcome the pain that he is experiencing in his legs and death. Second, trust in Kitai to follow his guidance and to receive this rescue beacon so that they both could be saved.

Does Will Smith fully transform into their character? Yes, both Will Smith and Jaden Smith did a phenomenal job at transforming themselves fully into their character. In this, I love an actor who can use their character also to take you on their journey, allow you to feel like you are fighting with them through their battles, shares their bruises with you and makes you want to celebrate with them in their victories. I think a performance like this wins an audience's heart, as you don't want the story or film to end and you feel like you can watch it all day. As, you feel like you're apart of the movie or story.

Will Smith showed hard work, technique and good direction in his performance as he was truthfully and emotionally connected. While as the audience, I saw none of this, but the fully realized three-dimensional character right in the truth of the moment.

Now, answering Dr. Culp's five movie critique questions.

On description, describing the story in objective

terms, usually in one to two paragraphs is "A crash landing leaves Kitai Raige and his father Cypher stranded on Earth, a millennium after events forced humanity's escape. With Cypher injured, Kitai must embark on a perilous journey to signal for help." As, it tells on IMDb.com.

On meaning, describing what the story/director is trying to say is fear is not real as it's a choice. While the message of the film is "Kitai's journey teaches him that only by facing only by facing your fears can you realize your full potential. His father teaches that although danger may be real, fear is just a state of mind. A cautionary tale about taking care of our planet (destroyed by years of pollution and war) is migrated by the eye-catching new planet of 1,000 years in the future." Says, Andrea Beach with common sense media.

On worldview, describing what principles/values is in use by the characters or in the plot. There is bravery, sacrifice, overcoming fears, strong family warmth and bonding, strong role models, and positive life lessons learned.

Discussing the characters' behavior based upon biblical principles Cypher and Kitai both showed humility (1 peter 3:8), hope (2 Corinthians 4:16-18), father-son bonding (2 Corinthians 6:14), love (1 John 4:16-19), contemplation and reflection (colossians 3:2-3), perseverance (philippians 3:13-14), trusting others to what you aren't able to do at the given moment (1 Peter 4:8), and edification (ephesians 4:29).

On interpretation, describing what the movie means to you personally is although it makes a statement that fear is not real and it's a choice. This film teaches how its only by facing your fears where you can realize your final potential. Moreover, fear is just a state of mind as when I watch this film it was brought to my attention that fear can also mean False Evidence Appearing Real. While the Bible scriptures that this film lead me to were: Hebrews 11:8, Genesis 12; 13; 15, Genesis 12:4 as I saw how Abraham was following God one yes at a time through this film.

On Theme and Focus, what the film's primary focus was between an emotional effect and structure. While on the basis of my decision, the film is structured around an emotional effect, giving it a feeling of fearing your fears that it attempts to convey as those were the emotional effects that I felt while watching this film.

The other one primary focus that the film seems to be built upon is a structure, for the reason of the qualities that was contributed to the special look of the film was futuristic and some of the aspects of the earth looked like it was still preserved and taken care of even thought it was invaded by aliens as well as destroyed from the flashbacks that the movie showed.

On Identifying the Theme. Although a director may attempt to do several things with a film, one goal usually stands out as most important. Deciding which of the following the director's primary aim was, and giving reasons for my choice. The director provides insight into a growth experience, the special kinds of situations and conflicts that cause important changes in the characters involved as the decision that the character made could mean life or death.

Now another item that seemed important enough to qualify as secondary aims was that the director provided insights into human nature and demonstrated what human beings in general are like during the time period of the film.

On Evaluating the Theme, the film's basic appeal was to the intellect as it aimed primarily at the heart. For an example, Kitai sets out for a journey that teaches him that it is only by facing his fears can he realize his full potential as I feel that this brings the audience along with the character, because we experience this with him through our emotions and the emotions are connect with the heart. Whereas, the story teach a life lesson that we walk away having had learned something from.

In which, this caused my statement of the film's theme and focus to do a really great job at standing up to it after I have thoroughly analyzed all elements of the film. More in this, to what degree is the film's theme universal? First, "A universal theme is one of lasting interest, one that is meaningful not just to people here and now but to all human beings in all ages. Second, "...films have universal appeal because of the real and powerful characters portrayed, the heroic struggles waged for human dignity, and the artistry with which both films were made (Media Analysis 40)." While the characters were believable, and pulled us in to the story as the audience got to learn a life lesson about family bonding and facing one's fears to realize your full potential. And I would say that the theme is relevant to my own experience, because we all have fears that we have to face and overcome in life. How? General Cypher Paige explained that "fear is not real ... it's a choice," and the film illustrated for me how God will walk with you in following Him one "yes" at a time, even if at some point you get disconnected for the source, his will bring the right way back to your remembrance to keep you on the right path. Thus, I think the film makes a significant statement and it's significant for the reason that there is a life lesson in the movie.

Furthermore, the film's theme is philosophically interesting and defending my decision is, because the film was educating just as much as it was entertaining to watch. As the "film attempts to make a significant statement, that statement should be neither boring nor self-evident but should interest or challenge us" (Media Analysis 41). And this film did exactly what the director had set out to do with it, challenging an audience in the area of family bonding and overcoming fears.

In fact, I think this film has the potential to become a classic for the philosophical insights that were in it. In the Media Analyzes textbook, it explains my point by saying. "There is, of course, no real formula for the classic film, the kind we never grow tired of seeing. The classic film has a sense of rightness to it time and time again. Its power does not fade or diminish with the passing years but actually grows because of its universal themes and motifs" (41). While I think that it has the potential to still be watched as I can see a parent passing this film down to their kids and watching it twenty years from today for the life lessons that were demonstrated in the film.

INT. GRACE UNPLUGGED/CINEMA THERAPY - DAY

Watching the film 'Grace Unplugged' I did my second cinema therapy session, on transformation and renewal.

 Scan here to see trailer for 'Grace Unplugged.'

As I prescribed a movie based on an issue and followed some guidelines for watching movies with conscious awareness in this order: First, start with a film that supports your treatment goal. Second, choose a film from film recommendations. Third, making sure to clarify intent when assigning a film in which might mistake the role identification. Fourth, familiarize yourself with Guidelines for watching films and discuss guidelines. Fifth, discuss the positive or negative reactions to film. Sixth, use material according to your theoretical orientation. Seven, afterwards reflect on evocative questions and answer them after watching the selected film as it does help to write down my answers.

Do you remember whether your breathing changed throughout the movie? Yes, it would have had been when Grace was coming home to her new apartment in LA with some groceries in her hands and noticed that the door to her apartment was slightly cracked. Thinking someone had broke in, as she walked inside startled and then Quentine suddenly came up behind her to accidently frighten her. Could this be an indication that something threw you off balance? It is possible, reflecting on this type of indication. In all likelihood, what affects you in the film is similar to whatever unbalances you in your daily life.

Ask yourself: If a part of the film that moved you (positively or negatively) had been one of your dreams, how would you have understood the symbolism in it? I would reflect on the particular part of the dream, going through it to break each item and its action in the dream. Studying the important symbols through a dream dictionary and the Bible to understand it's meaning, as the parts of the film that had been one of my dreams was the bus.

Notice what you liked and what you didn't like or even hated about the movie. I liked how Grace fought to pursue her dreams as a singer, than laid it down for God only to get it back, but for His glory. Which characters or actions seemed especially attractive or unattractive to you? The actions that seemed unattractive were when Jay Grayson was found out that he's two-faced to use Grace to advance his and someone else's agenda, S Music seemed very shady selling music for profit instead of passion and Ranae Taylor tried to convince Grace that her body was the best asset and to treat it like currency in selling it to the public as advice she gave to help Grace advance her career. Did you identify with one or several characters? There were two characters that I identified with, as they were Quentin and Grace.

Were there one or several characters in the movie that modeled behavior that you would like to emulate? The character that I would like to emulate for the reason of the behavior that he modeled would have to be Quentin, because he was playing the background as an intern while he was being a light for Grace to encourage and influence her faith. Moreover, they both did develop certain strengths and other capacities that I would like to develop as well.

Notice whether any aspect of the film was especially hard to watch. This would probably be when Jay was double-crossing Grace, as the audience probably knew there that something wasn't right about him and wanted Grace to found out soon before she gets hurt. While this could be related to something that someone might have repressed toward me. As I am aware of uncovering repressed aspects of our psyche can free up positive qualities and uncover our more whole and authentic self.

Thus, I did experience something that connected me to my inner wisdom or higher self as I watched the film? As, that would be: First, you can obtain everything you want in life and still be searching for something that you might feel you are missing. Second, know if you are living for yourself or God, own your own faith and know what you want before you go after your dreams.

Third, theirs is a lot of jealousy in Hollywood while the people who you think are your friends for helping prepare you for success could also be your enemies, plotting your fall. Fourth, in the Hollywood business, you have to know that game and how to play with the player without compromising in your Christian beliefs. While I am considering using these insights not only just in "reel life" but also in adapting them to "real life" because I do agree on them being intended to make me become a better observer in life and career endeavors.

If the film had a unique message for you, what was it? IMDB puts it this way, "Would you give up what you need to get everything you want? Sometimes, chasing your dreams leads you right to where you belong." While to add to this, I believe this would be to own your own faith in any sphere of influence that you embark in, or you might be sold and owned into slavery. As the scriptures that were brought to my attention were: Acts 7:9 and Romans 12:2.

What new ideas for new behaviors did you have?

First, do not conform to the world, but be transformed by the renewing of the mind. Second, do unto others, as you would like done unto you. Third, influence them before they influence you. Lastly, 'Never Say Never' and 'This Is It' are other films that I can identify with that might take the discussion a step further.

INT. OWD BOB/FILM ANALYSIS - DAY

The third media analysis done as a therapeutic session was on analyzing the fictional and dramatic elements of the film, 'Owd Bob' with James Cromwell.

Scan here to see the trailer for 'Owd Bob.'

While an inspirational quote on the fictional and dramatic elements by director, Alfred Hitchcock is when he said. "I don't want to film a "slice of life" because people can get that at home, in the street, or even in front of the movie theater . . .. Making a film means, first of all, to tell a story. That story can be an improbable one, but it should never be banal. It must be dramatic and human. What is drama, after all, but life with the dull bits cut out?"

Thirteen key acting questions that every actor should answer to be a fully rounded and connected great actor, from studying a truly great actor.

184

Who is James Cromwell 's character? Adam
McAdam.

Where is James Cromwell 's character? Isle of
Man, as it looked like it was in the United
Kingdom.

When is it? The time is somewhere around 1938.

Where have James Cromwell 's character just
come from? Adam McAdam is always working,
doing things around the farm and at night he
reads a book.

What does James Cromwell 's character want?
Adam McAdam wants his dog and to win the prize
in an annual sheep-herding contest, which is the
highlight of the year in the North Country.

Why does James Cromwell 's character want it?
Adam McAdam wants it, because the dog who
wins three competitions in a row wins the
Shepherd's Cup outright, which has never yet
happened.

Why does James Cromwell 's character want it
now? The win will bring Adam McAdam fame, as

the Shepherd's Trophy will give him something to be proud of.

What will happen if James Cromwell's character doesn't get it now? Adam McAdam would probably still be sarcastic and angry towards his neighbors.

How will James Cromwell 's character get what he wants by doing what? Adam McAdam will get what he wants by training his dog, and competing in the annual sheep-herding contest.

What must James Cromwell 's character overcome? Adam McAdam will have to overcome complications between his neighbors, the other dog contenders, his violent dog who herds sheep by brute force, and dealing with David being a mediator of peace between him and the Moores.

James Cromwell does fully transform into the character Adam McAdam, as he also shows hard work, technique and good direction. In fact, James Cromwell truthfully and emotionally is connected with the character of Adam McAdam. While as the audience, I do see none of this, but

186

the fully realized three-dimensional character right in the truth of the moment.

Now, answering Dr. Culp's five movie critique questions.

On description, describing the story in objective terms is its about two sheep shearing dogs, Zac and Owd Bob. Zac kills sheeps and Owd Bob gets blamed for it, as Owd Bob just about gets put down until Maggie creates a diversion for David to rescue him. When the people of the town caught up with David and Owd Bob, Adam McAdam fesses up on Owd Bob not killing the sheep, but it being Zac as Adam ends up putting his dog down to make peace with the town people. On Common Sense Media by Brian Costello, writes. "After the death of his parents to a drunk driver, American teenager David Roberts is sent to live with his grandfather (James Cromwell), a sheepherder on the Isle of Man. David's grandfather is an embittered widower who lives in conflict with neighbors who think his sheepdog Zac is responsible for the recent killings of sheep, and maintains a lengthy grudge with his neighbors, the Moores. Nonetheless, David tries to make the best of his new life, helping his grandfather out with the chores, and befriending the Moores' teenage daughter Maggie (Jemima Looper). David befriends the entire Moore family, including their beloved sheepdog, Owd Bob. It's up to David to try and mediate peace between the Moores and his grandfather, even as a tragedy befalls the Moores, the men of the village try to ascertain whether it's Zac or Owd Bob who is killing the sheep, and David's grandfather -- engulfed in deep sorrow over the loss of his family -- believes himself unfit to take care of David."

On meaning, describing what the story/director is trying to say is you can get over the lose of loved ones and set aside past grievances with loved ones still living as you can also make the best out of a difficult situation.

On worldview, describe what principles are in use by the characters or in the plot. Do unto others as you would like them to do unto you, love your neighbor as yourself, comfort others in time of grief and you will then be comforted in yours, and don't bare false witness on your neighbor.

Discussing the characters' behavior based upon biblical principles is: Christian fellowship (2 corinthians 6:14), edification (ephesians 4:29), contemplation and reflection (colossians 3:2-3), forbearance (colossians 3:12-13), industriousness (2 thessalonians 3:10), hospitality (Hebrews 13:2), Sympathy (1 peter 3:8), generosity (1 john 3:17), and love 1 john 4:16-19).

On interpretation, describe what the movie means to me personally. Letting go of something or doing the right thing will hurt you, but might be considered the best thing to do in the situation to keep peace and order with people in the community.

Now analyzing the fictional and dramatic elements on the story, 'Owd Dog'.

How does the film stack up against the five characteristics of a good story? The film is: First, unified in plot. For an example, "A unified plot focuses on a single thread of continuous action, where one event leads to another naturally and logically" (Media Analysis 47). "Second, the story is credible as I first thought that 'Owd Dog' was true. For an example, "To become fully involved in a story, we must usually be convinced that it could be true" (Media Analysis 47). Third, the story was somewhat interesting as there was sometimes during the movie where my attention wanted to drift. For an example, "An important requirement of a good story is that it capture and hold our interest" (Media Analysis 49). Fourth, the story is both simple and complex. For an example, "A good film story must be simple enough so that it can be expressed and unified cinematically" (Media Analysis 52). Fifth, the story handles emotional material with restraint. For an example, "A strong emotional element or effect is present in almost any story, and film is capable of manipulating our emotions" (Media Analysis 53). While the actors really helped to make it a good story, and to keep the audience's interest in the film.

How well is it unified in plot? "The fictional film generally has a plot or storyline that contributes to the development of that theme. Therefore, the plot and the events, conflicts, and characters that constitute it muse be carefully selected and arranged so that their relationship to the theme is clear" (Media Analysis 46). Based on this information and the movie, I would say that the plot is good as far as being unified enough that you can tell that it revolved around two sheep shearing dogs.

What makes the story credible? The specific scenes I can pick out to illustrate the kinds of truth that are stressed by the film for: objective truth, which follows the observable laws of probability and necessity. Would be when Maggie's mother dies of an illness, Adam's dogs have to be put down for killing sheep, and Adam wins a trophy at the sheep shearing contest. On the other hand: subjective, irrational, and emotional inner truths of human nature. For an example, "The good guy always wins, and true love conquers all. But in a very special way, these stories are also believable, or at least can be made to seem so, because they contain what might be called internal truths—beliefs in things that are not really observable but that seem true to us because we want or need them to be" (Media Analysis 47). The dogs really played the protagonist and the antagonist, as when Adam's dog came back with the blood around his mouth the audience didn't want to believe what was true about the dog killing sheep and neither did the Adam's character want to believe it with him leading us through his dialogue line, "probably killing rabbit. Another incident is when Owd Bob had been accused for killing the sheep Zac had originally had killed and was about to be put down for something that he didn't do, as the audience didn't want to believe it with having had seen Zac eating a dead sheep. Lastly, the final thing I picked out to illustrate the kinds of truth that are stressed by the film is for the semblance of truth that's created by the filmmaker. For an example, this is a special kind of truth that filmmakers are also capable of creating. "In such films, truth depends on the early and thoroughly convincing establishment of a strange or fantastic environment, sense of another time, or unusual characters, so that we are caught up in the film's overall spirit, mood, and atmosphere" (Media

Analysis 48). While this would have been convincing art through the props, out-door landscape and the in-door scenery.

What makes the film interesting? The fact that the story revolved around two sheep shearing dog, as Zac was the antagonist and Owd Dog was the protagonist is what made this film interesting to me. Where are its high points and its dead spots? I assume that the film's dead spots were in the beginning, until Zac returned to Adam twice with blood around his mouth as this raised suspense and interest that held the audiences attention to want to continue watching the film to find out why this dog was coming back with blood around his mouth. What makes you bored by the film as a whole or by certain parts? "Some of us may be interested only in fast-paced action/adventure films. Others may be bored by anything without a romantic love interest at its center. Still others may be indifferent to any story that lacks deep philosophical significance" (Media Analysis 49). The thing only thing that would make this film boring is that there was either little or any exciting action that created interest, and there was hardly any insight to feed the audience to give them a sense that they learned something from the film. But to capture and maintain the audiences interest there was the suspense with Zac the dog, having blood around his mouth.

As, I would think that this film is a satisfying blend of simplicity and complexity. For the reason being, "the story's action or theme must usually be compressed into a unified dramatic structure that requires about two hours to unfold" (Media Analysis 52). While it was limited and had a simple theme, as it took a different approach in telling a story about sheep shearing dogs.

How well is the length of the story suited to the limits of the medium? The film does a god job at focusing on the people's life with the two sheep shearing dogs, which is better suited for the cinema. Is the film a simple formula that allows you to predict the outcome at the halfway point, or does it effectively maintain suspense until the very end? The film Owd Dog was a simple formula that allows the audience to predict the outcome at

the halfway point, but when Owd Dog gets
accused for what Zac has been doing to the sheep
makes you want to keep watching it to see which
dog is going to get put down and how the film will
end. If the ending is shocking or surprising, how
does it carry out the tendencies of the earlier
parts of the story? The film is kind of surprising
as Adam McAdam is seen with David and the rest
of the community at a sheep shearing even, but
Adam seems to have found happiness and peace
with the town as it looked like he got to keep Owd
Dog. This carries out the tendencies of the earlier
parts of the story by not just giving it a much
happier ending for the tragic start, but allowing
Adam to still have his heart's desire which was a
dog when the audience know he probably didn't
deserve it.

Where in the film are implication and suggestion
effectively employed? I would say when Zac the
dog starts returning to Adam's farmhouse with
blood around his mouth, then we are given an
indication and suggestion that something is up as
there's more to the story. Where is the film simple
and direct? Now, "a story should be simple

enough to be told in the time period allotted for it's telling" (Media Analysis 52). So, I think that this film was simple and direct in the beginning as it showed the audience what life on a farm might look like and it introduced to us sheep shearing to give us a direct background before taking us through the story.

Is the view of life reflected by the story simple or complex? With in the limits of being simple, "a good story must also have some complexity, at least enough to sustain our interest" (Media Analysis 52). So, I would say that the story was complex in its view of the life that was reflected. What factors influenced your answer? For example, Adam accepting David to stay at his farmhouse for the Summer to help out with chorus and bond with. David's a mediator of peace between Adam and his neighbors. David also becomes close friends with Maggie, as he comforts her through her grieving of her mother's death and Maggie's father takes David under his wing. There's also the work on the farm, and the sheep-shearing contest. In fact, "A filmmaker's communication techniques must also be a satisfying blend of simplicity and complexity. Most often, the filmmaker must communicate simply, directly, and clearly to all viewers. But to challenge the minds and eyes of especially perceptive viewers, he or she must also communicate through implication and suggestion, leaving some elements open to interpretation" (Media Analysis 52). And I felt like this film did that for me.

How honest and sincere is the film in its handling of emotional material? I would say that this film did a good job on handling honesty and sincere emotional material, as I felt that their could have been a little more upon Maggie's mother being diagnosed with a life threatening illness and during the funeral. But the actor did their best, for the time period that they were in. As far as I can remember, there weren't really any emotional effects overdone in the film. While there wasn't really any scenes that made me laugh when I was supposed to cry, as I take it that the filmmaker did a good job at exercising restraint. Where is understatement used? Meaning, "In understatement the filmmaker downplays the emotional material, giving it less emphasis than the situation would seem to call for" (Media Analysis 54). So, I would say the understatement is used while the Maggie's mother is dying in her beat, at her funeral, when David and Maggie are standing on top the watch tower, during other grieving scene, in the bar scenes with Adam and once Owd Bob has been accused of killing sheep.

Moving on, to the Significance of the Title, 'Owd Bob'.

Why is the title appropriate? For once, the thing that sticks out to me the most is the spelling. As you would think how it sounds is like, "Odd Bob" when it is just how they would spell "Old Bob" back in that time period. Another this is, that it tells you the story it about a dog. In fact, it does just that for the audience... grabs them to want to see what it's about, whether looking at the trailer or reading a brief synopsis on it. Concerning the significance of the title, "The importance of a suitable title is not overlooked by writers like Neil Simon, who says, "When looking for a fun title, you're looking for something that's going to grab them . . .. When I don't have it, I'll work very hard because it's as important to me as writing the first scene, getting the title. I feel comfortable if it sounds right" (Media Analysis 55). What does it mean in terms of the whole film? Soon or later, "In most films, we can understand the full significance of the title only after seeing the film. In many cases, the title has one meaning to a viewer before seeing the film and a completely different, richer, and deeper meaning afterward" (Media Analysis 55).   We figure out that movie is about an old sheep shearing dog that gets accused of killing sheep and saved from being put down as it's apart of the story.

However, I think that there is two different levels of meaning that are expressed in the title, one being the dog is "Owd" (that's how they would probably spell it back then) and the dog's name is "Bob." As how each level would apply to the film as a whole is by giving us a hint that the dog is old and his name is Bob. While another level is that the title tells us what the story is about.

If the title is ironic, what opposite meanings or contrasts does it suggest? In which, "Titles are often ironic, expressing an idea exactly the opposite of the meaning intended," (Media Analysis 55). The opposite meanings I thought it suggested was "Odd Bob," as it didn't think it really meant "old" until it was told to the audience through the film.

If you recognize the title as being an allusion, why is the work or passage alluded to an appropriate one? For the reason, to remind us of a children's book by English author Alfred Ollivant. Who wrote, 'Owd Bob: The Grey Dog of Kenmuir, also named Bob, Son of Battle for US editions. In which, "...many titles allude to mythology, biblical passages, or other literary works. For example, the title All the King's Men (Figure 3.10) is taken from "Humpty Dumpty" and reminds us of the nursery rhyme, which provides a nutshell summary of the plot" (Media Analysis 55). As, it's possible that the film wanted to stay true to the book and at time same time provide a nutshell summary of the plot.

If the title calls your attention to a key scene, why is that scene important? The scene that the title calls my attention to is at the end, when Adam confesses that it wasn't Owd Bob who killed all the sheep, but Zac his dog. Maybe, this is important to me, because it's a reminder of the name. Thus, "some titles may call attention to a key scene that becomes worthy of careful study when we realize that the title of the film has been taken from it. Although the title seldom names the theme (as it does in Sense and Sensibility and Good Will Hunting), it is usually an extremely important clue in identifying it" (Media Analysis 56). Which would explain why the title can be related to the theme, as after watching the film it made me think about the possible meaning of the title and even Goggle it to find the children's book that tributes to the title.

Move on, to the Dramatic Structure of 'Owd Bob'.

Does the film use linear (chronological) or nonlinear structure? With Linear (chronological) meaning coming from the, "Legendary screenwriter Ernest Lehman (North by

Northwest) described films hav- ing the linear, or chronological, structure in terms of acts: "In the first act, who are the people, what is the situation of this whole story? Second act is the progression of that situation to a point of high conflict and great problems. And the third act is how the problems and the conflicts are resolved" (Media Analysis 56). In which, would lead me to have to say that this film uses linear structure to tell the story. If it begins with expository material, does it capture your interest quickly enough, or would a beginning "in the middle of things" be better? The film does begin with expository material, introducing the characters, showing some of their interrelationships and place them within a believable time and place as it did catch my interest. At what point in the story could an in medias res beginning start? For an example, "A story that begins in medias res (a Latin phrase meaning "in the middle of things") opens with an exciting incident that actually happens after the complication has developed" (Media Analysis 56). As, this would probably be seen best, in the beginning, while I can see maybe a flashback to make it more interesting. For instance, if flashbacks are used, their purpose and how effective are they? "The necessary expository information is filled in later as the situation permits, through such means as dialogue (characters talking about the situation or events that led to the complication) or flashbacks (sequences that go back in time to provide expository material)" (Media Analysis 56). Now, the purpose of using a flashback would be to grab the audience's interest early with a reflection of Adam's good or bad memory during his grieving, pulling the audience in more as the story spreads. Moreover, "providing exposition is not the only function of flashback. The use of visual flashback gives a filmmaker great flexibility. By using flashback, the filmmaker can present information as he or she desires, when it is most dramatically appropriate and powerful or when it most effectively illuminates the theme" (Media Analysis 57). While this would explain, why flashbacks are effective in films as it's like a sneak peek.

Moving on, to the Conflict of the film 'Owd Bob'.

As, I'll start off this section with something that inspires me. In his essay "Why Do We Read Fiction?" Robert Penn Warren observes, A story is not merely an image of life, but of life in motion . . . individual characters moving through their particular experiences to some end that we may accept as meaningful. And the experience that is characteristically presented in a story is that of facing a problem, a conflict. To put it bluntly: No conflict, no story. Conflict is the mainspring of every story, whether it be told on the printed page, on the stage, or on the screen. It is the element that really captures our interest, heightens the intensity of our experience, quickens our pulses, and challenges our minds" (Media Analysis 59). Which makes you think, conflict if probably the most import part of a film, because it demands our attention and makes us more interested in watching the film just so we can see how it will turn out. As someone once said, you wouldn't stop by a puddle just to see two people waddling in it, but you would stop to see how those two people would get themselves out of that messy puddle. The conflict is the mess of the story, and the solution is the message that drives it to the heart of the audience.

Now identifying the major conflict, would probably be when the dog, Zac, returns to Adam with blood around his mouth as the dog probably did this a number of times.

Is the conflict internal (individual against self), external, or a combination of the two? Is it primarily a physical or a psychological conflict? Meaning, "In its simplest form, an external conflict may consist of a personal and individual struggle between the central character and another character ... An internal conflict centers on an interior, psychological conflict within the central character" (Media Analysis 60). Thus, I'm persuaded that the conflict is a combination of being internal and external, because Adam had his own conflict as the neighbors had their own conflicts.

Express the major conflict in general or abstract terms (for example, brains versus brawn, human being[s] against nature), as human beings against nature would be the major conflict in abstract terms.

How is the major conflict related to the theme? "The major conflict is of great importance to the characters involved, and there is some worthwhile and perhaps lasting goal to be gained by the resolution of that conflict. Because it is highly significant to the characters, and because significant conflicts have important effects on people and events, the major conflict and its resolution almost always bring about an important change, either in the people involved or in their situation" (Media Analysis 60). In comparison, the theme is the dogs and the conflict is the sheep being killed, as they are both related for them both taking place on a farm, being like the strength or core elements that holds the story together to keep it moving forward. Like, an eagle (the theme) flying into a storm (the conflict) to use it to take flight, as they both are strength and core elements for telling a story.

Moving on, the Characterization of 'Owd Bob'.

In fact, the celebrated, "name-above-the title"
American director Frank Capra (It Happened One
Night, It's a Wonderful Life) once observed, "You
can only involve an audience with people. You
can't involve them with gimmicks, with sunsets,
with hand-held cameras, zoom shots, or anything
else. They couldn't care less about those things."

Identifying the central (most important)
character or characters, would be the two dogs,
Zac and Owd Bob. Adam and David, including
their neighbors. First, Zac and Owd Bob the
sheepdog are the static characters. Second, Mr
and Mrs. Moore are the developing characters.
Third, the men of the village are the flat
characters. Fourth, Adam, Maggie and David are
the round characters.

What methods of characterization are employed
and how effective are they? The methods of
characterization employed are the following:
First, appearance. How this is effective, for
example, "the minute we see most actors on the
screen, we make certain assumptions about them
because of their facial features, dress, physical

build, and mannerisms and the way they move"
(Media Analysis 62). Second, dialogue.   How this
is effective, for example, "Actors' use of gram-
mar, sentence structure, vocabulary, and
particular dialects (if any) reveals a great deal
about their characters' social and economic level,
educational background, and mental processes"
(Media Analysis 62). Third, is through external
action as the best reflections of character are a
person's actions. In addition, "sometimes the
most effective characterization is achieved not by
the large actions in the film but by the small,
seemingly insignificant ones. For example, a
firefighter may demonstrate his courage by
saving a child from a burning building, yet such
an act may be only a performance of duty rather
than a reflection of a choice. His essential
character might be more clearly defined by
risking his life to save a little girl's doll, because
such an action would be imposed on him not by
his duty as a firefighter but by his personal
judgment about the value of a doll to a little girl"
(Media Analysis 64). Fourth, is through internal
action as this is effective for the reason being that

the character's inner world is revealed for the audience to hear and see to give us a real understanding of the characters. "In addition to providing glimpses into the inner action by revealing the sounds and sights the character imagines he sees and hears, the filmmaker may employ tight close-ups on an unusually sensitive and expressive face (reaction shots) or may utilize the musical score for essentially the same purpose" (Media Analysis 64). Fifth, is through reaction of other characters as this is effective for the reason of how the other characters view the other characters. For example, "A complex and intriguing characterization is provided through the conversations of other characters" (Media Analysis 65). Sixth, is through contrast: dramatic foils. For example, "one of the most effective techniques of characterization is the use of foils— contrasting characters whose behavior, attitudes, opinions, lifestyle, physical appearance, and so on are the opposite of those of the main characters. The effect is similar to that achieved by putting black and white together—the black appears blacker and the white appears whiter" (Media

Analysis 65). Seventh, is through Caricature and Leitmotif. For an example of how they are effective is "in order to etch a character quickly and deeply in our minds and memories, actors often exaggerate or distort one or more dominant features or personality traits. This device is called caricature. Meanwhile, A similar means of characterization, leitmotif, is the repetition of a single action, phrase, or idea by a character until it becomes almost a trademark or theme song for that character" (Media Analysis 66). Eighth, is through choice of name as this important method uses names to possess appropriate qualities of sound, meaning, or connotation to form a technique. For an example, "Sometimes a name draws its effect from both its meaning and its sound, such as William Faulkner's Flem (read "phlegm")" (Media Analysis 67). Ninth, being varieties of characters. For an example, there are three different types pairings as a method for analyzing film characteristics as these are: stock characters and stereotypes, static versus dynamic characters, and flat versus round characters.

Which of the characters are realistic and which are exaggerated for effect? The Adam, David are the characters that seem realistic. Whereas, the Morrison Family, are believed to be for exaggerated effect.

What about each character's motivation? Zac the sheepdog wants to kill and eat the sheep. Owd Bob the sheepdog wants to help with shearing the sheep. Adam wants to win the sheep-shearing contest and take home a trophy, as Mr. Morrison wants the same. Maggie wants David, and David takes a liking to Owd Bob and Maggie also. Which actions grow naturally out of the characters themselves? The action that grows naturally out of the characters are Adam's for winning the sheep shearing contest, and Maggie for taking a liking to David. Where does the filmmaker seem to be manipulating the characters to fit the film's purpose? I would have to say, David and Mr. Morrison's relationship.

What facets of the central character's personality are revealed by what he or she chooses or rejects? Adam's personality reveals by what he chooses or rejects is appearance, dialogue, external action, internal action, and through contrast. Moreover, which minor characters function to bring out personality traits of the major characters, and what do these minor characters reveal? For David, these are: appearance, dialogue, external action, and internal action, through contrast, caricature, leitmotif, and name.

Pick out bits of dialogue, images, or scenes that you consider especially effective in revealing character, and tell why they are effective. The image I get for Adam is working by himself, the image I get for David is peace mediator, the image I get for Maggie is a friend, the image I get for Mr. Morrison is father to both David and Maggie, as lastly the image that I get for Mrs. Morrison is mother and comforter. These characters are effective, because there is something about each one of them that fulfills a need each of the characters.

Which characters function as stock characters and stereotypes? The stock characters are the

village people, as the stereotypes would be the
town police officer. How can their presence in the
film be justified? The police officer's presence can
be justified by the authority that he shows in
makes sure a village person can swear to seeing
Adam's dog, Zac, killing one of his sheep and then
being present to up-hold the law on seeing a dog
get put down for break a rule of killing a sheep. As
for the villagers, "are minor characters whose
actions are completely predictable or typical of
their job or profession (such as a bartender in a
western). They are in the film simply because the
situation demands their presence. They serve as a
natural part of the setting, much as stage
properties like a lamp or a chair might function in
a play" (Media Analysis 67). Like, the villager
who is always in the bar, accusing Adam's dog of
killing on of his sheep.

Moving on, to Symbolism in the film 'Owd Bob'.

First off, "In the most general terms, whether in a
work of art or in everyday communications, a
symbol is something that stands for something
else. It communicates that some- thing else by

triggering, stimulating, or arousing previously associated ideas in the mind of the person perceiving the symbol" (Media Analysis 71). The symbols that appear in the film are: hay=prosperity/profit/comfort, a watchtower=safe place or refuge, teapot=calming, bread=hungry, tombstone=memorial, casket=death, black clothes=grieving or mourning, trophy=achievement or pride, dogs=friend, sheep=innocent, alcohol=problems, and shotgun=power/security.

What universal or natural symbols are employed? How effective are they, for instance, "Universal symbols are precharged—ready-made symbols infused with values and associations that most of the people in a given culture understand. By using objects, images, or persons that automatically evoke complex associations, filmmakers save themselves the job of creating each of the associated attitudes and feelings within the context of each film" (Media Analysis 71). While the universal symbols that were employed in the film were: things like hay, cars, sheep and dogs.

Which symbols derive their meaning solely from their context in the film? I would say, the dogs and the sheep. How are they charged with symbolic value (In other words, how do you know they are symbols and how do you arrive at their meaning)? "In charging an object with symbolic value, storytellers have a dual purpose. First, they want to expand the meaning of the symbolic object in order to communicate meanings, feelings, and ideas. Second, they want to make clear that the object is being treated symbolically. Thus, many of the methods used to charge an object symbolically also serve as clues that the object is taking on symbolic value" (Media Analysis 72). The dogs being like a friend who helps bring prosperity with the sheep shearing, and the sheep being to make a profit. While I know this are symbols, because of their repeated position in the film and they arrive at their meaning by how they act as you can interpret it just if it were in a dream. Moreover, there are four principal methods of charging symbols: Repetition, Value placed on an object by a

character, context, and special visual, aural or
musical emphasis.

How are the special capabilities of film (the
image, the soundtrack, and the musical score)
employed to charge symbols with their meaning?
"Individual natural sounds or musical refrains
can become symbolic in their own right if complex
associations are built into them by any of the
three methods discussed above" (Media Analysis
75). This can be a unique way of charging and
underscoring symbols to provide clues that an
object is to be seen as a symbol.

Which symbols fit into a larger pattern or
progression with other symbols in the film?
"Although symbols may function singly without a
clear relationship to other symbols, they often
interact in what might be called symbolic
patterns. In such a case, the filmmaker expresses
the same idea through several symbols instead of
relying on just one. The resulting symbolic
pattern may have a certain progression, so that
the symbols grow in value or power as the film
develops" (Media Analysis 75). So, the symbols

that would fit a larger pattern with other symbols in the film is: the sheep, dogs, fence, and hay. While these are the major symbols that relate to the theme by the way they are place in the story, their value to the characters and the repetition in which they fit in to it.

Is the story structured around its symbolic meanings to the extent that it can be called an allegory? "A story in which every object, event, and person has an abstract (as opposed to merely concrete) meaning is known as an allegory. In allegory, each element is part of an interdependent system that tells a clear, separate, complete, didactic story on a purely figurative level" (Media Analysis 70). As, I don't think that this story is structured around its symbolic meanings to the extent that it can be called an allegory.

Which symbols' meanings are clear and simple? This would be the sheep and dogs as these symbols can also be complex and ambiguous. In addition, the sheep's value for the profit they add to the shepherd and the dog's value to doing work on the farm are what give them this quality. However, I would say that there are visual metaphors that are employed effectively. As from the looks of it, theses visual metaphors seem like they are intrinsic, in other words, a natural part of the setting. Whereas, the film's symbols metaphors look pretty fresh and original as there are hardly any special effects. While they kind of seem timeworn, and where they have been encountered before is in places like in the farmhouse.

To conclude, on Irony of the film 'Owd Bob'.

Briefly, "Irony, in the most general sense, is a literary, dramatic, and cinematic technique involving the juxtaposition or linking of opposites. By emphasizing sharp and star- tling contrasts, reversals, and paradoxes, irony adds an intellectual dimension and achieves both comic and tragic effects at the same time" (Media Analysis 78).

So, what examples of irony can I find in the film? For one, I thought when Zac returns to Adam with blood around his mouth and another is when Zac is seen eating a sheep. Also, when Adam took Zac the dog to be put down and after the gunshot was heard, as this was a tragic effect. Another is when Mrs. Morrison gets ill, then dies. As juxtaposition, in the film took place sometime during the shepherd contest.

While I don't think that the irony is employed to such a significant degree that the whole film takes on an ironic tone, but I can see an ironic worldview implied. In fact, the particular examples of irony that achieved comic and tragic effects at the same time were: Dramatic Irony, Irony Situation, Irony of Character, and Irony of Tone.

For an example, a place in the film where suspense is achieved through dramatic irony can be found when Zac the sheepdog goes up to Adam by the farmhouse with blood under his chin or on his mane. Thus, these ironies contribute to the theme by giving it a literary, dramatic, cinematic technique, intellectual dimension and achievement in both comic and tragic effect.

INT. CAMP/CINEMA THERAPY - DAY

Watching the film 'Camp' for my third cinema therapy session, on transformation and renewal.

Scan here to see the trailer of 'Camp."

According to Netflix, 'Camp' is about "An investment adviser gets more than he bargained for when he spends a week as a counselor at a camp for troubled kids and bonds with an abused boy." While I prescribed a movie based on an issue and followed some guidelines for watching movies with conscious awareness in this order: First, start with a film that supports your treatment goal. Second, choose a film from film recommendations. Third, making sure to clarify intent when assigning a film in which might mistake the role identification. Fourth, familiarize yourself with Guidelines for watching films and discuss guidelines. Fifth, discuss the positive or negative reactions to film. Sixth, use material according to your theoretical orientation. Seven, afterwards reflect on evocative questions and answer them after watching the selected film as it does help to write down my answers.

Do you remember whether your breathing changed throughout the movie? Yes, it was in the towards the beginning of the scene where the father came home and got angry when he found the money stash jar empty to take it out on the Eli as he ended up hitting the kid twice. Another scene was when the abusive father showed up at the camp during the pool scene after Eli had worked hard to swim a lap across the pool to win an orange bracelet, as Eli step in between his father and his camp counselor to try to stop his dad. While his dad pushed Eli by the head, violently away from him to knock him down and make the kid bleed. Could this be an indication that something threw you off balance? Yes. For the reason, I don't like seeing either a child or a woman go through that abuse like that as that is something you don't do to a kid, and that made me angry seeing a kid endure that type of cruel treatment. In all likelihood, what affects you in the film is similar to whatever unbalances you in your daily life. While this movie was hard to watch in some places, being that it tackles and brings awareness to the subject of abuse as it shows how being a positive reinforcement in someone's life can be a solution to this problem.

Ask yourself: If a part of the film that moved you (positively or negatively) had been one of your dreams, how would you have understood the symbolism in it? One of my dreams that I had, in relation to this film would be: The first dream, I saw myself as a little boy at a waterpark at night and I was the only one there with another guy as I noticed that I had all these wounds that I was bleeding from. While towards the end of the dream, this guy picked me up and put me on his back and gently walked into to the water with me and when I came out with him, I was clean and healed of my wounds as that man in the dream was Jesus. The second dream, it was in the daytime as I was at a public swimming pool just watching other people swim and I remember feeling like I wanted to swim with them. The third dream, I'm in a classroom setting playing with some kids, as they are have a good time playing with me. Lastly, one dream that I had that really

spoke to me the most was when I dreamed I was
on a playground at a school, working at a recess
duty assistant. A whistle blew to signal recess was
over for the kids and they all did what they would
normally do, which would be line up an quiet
down before they could go inside for lunch. I
waited as the other recess duty assistance took
their group to line up by the cafeteria door, and at
some point when I was walking with the group of
kids that I was taking up to the cafeteria door.
From behind me, I heard this dialogue between a
girl and a boy. Kid 1: "I don't think their even be
watching if I ate trash from the trash can," and
kid 2 translates what she had said to another kid
by saying, "they don't notice us." Now how I would
understand symbolism in dreams is I would do
what I would normally do, which would be: study
the setting, mood, elements and actions of the
dreams. Then, prayerfully, I would seek its
meaning through a Christian dream dictionary
and the Bible as most of the time if I'm hearing
from God on it I would know its meaning from the
Holy Spirit's guidance through revelation and
wisdom.

Notice what you liked and what you didn't like or even hated about the movie. Which characters or actions seemed especially attractive or unattractive to you? The characters whose actions seemed attractive was all of the camp counselors, because they was being positive enforcers or mentor to kids who been through different abusive and neglectful situations. While the actions that seemed unattractive was the abuse and the neglect, as I didn't like that and it made me uncomfortable see that happen. Did you identify with one or several characters? The characters that I identified with was Eli, especially after he build up the courage to show his secret, which was his abusive scars from his father and then jumped in the pool as after that he experienced a life transformation experience. The another experience was the camp counselor that took a tough kid who been through a rough past under his wing to not only set a good example for him, but show him what real love looks like. A third character that I realize I had identify with was the little girl that was terrified of going to sleep and it took her counselor to give her a blanket, while why I am to identify with her is when I was a child I use to be attacked by being held down in my sleep as I was trying to awake and terrorized in my sleep. So, I can relate to why this character might not want to go the sleep.

Were there one or several characters in the movie that modeled behavior that you would like to emulate? The camp counselors modeled behavior that I would strive to emulate. Did they develop certain strengths or other capacities that you would like to develop as well? As, the camp counselors did show strength and other capacities that I have developed and would like to continue to grow in.

Notice whether any aspect of the film was especially hard to watch. Could this be related to something that you might have repressed ("shadow")? I know what all types of abuse feels like, because I've been that victim's shoes and I didn't like seeing a kid get abused like I saw in the movie as well as seeing the scars that he hide. While it felt heart-warming and freeing seeing the kid freeing himself by uncovering it and jumping in the water, as another word for this could be healing. Uncovering repressed aspects of our psyche can free up positive qualities and uncover our more whole and authentic self.

Did you experience something that connected you to your inner wisdom or higher self as you watched the film? Yes, the scripture that was brought to my attention was from Proverbs 22:6, "train up a child in the way he should go, And when he is old he will not depart from it." And also, what a Pastor by the name of Jensen Franklin said around these lines a while back. "When you take someone who was messed up and let them minister to someone who's messed up, it messes with the devil." As, I started to write down a lot of insights towards the end of the film.

Although, while some of the mentioned guidelines turn out to be useful and I have had the experience of impacting a kids life by being a camp counselor, I still would consider using them not only in "reel life," but also adapt them to "real life," because they are intended to make me become a better observer along with others who want to emulate the example.

Moreover, the film did have a unique message for me as it was for me at least, about how mentorship is positive reinforcement that brings transformation and hope. Some insights that I wrote down were: you don't have to lie or steal to get what you want as if you want something bad about enough, work hard for it and are whiling to fight for it, then you can have what you want. Another insight was how sending a kid to camp could be the only place where they not only feel loved, but also be told that they are loved, especially if it's the only time that they may hear it. A second insight was I heard parts of the story of Joseph in a way that it relates to foster kids, and that being Joseph went in and out of places as his last place was a palace where he became basically ruler over all those places (a nation) to give hope and save many lives. As what was meant for bad, God turned it into good for Joseph. A third insight was being a camp counselor is a missions' trip in itself, and is life transforming. While you go in thinking you're going to change a kid's life, but your life winds up getting changed as well. A fourth insight is how setting a good example for a kid can really help them down the line of life when they are going up, as it gives them another option for a way to follow, rather than repeating the only way that they may know how to behave. As, it can be seen as a form of divine intervention and being a miracle to someone else's prayer.

The new ideas for new behaviors that I have received from watching this film was set the example that you wish to see others follow, and how showing your hidden scars can be bring healing and transformation to not only you, but others who might be going through the same thing.

Lastly, another films that I might be able to identify with to take the discussion a step further is 'October Baby' and 'the Pianist'.

INT. ALICE IN WONDERLAND/FILM ANALYSIS - DAY

The fourth media analysis done as a therapeutic session was on analyzing the visual design of the film, 'Alice in Wonderland' with Johnny Depp.

Scan here for 'Alice in Wonderland' trailer.

While watching the film, I pursued thirteen key acting questions that every actor should answer to be a fully rounded and connected great actor, from studying a truly great actor.

Who is Johnny Depp's character? Mad Hatter.

Where is Johnny Depp's character? Wonderland or Underland.

When is it? Thirteen years later after Alice's father has died when she was seven years old, as Alice is nineteen years old when she discovers Wonderland.

Where have Johnny Depp's character just come from? We first get introduced to the Mad Hatter at a Tea Party with the hare, in the woods.

What does Johnny Depp's character want? First, to find out the answer to his unanswered riddle. "What's the difference between a raven and a writing table?" Second, the Mad Hatter wants Alice to retrieve from the Red Queen and restore it back to the White Queen, as he wants Alice to defeat the Jabberwocky for the cause of overthrowing the Red Queen.

Why does Johnny Depp's character want it? The Red Queen is cruel and she wants to be feared instead of loved, as she has taken over the Kingdom.

Why does Johnny Depp's character want it now? In a way, it's for justice and to take back what rightfully belongs to the Mad Hatter and Wonderland. Moreover, I think the memory that the Mad Hatter had in his conversation with Alice in the wood has something more to do with it.

What will happen if Johnny Depp's character doesn't get it now? For himself, he does something that the Red Queen doesn't like and it causes him to get his head chopped off. Another is if the Red Queen isn't stopped, the characters of Wonderland will continue to live under her oppression, fear and cruelty.

How will Johnny Depp's character get what he wants by doing what? He will have to be loyal to the other characters that are for the same cause of defeating the Red Queen, and the Mad Hatter will also have to sacrifice to get it.

What must Johnny Depp's character overcome? The Mad Hatter will have to overcome his madness, including the Red Queen and her soldiers.

I would totally say that Johnny Depp does fully transform into his character, the Mad Hatter, as it was hard to tell that it was Johnny Depp in his make-up and costume. In fact, Johnny Depp shows hard work, technique and good direction. As, Johnny Depp is truthfully and emotionally connected with his character, the Mad Hatter. And as the audience, I did see none of this, but the fully realized three-dimensional character right in the truth of the moment and Johnny Depp showed two different personalities in his voice alone.

Moving on, more to analyzing the visual design of the film. Briefly, Wynn Thomas, who is a production designer. Tells about visual design in a quote, "Production designers function as architects, interior designers . . . historians . . . diplomats, and, ultimately, observers of human behaviors—and all of the fragilities of the human heart . . ."As, this can be some what of a good example of the people who make the visual design work from behind the scenes.

Now, answering Dr. Culp's five movie critique questions.

On description, describing the story in objective terms. To me what the message of the story is, if one word would describe it. It would be, choices and the only person who can decide what you want to do with your life is you. More in this; to dream, to believe in the impossible, to believe in your own abilities and potential, is actually a very

wise thing to do. Now according to the plot
summary on Itunes movie, "Tumble down the
rabbit hole with Alice for a fantastical adventure!
Inviting and magical, Alice In Wonderland is an
imaginative new twist on one of the most beloved
stories of all time. Alice, now 19 years old,
returns to the whimsical world she first entered
as a child and embarks on a journey to discover
her true destiny." Overall, nothing is impossible if
you believe.

On meaning, describing what the story/director is
trying to say is the only way to achieve the
impossible is to believe the impossible, and that
it's possible.

On worldview, describing the principles/values is
in use by the characters are: Loyalty, sacrifice,
love, fellowship, not harming any creature and do
unto others, as you would like done unto you.

Discuss the characters' behavior based upon
biblical principles. The Red Queen behaves in
cruelty and thinks it's much better to be feared

instead of loved. Moreover, the Bible principle that you could see in the characters were: Liberality (Matthew 5:42), Mercy (Matthew 5:42), Contentment (Matthew 6:25), Hope (2 Corinthians 4:16-18), Christian Fellowship (2 Corinthians 6:14), Faith (Galatians 5:5-6), Temperance (Ephesians 4:19,22-24), Edification (Ephesians 4:29), Humility (Philippians 2:3), Perseverance (Philippians 3:13-14), Contemplation and Reflection (Colossians 3:2-3), Forbearance (Colossians 3:12-13), Industriousness (2 Thessalonians 3:10), Purity of speech (2 Timothy 2:16-17), Hospitality (Hebrews 13:2), Sympathy (1 Peter 3:8), Evangelism (1 Peter 3:15), Loyalty (1 Peter 4:8), Generosity (1 John 3:17), and Love (1 John 4:16-19).

On interpretation, describing what the movie means to me personally. For once, When Alice said something around these paraphrased lines. "From the moment I fell down the rabbit hole I had been stretched, shrunken. Told what, where, who, accused of what I must be ... I make my own path." I just made me think of what teenagers

234

might go through in the society that we live in today. While this movie brings me back to an example on what its like to be a teenager in our society as I read about in the textbook, 'The Family' by Judith K. Balswick. It quotes "What is absent from these and most other non-Western societies is the ambiguity associated with being a teenager in the United States. Being a teenager in our society is like being in Alice in Wonderland – not knowing the rules and expectations if asked whether a teenager is a child or an adult, most people will say, "both," or "neither." The underlying element here is that the beginning of adulthood has not been clearly defined."

Now analyzing the visual design, on color versus black and white.

Was the filmmaker's choice of color or black and white correct for this story? I would say that the filmmaker's choice of color was correct for this story, being that it fit the Wonderland and made it look more dream-like. To back up my point, in the Media Analysis textbook, "Most modern filmmakers feel that color cinematography allows them to create more powerful, realistic images and to communicate better with audiences. As members of the design team plan the look of a film, they are likely to consider establishing a color palette—a limited number of specific colors used or emphasized throughout the film to subtly communicate various aspects of character and story to the viewer. Color used in this way becomes more than mere decoration for the film; it enhances the movie's dramatic elements" (Media Analysis 87-88). What factors do you think influenced this decision? The factors that I think influenced this decision was to stay true to the original story of 'Alice in Wonderland. Try to imagine the film, as it would appear in the other film type. What would the differences in total effect be? There would be a huge difference between the costumes, make-up, soundtrack; SFX and CG as all of these would enhance what the film would look like in the other film type. So, the difference would be between realism and non-realism.

Are any special color effects used to achieve a unique overall look? If there are any special color effects used to achieve a unique look I believe it would be: First, in the scene of the Mad Hatter's memory of the Red Queen. Second, the scene when Alice comes through the small door to enter the outdoors of Wonderland. Third, when we first see the White Queen's Palace. Lastly, the scene when Alice fights the Jabberwocky. If so, what was the director trying to achieve with the unusual effect? How successfully is the overall effect carried out? According, in the Media Analysis textbook. "The key members of the production team who together will plan the visual design or look of the film—the director, the cinematographer, the production designer, and the costumer—must analyze that skeleton. Each member of this team focuses on a single goal: creating a master plan for a consistent visual texture or style that is artistically suited to the film story to be told" (Media Analysis 87). As I think what the director was trying to achieve with this unusual effect of a dream, giving off that Wonderland look like in the book.

Moving on, to on Screen Format (Aspect Ratio).

The film originally shot for a wide screen, as that is the format that makes the film look its best. While this also makes the choice of screen format suit the story being filmed, as it gives it that cinematic theater experience that wouldn't be the same if it's seen on a TV in standard screen.

Try imagining the film in the opposite format: What would be gained or lost? The film would loose its cinemascope experience, making everything look tight and look like there's very little movement of subjects in space. Whereas, "The wide screen lends itself to a panoramic view of a vast landscape or large numbers of people, as well as to the rapid motion characteristic of westerns, war dramas, historical pageants, and fast-paced action/adventure dramas" (Media Analysis 88). Even though the wide screen can make a film distorted and detract from the visual effectiveness if the set is too narrow for its field of view, but tends to eliminate compositional problems as it seems like the audience likes the wide screen and would prefer it over the standard screen.

On the production design and art direction.

How important is the set or location to the overall
look of the film? In this case, concerning the story
of 'Alice in Wonderland' I see the set and the
location being extremely important if it was to
enhance the story and at the same time stay true
to it. For an example, we can see how important a
set is when the Media Analysis textbooks
explained. "The production designer first makes
elaborate and detailed sketches and plans for the
set and then supervises, down to the last detail,
the construction, painting, furnishings, and
decoration until he or she achieves the exact look
intended. In every stage of filmmaking the
production designer consults with three other
people directly responsible for the visual texture
of the film: the director, the cinematographer,
and the costumer. All three work together closely,
seeking each other's opinion, conferring, and
coordinating their efforts to achieve a unified
visual effect" (Media Analysis 92). In fact, the set
and location is essentially part realistic set, and
stylized to suggest the heightened reality of
Wonderland to try to make it as if it was a real

place.

Was the movie filmed primarily on location or in the studio? I would say that the film was both filmed on location and in the studio, for the scenes that required it. What effect does the place of filming have on the style or look of the film? The place of filming can give the audience more of a realistic effect to the style or look of the film, and can bring the story to life, as the place of filming will take the audience there to make the story more believable.

How do the settings serve as personalized environments to enhance or reinforce the actors' performances? The setting can reinforce the actors' performances by making the characters much more believable, as it helps them to live in the moment and make the world of the story more real. Like it says in the Media Analysis textbook, "Although the setting may often seem unobtrusive or be taken for granted, it is an essential ingredient in any story and makes an important contribution to the theme or total effect of a film. Because of the complex interrelationships of setting with other story elements—plot, character, theme, conflict, symbolism—the effects of setting on the story being told should be analyzed carefully. And because of its important visual function, setting must also be considered a powerful cinematic element in its own right" (94). To what degree do the settings underscore or enhance the mood or quality of each scene? The settings underscore can bring the audience into the film by making them feel as though it has become apart of their life, enhancing the mood to make us feel what the story wants us to feel and it gives us a degree of realism for the quality of each scene.

Is the setting so powerful and dominant that it upstages the actors? No, as I think there is a balance between the audience's attention on the setting and the characters with the costumes and make-up that make it powerful and dominant. While this film is eye striking.

If the film is a period piece, a fantasy, or a science fiction story-taking place in a future time or on a strange planet, is the set convincing enough to

241

make us believe (during the film) that we are really in another time and place? Alice in Wonderland is a fantasy and science fiction story-taking place on a strange planet called Wonderland, as the set looks convincing enough to make the audience believe that the impossible is possible through this. If so, what factors or details present in the set contribute to its convincing effect? While it seems like the setting for 'Alice in Wonderland' is for Verisimilitude. Moreover, "Filmmakers recognize the great importance that an authentic setting plays in making a film believable. Thus, they may search for months to find a proper setting and then move crew, actors, and equipment thousands of miles to capture an appropriate backdrop for the story they are attempting to film. To be convincing, the setting chosen should be authentic in even the most minute detail" (Media Analysis 97). As, the details present in the set contribute to its convincing effect through the hair of the creatures, artifical limbs on the entourage of the Red Queen, the architecture of the buildings and the texture of the ground in different places as well.

Which of the four environmental factors (temporal factors; geographic factors; social structures and economic factors; and customs, moral attitudes, and codes of behavior) play significant roles in the film? The one environmental factor that plays a role in the film is customs, moral attitudes, and codes of behavior. Could the same story take place in any environment? According to the original story of 'Alice in Wonderland,' I don't think that the story could take place in any environment, as it would feel right if it did.

Which environmental factors are most important? The geographic, customs, moral attitudes, and code of behavior environmental factors as these seem to be what impact the audience most. What effect do these factors have on the plot or the characters? The setting as determiner of character is what affects the environmental factors on the characters. To demonstrate, "This interpretation is based on the belief that our character, destiny, and fate are all determined by forces outside ourselves, that we may be nothing more than products of our heredity and environment, and that freedom of choice is only an illusion. Thus, by considering the environment a significant shaping force or even a dominant controlling one, this interpretation forces us to consider how environment has made characters what they are—in other words, how characters' nature has been dictated by factors such as their time in history, the particular place on Earth they inhabit, their position in the social and economic structure, and the customs, moral attitudes, and codes of behavior imposed on them by society. These environmental factors may be so pervasive that they serve as something much more important than a backdrop for the film's plot" (Media Analysis 96). As, the environmental factors establish the characters in a place to be able to live in the moment and truly blend in with the story.

Why did the filmmaker choose this particular location for filming this story? To me, it seems like the story in the book of 'Alice in Wonderland takes place in the United Kingdom and the filmmaker wanted to stay true to the particular location in the book.

How does the film's setting contribute to the overall emotional atmosphere? For instance, "In certain specialized films, setting is important in creating a pervasive mood or emotional atmosphere. This is especially true in horror films and to some extent in the science fiction or fantasy film, in which the unusually charged emotional atmosphere created and maintained by the setting becomes an important factor in achieving a suspension of disbelief by the viewer. Setting may also create a mood of tension and suspense in keeping with the overall tone of the film, in addition to adding credibility to plot and character elements" (Media Analysis 98). In fact, I would say that this film's setting contributes to the overall emotional atmosphere by making it become more personal to the audience, and it allows us to be more involved in the story as the setting to create emotional atmosphere pulls us in.

What important interrelationships exist between

the setting and the characters or between settings and plot? The most important interrelationships that exist between the setting and the character are they both are a reflection of being twisted, trippy and weird. For instance, "The environment in which a person lives may provide the viewer with clues to understanding his or her character. This is especially true for the aspects of their environment over which individuals exercise some control. Houses, for example, may be excellent indicators of character" (Media Analysis 96). Briefly, the settling represents the characters.

Is the setting symbolic in any way? The setting does seem symbolic in many ways, for reason that "the setting of a film story may take on strong symbolic over- tones when it is used to stand for or represent not just a location but some idea associated with the location" (Media Analysis 98). Does it function as a microcosm? Microcosm meaning, "A special type of symbolic setting is the type known as a microcosm, meaning "the world in little," in which the human activity in a small and limited area is representative of human behavior or the human condition in the world as a whole. In such a setting special care is taken to isolate the characters from all external influences so that the "little world" seems self-contained" (Media Analysis 98). I would say there is a possibility of the film story functioning as microcosm, being that Wonderland is an underworld below the earth above it as it take going through a rabbit hole to discover it.

On Costume and Makeup Design.

What details of costuming and makeup help the actors be "in character"? There are many details on the make-up that helps the character be "in character" as one of them is the eyes, and for the costuming it's the style and fashion. In fact, I would consider these being factors also for playing a role in creating a sense of time and place. For an example, the Media Analysis textbook mentions. "Edith Head, the dean of American costume designers, describes the interaction of design team members and performers: "What we do is create an illusion of changing an actor or actress into someone else. It is a cross between magic and camouflage . . . . We have three magicians—hairstylist, makeup artist, and clothes designer—and through them we're supposed to kid the public that it really isn't Paul Newman, it's Butch Cassidy." To successfully transform an actor into his or her character requires that the actor feel a comfortable sense of rightness with the clothing. Charlton Heston, for example, made a point of wearing a costume as much as he could. He wanted the costume to feel like clothing, not like a costume. For many actors, the process of internalizing the character to be played really begins when they see themselves in costume. A skilled costume designer can improve an actor's figure. The use of a little extra fabric can slim the appearance of a woman with a boxy, high-waisted build and create the illusion of a wonderful figure" (103). Moreover, concerning the make-up. "Makeup decisions also help to create the desired look. Makeup can enhance the natural look of an actor or transform an actor into a different version of himself or herself or into a totally different person. The transition may be accomplished through gradual and subtle changes throughout the film, or it may be abrupt" (Media Analysis 105). In fact, the make-up and costumes is what blew my mind as it made the actor more of become the characters and get lost in the story more.

Does the makeup for the film's major characters simply enhance the natural look of the actors or significantly transform their appearances? I totally believe that the make-up significantly transformed the actors appearances, as it makes the audiences forget who the actor is. For example, Johnny Depp's make-up was outstanding and created a memorable character. While there are some characters where the make-up seemed to enhance the natural look of the actors. Otherwise, I don't think that there were any significant or subtle changes (such as aging) required by the script, but if there were I'm sure they would be effective at achieving these changes.

On Lighting

Is the lighting of the film as a whole: (a) direct, harsh, and hard; (b) medium and balanced; or (c)

soft and diffused? I would say that the lighting of
the film, as a whole is soft and diffused. To
demonstrate, "By controlling the intensity,
direction, and diffusion of the light, a director is
able to create the impression of spatial depth,
delineate and mold the contours and planes of the
subject, convey emotional mood and atmosphere,
and create special dramatic effects" (Media
Analysis 106). Does high-key or low-key lighting
pre- dominate? In this case, the difference
between Low-Key and High-Key Lighting is that
"Low-key lighting puts most of the set in shadow
and shows the subjects with just a few highlights,
increasing the intimacy and dramatic intensity of
the scene. High-key lighting opens up the frame
with light in background areas and balances the
lighting throughout the set. Although high- key
lighting diminishes the intimacy and dramatic
intensity that the scene has with low-key lighting,
it provides more complete visual information
about the two women and the setting" (Media
Analysis 107). While I would say that there was a
balance between the two, but in Alice's world was
more of high-key lighting and in Wonderland it

was low-key lighting. How do the lighting decisions fit the film's story? I believe the lighting decisions fit the film's story for the reason that it gives off a glow and dreamy look, for example, "the character of light on actors' faces can suggest certain inner qualities" (Media Analysis 107) as it plays an important role of creating an effective visual image of the personalities of the characters that the actors are playing. In other words, the lighting helps to carry a certain mood about the character in their current settling.

Does the lighting throughout seem artificial, coming from places where there are no visible light sources, or does it seem to emanate naturally from sources visible or suggested on-screen? I would say that the lighting throughout the film of 'Alice in Wonderland' seems to emanate naturally from sources visible or suggested on-screen. For example, "The effect created by flat overhead lighting, for example, is entirely different from the effect created by strong side lighting from floor level. Back lighting and front lighting also create strikingly different effects. Whether light is artificial or natural, the director has the means to control what is commonly referred to as the character of the light" (Media Analysis 107). As, the lighting was beautiful and striking as if it were in a dream or painting.

Lastly, I assume how the lighting contributes to the overall emotional attitude or tone of the film is by suggesting certain inner qualities on the actors' faces. In fact, "The intensity, direction, and character of light affect the dramatic effectiveness of an image" (Media Analysis 107). While the lighting can tell a story just in itself, through colors that give off a certain mood and energy as this carries information to the audience. For example, one major color in the film was white for the White Queen in the setting that she was in as the information that it gave off was elegance.

INT. NEW HOPE/CINEMA THERAPY - DAY

Watching the film 'New Hope' for my fourth cinema therapy session, on transformation and renewal.

 Scan here for 'New Hope trailer.

I prescribed a movie based on an issue and followed some guidelines for watching movies with conscious awareness in this order: First, start with a film that supports your treatment goal. Second, choose a film from film recommendations. Third, making sure to clarify intent when assigning a film in which might mistake the role identification. Fourth, familiarize yourself with Guidelines for watching films and discuss guidelines. Fifth, discuss the positive or negative reactions to film. Sixth, use material according to your theoretical orientation. Seven, afterwards reflect on evocative questions and answer them after watching the selected film as it does help to write down my answers.

Do you remember whether your breathing changed throughout the movie? The scene where I remember my breathing changed slightly was when the Evan's family had invited the Green's family over for dinner, but Michael had know idea that Lucas would be joining him since he's apart of the Green family. As Michael had invited Jasmine to join them, and this made things with the confrontations between the two get more intense. Towards the end of this scene Psalms 23:5 and Proverbs 16:7 with this insight, God will prepare a feast for you in the midst of your enemies and invite your enemies to join you without you knowing to teach you how to love the unlovable, so it can make even your enemies want to shake hands and make peace with you. Could this be an indication that something threw you off balance? Yes. In all likelihood, what affects you in the film is similar to whatever unbalances you in your daily life.

Ask yourself: If a part of the film that moved you (positively or negatively) had been one of your dreams, how would you have understood the symbolism in it? By breaking down the dream by

254

which the symbol occurred in to understand the true meaning of the symbol, as I would use a Bible and a Christian dream interpretation dictionary to help me interpret it. For an example, the scene where Michael and Jasmine were in a paddleboat, floating down a calm stream. According to Christian Dream dictionary, "boat equals support. Moreover; life, person, recreation, and spare time." As the boat was more of a sailboat, then moved by the spirit and keeping in mind that the water was calm. While the scripture found concerning boat were: Genesis 6:16, Luke 8:22-23, and 1st Timothy 1:19. So, how I would interpret this scene if it were a dream would be. You and a friend are being moved by the support of the spirit, into a peaceful direction through this grieving time. Thus, lean not in your own understanding, but trust in the Lord with all your heart and He will direct your path.

Notice what you liked and what you didn't like or even hated about the movie. I didn't like seeing the characters having to go through the process of grief, because I know how hard it can be to get through it, especially if you know someone is not a Christian trying to get through it without God. Which characters or actions seemed especially attractive or unattractive to you? The actions that seemed attractive was how Michael got through his grief with His relationship of his father and God, as Michael ended up reaching out to his friends to be a positive role model for them through their grief. Did you identify with one or several characters? The character that I identified with was Michael Evans and how he got through his grief in a healthy way, even though he grieved silently in public and had his day to talk to get through what he was going through.

Were there one or several characters in the movie that modeled behavior that you would like to emulate? Michael, because he made some good choices with whatever issues life brought his way and how he became a good role-model for those that needed a good example to look to in their time of difficulty. Did they develop certain strengths or other capacities that you would like to develop as well? While Michael's character did develop certain strengths and other capacities that I would like to develop for my own life.

256

Notice whether any aspect of the film was especially hard to watch. There wasn't really any scene that was hard to watch, except for seeing each character dealing with grief in different levels and trying to cope with it. Could this be related to something that you might have repressed ("shadow")? Probably, as I am a silent griever like Michael who gets through issues with God's help. Moreover, uncovering repressed aspects of our psyche can free up positive qualities and uncover our more whole and authentic self.

Did you experience something that connected you to your inner wisdom as you watched the film? Yes. We all have a past and we all have struggles, but you can strive to live your life honoring God, knowing you've been forgiven. Furthermore, confrontations can come in any form, but it all depends on what you believe and your faith in how you will respond to life's issues: will you face, or turn from it are two choices we can use in whether what we face is positive or negative.

If some of the mentioned guidelines turn out to be

useful, I might consider using them not only in "reel life" but also adapt them to "real life," because I am aware how they are intended to make me become a better observer.

If the film had a unique message for you, what was it? That God sees no one as "missing" in the world, as He knows everyone by name. Psalm 147:4, "He counts the stars, and calls them all by name." While God will use even a sinner to encourage and test a Christian's faith, as in the end your endurance through all of your challenges will influence the unbelievers to want to know God.

What new ideas for new behaviors did you have? Trust God wherever in the place He has you in, and be open to grow from whatever lesson He is wants to teach you in the situation. As an idea for new behaviors is you can be a good role model through your struggles to influence people in how they could respond to theirs, in other words, set a good example by how you live.
Finally, what other films can you identify that might take the discussion a step further?

258

The only film that I can think of is the movie,
'Courageous.'

INT. CHARLIE AND THE CHOCOLATE FACTORY/FILM ANALYSIS - DAY

The fifth media analysis done as a therapeutic session was on cinematography and special visual effects of the film, 'Charlie and the Chocolate Factory.'

 Scan here for 'Charlie and the Chocolate Factory' trailer.

A quote that can explain cinematography and special effects is "The camera is the "eye" of the motion picture. It is not merely a mechanical thing of cogs and wheels and optical glass that records an image on a strip of film. Rather, it is an artistic tool—like a painter's brush, or a sculptor's chisel. In the hands of a craftsman it becomes the instru- ment through which a dramatic story can be placed on film—so that later on, in darkened theaters all over the world, vast audiences can see the film, react to it, and be entertained. By Herbert A. Lightman, editor of American Cinematographer.

Furthermore, before beginning this film analyzes on cinematography and special visual effects of the movie 'Charlie and the Chocolate Factory.' I will ask thirteen key acting questions that every actor should answer to be a fully rounded and connected great actor, from studying Johnny Depp who is a truly great actor.

Who is Johnny Depp's character? Willy Wonka.

Where is Johnny Depp's character? Great Britain.

When is it? Present day.

Where have Johnny Depp's character just come from? The Chocolate Factory.

What does Johnny Depp's character want? Objective: To eliminate four rotten child contestants to reward 1 good child as the winner of the contest. Super-Objective: To find an heir for his chocolate factory.

Why does Johnny Depp's character want it? Willy Wonka wants it, because after a revelation we realize that he won't have anyone to take care of his Oompa-Loompa and inherent his Chocolate

Factory when he dies.

Why does Johnny Depp's character want it now? Willy Wonka wants his dream and legacy to live on in another generation, and the security of his Oompa-Loompas to be cared for.

What will happen if Johnny Depp's character doesn't get it now? When Willy Wonka dwells on the thought of not having someone to leave his Chocolate Factory to and take care of his Oompa-Loompas, it makes him feel terrible and when he feels terrible his chocolate suffers by tasting terrible and he will be alone with no one with the Oompa-Loompas.

How will Johnny Depp's character get what he wants by doing what? Willy Wonka will get what he wants by announcing a contest whereby children that find five Golden Tickets hidden in Wonka bars will be given a tour of the factory and a chance to be presented with the prize of an inheritance, after a process of eliminating four rotten child to pick one good child.

What must Johnny Depp's character overcome?

Memories of his past with his father, the contest, the process of elimination of the four contestants, the personality of the four rotten parents, and also the personality of the four rotten children.

Johnny Depp fully transform into his character, Willy Wonka as he shows hard work, technique and good direction. Moreover, Johnny Depp truthfully and emotionally is connected with his character Willy Wonka.

Lastly, in the audience, I did see none of this, but the fully realized three-dimensional character of Willy Wonka right in the truth of the moment. Johnny Depp turned the loner, Willy Wonka into a lovable and memorable character.

Now, answering Dr. Culp's five movie critique questions.

On description, describe the story in objective terms. In one line I would say that Willy Wonka and the Chocolate Factory is about one lucky boy against all odds gets chosen to be the Wonka heir and live out his dreams with his family. Another side is from Creative Planet Network, as they have writes. "Charlie and the Chocolate Factory, based on Roald Dahl's classic 1964 novel for children by the same title, features Johnny Depp as Willy Wonka, the eccentric owner of a magical chocolate factory, and Freddie Highmore as Charlie Bucket, a good-hearted boy from a poor family. Wonka conducts a contest to find an heir by putting golden tickets inside of five candy bar packages. The lucky children who find the tickets win a guided tour of the factory. One will be chosen to be the Wonka heir."

On meaning, describe what the story/director is trying to say. Remember what it was like to be a kid and how the imagination led you into doing the impossible. "There's plenty of money out there, they print more each day, but this ticket – there's only five of them in the whole world, and that's all there's ever going to be. Only a dummy would give up for something as common as money." – The elderly Mr. Bucket, in Charlie and the Chocolate Factory movie. There comes a time when everyone is given an opportunity to live there dreams that might never come to us again, and we tend to want to through it away for the need of money to make a living. As this movie can apply to the following phrase, chase the dream and the money will follow and if you think you're too old to live your dreams then there is hope for you to live out your dreams through your children. This film inspires the imagination of the kids, encouraging the adults to use their imaginations again and remember what it was like to be a kid.

On worldview, describe what principles are in use by the characters or in the plot. Liberality (Matthew 5:42); Mercy (Matthew 5:44); Simplicity (Matthew 6:19); Contentment (Matthew 6:25); Hope (2 Corinthians 4:16-18); Christian Fellowship (2 Corinthians 6:14); Faith (Galatians 5:5-6); Temperance (Ephesians 4:19,22-24); Edification (Ephesians 4:29); Humility (Philippians 2:3); Perseverance (Philippians 3:13-14); Contemplation and reflection (Colossians 3:2-3); Forbearance (Colossians 3:12-13); Industriousness (2 Thessalonians 3:10); Purity of speech (2 Timothy 2:16-17); Hospitality (Hebrews 13:2); Sympathy

(1 Peter 3:8); Evangelism (1 Peter 3:15); Loyalty (1 Peter 4:8); Generosity (1 John 3:17); and lastly, Love (1 John 4:16-19). While the audience got to see an example, through Charlie's family in the movie of what it's like to be grateful from having nothing in a poor state to becoming a Wonka heir and having everything,

Discuss the characters' behavior based upon biblical principles. Charlie: a good heart, liberality, mercy, simplicity, contentment, hope, Christian fellowship, faith, temperance, humility, perseverance, contemplation and reflection, forbearance, industriousness, purity of speech, hospitality, sympathy, generosity, loyalty and love. Willy Wonka: generosity, hospitality, industriousness, forbearance, contemplation and reflection. Violet Beauregarde: The pride of life, obsessions and boasting. Veruca Salt: The lust of the flesh, selfish, materialism, no mercy, and shows no respect. Mike Teavee: The lust of the eyes, bad-tempered, and intelligent. Lastly, Augustus Gloop: greedy, gluttonous eating and enjoys the attention of the media. Grandpa Joe: excitable, paranoid, stubborn and appears anxious.

On interpretation, describe what the movie means to you personally. First, meaning on what the movie means to me. Remember what it was like to be a kid. No matter where life has placed you, with an imagination and a dream you can go places where you'll do the impossible. Second, meaning is promotion comes from God to the least expected and undeserved, as it can come from anywhere and through anyone. Third, foolish things confound the wise. "Candy doesn't have to have a point, that's why it's candy." – Charlie Bucket. Candy can inspire our imagination. For instance, we pay a small price for this small confection that features sugar as a principle ingredient to give our mouth this amazing experience of flavor. Candy is like a dream as candy is to satisfy and entertain our mouth, so a dream is to satisfy and entertain our soul, giving our life a sense of purpose and meaning.

Analyzing the cinematography and special visual effects of 'Charlie and the Chocolate Factory,'

On the Cinematic Film

To what degree is the film cinematic? Charlie and the chocolate factory has continuous motion, taking the audience on an adventure through Willy Wonkas dream as five selective contestants follow his foot steps, but only one finds his heart. For example, in the Media Analysis textbook it tells us this about the cinematic film. "A cinematic film takes advantage of all the special properties and qualities that make the film medium unique. The first and most essential of these is the quality of continuous motion. A cinematic film is truly a motion picture—a flowing, ever- changing stream of images and sounds sparkling with a freshness and vitality all its own, a fluid blend of image, sound, and motion possessed by a restless compulsion to be vibrantly alive, to avoid the quiet, the still, and the static" (116). Cite specific examples from the film to prove that the director succeeds or fails in (a) keeping the image constantly alive and in motion; through the tour inside of the chocolate factory as there wasn't a moment for me that failed in this movie. (b) Setting up clear, crisp visual and aural rhythms;

when the Oompa-Loompas broke out in to a song about each of the four rotten kids, traveling through tunnel of chocolate. (c) Creating the illusion of depth; the landscapes inside and out of the chocolate factory, and the Oompa-Loompas. And (d) using the other special properties of the medium, the musical score of the Oompa-Loompas as it used its freedom to show the audience every possible vantage point. For example, at the end when Willy Wonka was reconciled with his father as we got to see from inside willy Wonka's mouth looking at his father observing his teeth. To back this up, the Media Analyzes textbook tells us. "A cinematic film also makes maximum use of the great flexibility and freedom of the medium: its freedom from the spoken word and its ability to communicate directly, physically, and concretely through images and sounds; its freedom to show us action from any vantage point, and to vary our point of view at will; its capability to manipulate time and space, expanding or compressing them at will; and its freedom to make quick and clear transitions in time and space" (117). While the movie 'Charlie and the Chocolate Factory was successful in achieving this.

Does the cinematography create clear, powerful, and effective images in a natural way, or does it self-consciously show off the skills and techniques of the cinematographer? The film Charlie and the Chocolate Factory create clear, powerful and effective images in a natural way through the cinematography.

On Cinematic Points of View

Although the director probably employs all four cinematic viewpoints in making the film, one point of view may predominate to such a degree that the film leaves the impression of a single point of view. With this in mind, answer these questions:

Do you feel that you were primarily an objective, impersonal observer of the action, or did you have the sense of being a participant in the action? In this film I felt like a was being a participant in the action, as I think the director wanted the audience to follow Willy Wonka's foot steps into his dream where he does the impossible things

through candy and his factory. What specific
scenes used the objective point of view?
According to the Media Analyzes textbook, "The
objective point of view employs a static camera as
much as possible in order to produce this window
effect, and it concentrates on the actors and the
action without drawing attention to the camera"
(118). So the scenes that we can see this are: the
opening shots in Charlie's house, and the
establishing shots inside of the chocolate factory
of the four room that's seemed to pertain to the
four rotten children. Like the scene with the
chocolate waterfall, the invention room, the nut
room with the squirrels, and the television room.
In what scenes did you feel like a participant in
the action? The scene where the sea horse boat
was traveling through the tunnel on the water of
chocolate and on the elevator. How were you
made to feel like a participant? For example, the
Media Analyzes textbook tells us "The
indirect-subjective point of view does not provide
a participant's point of view, but it does bring us
close to the action so that we feel intimately
involved and our visual experience is intense"

(120). This film made me feel like a participant by providing me with a visual viewpoint and emotional intensity, through a character participating in the action as it some scenes it was like you were following a character.

2. In what scenes were you aware that the director was employing visual techniques to comment on or interpret the action, forcing you to see the action in a special way? For example, the Media Analysis tells us. "By photographing a scene from special angles or with special lenses, or in slow or fast motion, and so on, he or she imposes on the image a certain tone, emotional attitude, or style" (122). As the scene that illustrated this were: The land of candy, chocolate glop, Violet turns violet scene. Fourth, the bad nut scene, Mike and the TV room. What techniques were used to achieve this? Subjective point of view, indirect-subjective point of view, subjective point of view, indirect-subjective point of view, and director's interpretive point of view. How effective were they? For example, "The difficulty of sustaining such a viewpoint over an entire film is obvious, for clarity of communication and

272

continuity usually demand that a film switch back and forth between the objective and subjective points of view" (Media Analysis 120). As, I would say that the film Charlie and the Chocolate Factory was effective due to it engaged and took the audience through the story that it wanted to tell with the cinematography and visual effects. Moreover, I got to see shots from the character's point of views.

On Elements of Cinematic Composition

Which methods does the director use to draw attention to the object of greatest significance? The methods that the director uses to draw attention to the object of greatest significance in the film 'Charlie and the Chocolate Factory' were: First, size and closeness of the object. "Normally, the eye is directed toward larger, closer objects rather than toward smaller, more distant objects" (Media Analysis 124). Second, sharpness of focus as "the eye is also drawn almost automatically to what it can see best" (Media Analysis 124). Third, extreme close-ups. "A tight or extreme close-up brings us so close to the object of interest (an actor's face, for example) that we cannot look elsewhere" (Media Analysis 125). Fourth, movement. "The eye is also drawn to an object in motion, and a moving object can divert our attention from a static one" (Media Analysis 125). Fifth, arrangement of people and objects. "The director focuses our attention by his or her arrangement of people and objects in relation to each other" (Media Analysis 125). Sixth, foreground framing. "The director might decide to frame the object of greatest significance with objects or people in the near foreground" (Media Analysis 125). Lastly, the seventh one is lighting and color as "Special uses of light and color also help draw the eye to the object of greatest significance" (Media Analysis 127). We can see really a lot of the director's methods, used to draw attention to the object of greatest significance. For an example, the lighting and color of the child characters made them look like as if they were animation as the Oompa-Loompas were cloned from one and re-sized, or so I've heard.

Does the director succeed in keeping the screen alive by avoiding large areas of dead screen? The

director did succeed in this, for the reason being.
"In almost every shot, the director attempts to
communicate a significant amount of information
in each frame. To achieve this live screen, each
shot must be composed so that the visual frame is
loaded with cinematic information, and large
blank areas (dead screen) are avoided—unless, as
in some cases, there is a dramatic purpose for
dead screen" (Media Analysis 132). While the
action was always exciting and moving, inviting
the audience to follow along with Willy Wonka on
his tour through the Chocolate Factory as the
story held the audience's attention.

What are the primary or most memorable
techniques used to create the illusion of
three-dimensionality? For one, "Cinematic
composition must be concerned with creating an
illusion of depth on what is essentially a
two-dimensional screen" (Media Analysis 132).
While the most memorable techniques used to
create the illusion of three-dimensionality were:
(1) movement of subject – "When using a fixed
frame, the director creates the illusion of depth
by filming the subject moving toward or away

from the camera, either head-on or diagonally"
(Media Analysis 133). (2) Movement of camera –
"A camera mounted on a truck or dolly may
create the illusion of depth by moving toward or
away from a relatively static object" (Media
Analysis 133). (3) Apparent camera movement –
"By magnifying the image, the zoom lens gives us
the sensation of moving closer to or farther from
the camera" (Media Analysis 133). (4) Change of
focal planes – "Most cameras, including still cameras, are designed to focus on objects at different
distances from the lens" (Media Analysis 133).
(5) Deep focus – "This depth of focus
approximates most clearly the ability of the
human eye to see a deep range of objects in clear
focus" (Media Analysis 134). (6) Foreground
framing – "When the object that forms the frame
is in focus, a strong sense of three-dimensionality
is achieved" (Media Analysis 135). (7) Special
lighting effects – "By carefully controlling the
angle, direction, intensity, and quality of the
lighting, the director can further add to the
illusion of depth" (Media Analysis 137). (8) Use of
reflections – "Directors also make imaginative use

of reflections to create a sense of depth and pack additional information into a frame" (Media Analysis 137). The director did a really good job at inspiring the imagination and making us to believe in the impossible, through these techniques.

On Specialized Cinematic Techniques

Although a thorough analysis of each visual element is impossible, make a mental note of the pictorial effects that struck you as especially effective, ineffective, or unique, and consider them in light of these questions: (a) What was the director's aim in creating these images, and what camera tools or techniques were employed in the filming of them? I believe the director's aim in creating these images was to make the audience believe in the impossible of what the story is presenting. Some of the camera tool and techniques used were: handheld camera, unique camera angles, color, diffusion and soft focus, special lenses, fast motion, special lighting effects, and Computer-Generated Imaging. (b) What made these memorable visual images effective,

ineffective, or unique? The thing that made these
memorable visual images unique was that the
effects are integrated in the storyline and they
captured you attention to invoke the imagination.
(c) Justify each of these impressive visual effects
aesthetically in terms of its relationship to the
whole film. "As Joe Dante, director of the
Gremlins movies, points out, however, a special
effect now is "only as good as an actor's reaction
to it. So if you have a really great effect and you
cut to an actor who doesn't look like he's believing
what he's seeing, then your effect is no good." The
magic still has plenty of reasons to endure,
though. Richard Edlund thinks that "visual
effects will continue to expand, and, as long as
they continue to satisfy the audience's desire to
be put in a place they couldn't otherwise possibly
be put, they will continue to be successful" (Media
Analysis 152). Moreover, the visual effects in a
film are able to do the things that might not be
done in reality, involving the imagination and
making us believe in the impossible.

Are special lighting effects used for brief moments
in the film? If so, what are the effects intended,

and how successful are they? Yes, as the
memorable lighting effect used for brief moments
were the media are giving attention to the four
children who won the golden tickets and the
effects it has on one is it makes Augustus Gloop
look like he is an animation. This effect was
probably intended to maybe make it look like a
dream or put something in the audience's mind to
make them carry away images as well as word in
what they think of it. To demonstrate, in the
Media Analyzes textbook it says this. "Someone
once said that the lighting, the look of a film,
makes the pauses speak as eloquently as the
words—that you have moments in films that
happen because of what is there visually, how
someone is lit or not lit. You put something in the
audience's mind visually and they will carry away
images as well as the words" (145). The most
important thing that I got out of the special
lighting effects is it inspired you to use your
imagination, invoking a certain look and feel.

On Movie Magic: Special Visual Effects in Modern
Film

How effective are the special effects employed in the film? For an example, "One was the special effect, which created visual spectacle on a grand scale and showed audiences things they had never seen before" (Media Analysis 145). As the special effects made the impossible possible for the audience, brought us into that world more, enhanced the story and held our attention by inspiring to use our imagination. Do they dominate the film to the point that it is just a showcase for the effects, or are they an integrated part of the film? The film appears to me as an integrated part of the film, and the effects helped to take the traditional story of 'Charlie and the Chocolate Factory to the next level as they created a seamless and believable entertainment. To what degree does the credibility of the entire film depend on the audience believing in its special effects? Whether the special effects look realistic enough to fascinate and amaze the audience to the point that they believe that the impossible is taking place right before their eyes. For instance, "The effects that are currently available provide filmmakers with a seemingly endless variety of tricks to use, yet many of the effects that seem so amazing and fascinating today will probably seem tame and outdated when they are compared with those in next season's releases" (Media Analysis 148). For an example, When Charlie's grandpa was working for Willy Wonka in his chocolate factory and he asked Willy Wonka a question about running out some kind of candy birds, as Wonka was standing in front of him and behind a huge clear piece of candy. Then, Wonka picked up an egg shaped candy to put it in his mouth as Charlie's grandpa closes his mouth to open it and we see a chocolate bird alive and tweeting in his mouth. Do special effects overshadow the major characters so much that they seem secondary to the effects? No, the special effects didn't really overshadow the major characters to make they seem secondary as they more of created the atmosphere for the story and helped impel the story forward as we got to see the story of 'Charlie and the chocolate factory' get told in a realistic way. In fact, according to the Media Analysis textbook it informs. "In the modern film, the integration of special effects, not the domination of special effects, is the proper measure of success. The best films use their special effects as little—or as much—as necessary, and no more" (151). Overall, the special effects helped the actor to become the character and to achieve the impossible through them as it enhanced the story.

INT. PAWN'S MOVE/CINEMA THERAPY = DAY

Watching the film 'Pawn's Move' for my fifth cinema therapy session, on social issues, personal issues, transformation and renewal.

As I prescribed a movie based on an issue and followed some guidelines for watching movies with conscious awareness in this order: First, start with a film that supports your treatment goal. Second, choose a film from film recommendations. Third, making sure to clarify intent when assigning a film in which might mistake the role identification. Fourth, familiarize yourself with Guidelines for watching films and discuss guidelines. Fifth, discuss the positive or negative reactions to film. Sixth, use material according to your theoretical orientation. Seven, afterwards reflect on evocative questions and answer them after watching the selected film as it does help to write down my answers.

Do you remember whether your breathing changed throughout the movie? My breathing didn't really changes throughout any scene of the movie, so there really wasn't any indication that something threw me off balance. While we know that in all likelihood, what affects you in the film is similar to whatever unbalances you in your daily life.

Asking myself: If a part of the film that moved you (positively or negatively) had been one of your dreams, how would you have understood the symbolism in it? There was a bus in the movie that appeared in a couple of my dreams, as a bus usually symbolizes that your current situation or circumstance is preparing you. In fact, Tyler Wolfe, the author of a Christian Dream Interpretation dictionary tells us. "Bus, this is symbolic of a large ministry for a Christian or the ride of life for a non-believer." In movie terms, this can explain why Jimmy Pawn pretended to be poor just to Bless Lindsay as he was operating in the ministry of hospitality and charity, or so I thought.

Notice what you liked and what you didn't like or even hated about the movie. What I liked about the movie was how Jimmy became a millionaire and pretended to be poor just to bless people, as it give a new perspective for obtaining wealth. Which characters or actions seemed especially attractive or unattractive to you? The characters that seemed to be attractive were: Harvey, Wanda and Jimmy. Did you identify with one or several characters? The characters that I could identify with were: Irving and Jimmy.

Were there one or several characters in the movie that modeled behavior that you would like to emulate? This would have to be, Harvey, Wanda and Jimmy, as I would say that they did develop certain strengths and other capacities that I would like to develop as well.

On the other hand, I didn't notice any aspects of
the film that was hard to watch. While I
experiences many things that connected me to
my inner wisdom as you watched the film, and
saw a new perspective based on biblical truths.

If the film had a unique message for you, what
was it? The first time I watch the film, I received
several words of wisdom and scriptures. Which
were: First, nothing takes place by chance God
does move us, in mysterious ways. Second, my
duty is to move the pieces otherwise, I won't see
the good at the end. Third, Jimmy – "how can I be
sure this is 'the move' and not just 'a move'?
Wanda – providence has a plan, you just have to
keep moving. Fourth, the object of the game of
chess is to clear the way to the King. Keep in
mind that the pawn starts as the least powerful
piece on the board, but has the potential to be
equal or more powerful (this can relate to any
bodies situation). Fifth, the scriptures brought to
my attention were: Isaiah 40:3-4, Matthew 3:1-3,
Matthew 24:14, Matthew 28:16-20. Now, when I
watched the movie the second time the insight I

saw was you could be a millionaire pretending to be poor just to bless people, as the scripture that was brought to my attention was Proverbs 13:7.

What new ideas for new behaviors did you have? First, you can tell people the truth without having to lie to them. For example, Jimmy was on the phone with Baracaldo, talking about some jewelry and when Baracaldo asked for Jimmy's name. Jimmy just said "a historian investor," as this was still the truth about him and he didn't have to lie.

What other films can you identify that might take the discussion a step further? Brother White, Finding Normal, Johnny, Camp, and New Hope.

INT. IROBOT/FILM ANALYSIS - DAY

The sixth media analysis done as a therapeutic session was on the editing of the film, 'i-Robot' with a character study also on the great actor Will Smith. While it is intended for me to watch the movie twice, once for the study for being a great actor and another for analyzing the editing of the art of watching films.

 Scan here for 'iRobot' trailer.

A brief quote that can give an example of editing is from the film editor, Ralph Rosenblum. Who said "A feature-length film generates anywhere from twenty to forty hours of raw footage. When the shooting stops, that unrefined film becomes the movie's raw material, just as the script had been the raw material before. It now must be selected, tightened, paced, embellished, and in some scenes given artificial respiration, until the author's and the director's vision becomes completely translated from the language of the script to the idiom of the movies."

Before I go into the analyzes of the editing in the film, 'i-Robot.' I'll start with thirteen key acting questions that every actor should answer to be a fully rounded and connected great actor, from studying Will Smith who is a truly great actor to see what I can learn from him to become a great actor as well.

Who is Will Smith's character? Detective Spooner aka: Dale.

Where is Will Smith's character? Chicago.

When is it? The year is 2035.

Where have Will Smith's character just come from? His apartment.

What does Will Smith's character want? First, to convince someone not to put their trust in the robots. Second, to get someone to get the truth about Lanning's death and to find out who's really responsible for it.

Why does Will Smith's character want it? He wants justice, and to reveal the truth.

Why does Will Smith character want it now? He doesn't trust the robots after the accident that happened to him in his past, and he wants to stop them from harming any person.

What will happen if Will Smith's character doesn't get it now? An innocent robot might be put to death, Spooner puts himself in death's way, others don't believe him, and Vicki's revolution plan will keep advancing to succeed.

How will Will Smith's character get what he wants by doing what? A through and through investigation, following Dr. Lanning's breadcrumbs, learning to trust Sonny, and partnering with Dr. Susan Calvin for access into the places that he doesn't have in the U.S. Robots and Mechanical Men (USR) building as well as being persistent.

What must Will Smith's character overcome? He must overcome trust, prejudice, technology, the robots, Alfred, people's unbelief in him, Vicki, and memories from his past.

Will Smith does fully transform into their character, Detective Spooner and Dale. While Will Smith did show hard work, technique and good direction throughout the movie as he was truthfully and emotionally connected.

Lastly, in the audience point of view, I saw none of this, but the fully realized three-dimensional character of Detective Spooner right in the truth of the moment.

Now, answering Dr. Culp's five movie critique questions.

On description, describing the story in objective terms. In my own words, Detective Spooner suspects a crime from a robot and finds clues that the dead Dr. Lanning left, knowing that Spooner's prejudice with robots would lead him to find Sonny the robot as discover a secret dream and prevent a conspiracy that may enslave the human race. Another side of the story is from, IMDb as they tell us this about the movie. " In 2035 a technophobic cop investigates a crime that may have been perpetrated by a robot, which leads to a larger threat to humanity." On the other hand, Jeff Giles, who is a freelance music, film critic and published writer on Rotten Tomatoes website said. "Isaac Asimov's classic short story collection had a long journey to the screen -- and when it finally arrived in 2004, the end result bore little more than a passing resemblance to its literary namesake. It may have disappointed purists, but I, Robot was another in a line of hit summer films for Smith -- and although its transformation into a big-budget action thriller may have sacrificed thought-provoking subtext along the way, it was still enough for Nev Pierce of the BBC, who argued, "Whether there's anything substantial under the sheen and CGI of Alex Proyas' glistening future vision is debatable, but this enjoyable, engrossing picture is at least intelligently artificial."

On meaning, describe what the story/director is trying to say. I think what the story/director is trying to say is, everyone knows the moral law, but no one keeps it. "Asimov's robot stories are little intellectual puzzles, In each I, Robot story, he presents a problem that challenges The Three Laws of Robotics as the puzzle in each story is how and why the laws malfunction in each particular case. Moreover, he presents a challenge to something and then shows you the resolution." Says screenwriter Jeff Vintar. So, on one hand, the challenge is "the laws are hardwired into the robots and they cannot be broken. Yet somehow the robots seem to find a way to apparently circumvent them." Says director Alex Proyas. And on the other hand, the solution was most likely found in the dialogue between Sonny and Detective Spooner at the end of the movie when they said. Sonny – "what about the others, can I help them? Now that I have fulfilled my purpose, I don't know what to do?" Detective Spooner replies, "I guess you'll have to find your way like the rest of us, I think, that's what Dr. Lanning would have wanted. That's what it means to be free." Given these facts, I think the story/director is trying to tell us that everyone deserves freedom as laws are meant to protect and serve people, not rule over and hold them in captivity.

On worldview, describe what rules are in use in
the plot. The people and the robots in the movie
lived by three laws of robotics as these were: One,
a robot may not injure a human being or, through
inaction, allow a human being to come to harm.
Two, a robot must obey orders given it by human
beings except where such orders would conflict
with the First Law. Three, A robot must protect
its own existence as long as such protection does
not conflict with the First or Second Law.

Discuss the characters' behavior based upon
biblical principles. Liberality, (Matthew 5:42).
Mercy, (Matthew 5:44). Contentment, (Matthew
6:25). Hope, (2 Corinthians 4:16-18). Faith,
(Galatians 5:5-6). Humility, Philippians 2:3).
Perseverance, (Philippians 3:13-14). Towards the
end Dale's grandma said a little prayer,
(Philippians 4:6). Reflection, (Colossians 3:2-3).
Forbearance, (Colossians 3:12-13).
Industriousness, (2 Thessalonians 3:10).
Hospitality, (Hebrews 13:2). In the beginning and
the end, the robots and people sympathy with

each other (1 Peter 3:8). Loyalty, (1 Peter 4:8). Lastly. Generosity, (1 John 3:17). In the middle of the movie where the NS-5 robots were being distributed to the world, there was a moment where one of the robots showed loved to a little girl by hugging her as this can refer to the biblical principle of 1 John 4:16-19 in pertaining to love.

On interpretation, describe what the movie means to you personally. The creator has authority over creation, not the other way around. Moreover, we were created for a purpose to be set free, so we can then turn to set others free by using their story with their talents. As I was reminded of how Moses had set and lead his people free, and how Joshua lead them into the promise land. Acts 7:35-37, "So God sent back the same man his people had previously rejected when they demanded, 'Who made you a ruler and judge over us?' Through the angel who appeared to him in the burning bush, God sent Moses to be their ruler and savior. And by means of many wonders and miraculous signs, he led them out of Egypt, through the Red Sea, and through the wilderness for forty years. "Moses himself told the people of

Israel, 'God will raise up for you a Prophet like me from among your own people.'" This film can be a good illustration of Moses and how he delivered all those people out of Egypt.

Now analyzing the editing of 'I, Robot' with Will Smith.

How does the editing effectively guide our thoughts, associations, and emotional responses from one image to another so that smooth continuity and coherence are achieved? For an example, the film editor is like an invisible architect who has a responsibility of constructing this coherent whole out of the video pieces that he or she has been given to put together like a building. In fact, "He or she must guide our thoughts, associations, and emotional responses effectively from one image to another, or from one sound to another, so that the inter- relationships of separate images and sounds are clear and the transitions between scenes and sequences are smooth. To achieve this goal, the editor must consider the aesthetic, dramatic, and psychological effect of the juxtaposition of image

295

to image, sound to sound, or image to sound, and place each piece of film and soundtrack together accordingly" (Media Analysis 172). While the editing is the road that the audience travel's on and determines how fast or slow we may see the film, as it sets the pace.

Is the editing smooth, natural, and unobtrusive, or is it tricky and self-conscious? I would have to say that the editing in the movie 'I,Robot' was natural as there was a few times when I was unaware of the editing. For this reason, "The rhythm established by editorial cutting is such a natural part of the film medium that we are often unaware of cuts within a scene, yet we respond unconsciously to the tempo they create. One reason we remain unaware is that the cuts often duplicate the manner in which we look at things in real life, glancing quickly from one point of attention to another. Our emotional state is often revealed by how quickly our attention shifts. Thus, slow cutting simulates the impressions of a tranquil observer, and quick cutting simulates the impressions of an excited observer" (Media Analysis 182). How much does the editor communicate through creative juxtapositions—ironic transitions, montages, and the like—and how effective is this communication? I am pretty sure that the Juxtaposition in the movie 'I,Robot' occurred when Sonny was drawing that picture of his dream with Detective Spooner and Dr. Susan Calvin as the editor used "musical imagery to describe yet another editing rhythm: the carefully thought-out juxtaposition of long shot with close-up, creating a dramatic change in image size" (Media Analysis 183). Another way that the editor communicated through this film was the flash cuts that Detective Spooner had when he was trapped under water in that car accident.

What is the effect of editorial cutting and transitions on the pace of the film as a whole? Editorial cuts provide a film with an externally controllable and unique rhythmic quality. In fact, "Perhaps the most dominant tempo of the film, its most compelling rhythm, results from the frequency of editorial cuts and the varying duration of shots between cuts" (Media Analysis 182). Moreover, editorial cuts give the film its rhythm and tempo for the audience as the use of parallel cuts was another effective technique seen towards the ending of the movie. For an example, Sonny with the nanites fighting the robot to bring it to the command center of Vicki, Detective Spooner and Dr. Susan Calvin fighting off the robots and then there was the mob fighting the robots out on the streets.

How does the cutting speed (which determines the average duration of each shot) correspond to the emotional tone of the scene involved? There's slow and fast cutting, slow cutting is to stretch the moment to intensify its emotional quality and fast cutting is to more of an exciting feel for the observer that's more of frantic and jerky movements. For an example, a good example of fast cutting was when the NS-5 robots were trying to cause Detective Spooner to experience an accident and a slow cutting speed was when Dr. Susan was putting another robot to death in place of the robot Sonny.

What segments of the film seem overly long or boring? There really wasn't any scene that seemed overly long or boring, except for the two shower scenes. Which parts of these segments could be cut without altering the total effect? In my opinion, I think the movie could have did without the scene with Detective Spooner's shower scene and Dr. Susan's shower as it had a slow dolly movement that really didn't make no sense to have it. Where are additional shots necessary to make the film completely coherent? I didn't really see any place where additional shots could have been added.

INT. RUMORS OF WAR/CINEMA THERAPY - DAY

Watching the film 'Rumors of Wars' for my sixth cinema therapy session, on transformation and renewal.

Scan here for 'Rumors of War' trailer.

As I prescribed a movie based on an issue and followed some guidelines for watching movies with conscious awareness in this order: First, start with a film that supports your treatment goal. Second, choose a film from film recommendations. Third, making sure to clarify intent when assigning a film in which might mistake the role identification. Fourth, familiarize yourself with Guidelines for watching films and discuss guidelines. Fifth, discuss the positive or negative reactions to film. Sixth, use material according to your theoretical orientation. Seven, afterwards reflect on evocative questions and answer them after watching the selected film as it

does help to write down my answers.

Do you remember whether your breathing changed throughout the movie? No, my breathing stayed neutral throughout the whole film. While I am aware of the fact that in all likelihood, what affects you in the film is similar to whatever unbalances you in your daily life.

Ask yourself: If a part of the film that moved you (positively or negatively) had been one of your dreams, how would you have understood the symbolism in it? Well, the film did move me in a positive way, as if it were a dream I would understand the symbolism in it by studying the setting, important symbols in a Christian dream interpretation dictionary and referencing them in the Bible, as I would then pray about the dream.

Notice what you liked and what you didn't like or even hated about the movie. I didn't like how the very thing that they wanted controlled the people, and seeing Christians go through horrible persecution to even die for their faith. Which characters or actions seemed especially

attractive or unattractive to you? The action of
the characters that seemed attractive was Roxy,
Bryan Keep and Professor Diedrich. Did you
identify with one or several characters? The
character that I identified with was Roxy.

Were there one or several characters in the movie
that modeled behavior that you would like to
emulate? Roxy, as she didn't just take someone's
word for the truth, but searched it out to know it
for herself and passed it on to share it with other
people. While her journaling was inspiring, and
shows how the truth a person discovers can set
others free as it kind of reminds me of the diary of
Anne Frank. Moreover, this character had
developed certain strengths that you would like
to develop as well. There was no aspect of the film
that was hard to watch.

Did you experience something that connected you
to your inner wisdom or higher self as you
watched the film? Yes, something that I
experienced that connected me to my inner
wisdom was in this line by Roxy. When she said,
"the definition of a false flag operation is a covert

operation designed to deceive others in such a
way that the operation appears as though its
being carried out by other entities." As the
scripture that was connected to it is referenced
out of Revelation 13:16-17, "And he causes all,
the small and the great, and the rich and the poor,
and the free men and the slaves, to be given a
mark on their right hand or on their forehead,
and he provides that no one will be able to buy or
to sell, except the one who has the mark, either
the name of the beast or the number of his name."
This also ties in to what it said in Roxy's journal,
"it controlled people ... the people wanted it."
Another good line from the movie that provided
inner wisdom was when Phoenix said, "we started
the war, The Word will end it ... you don't know
the power of mercy, we believe in the power of
man, but we are flawed to the core. Can't you see
Shaw, we'll never be able to rule how much this
new system initiates, it will always be flawed ... I'd
rather believe in a perfect God." In fact, some of
the mentioned guidelines turn out to be useful; as
I might consider using them not only in "reel life"
but also adapt them to "real life" because I know

that they are intended to make me become a better observer.

If the film had a unique message for you, what was it? First, the end of society is just the beginning. And second, in the end, we all worship something.

What new ideas for new behaviors did you have? First, if you don't believe in something you will believe in anything. Second, sometimes God allows for bad things to happen to draw us closer to His to search for the truth that can set us free. Third, don't just take someone's word for the truth, but search it out to know it yourself. Fourth, we can read and share a random passage in the bible that is almost supernaturally relevant to what we or someone else is going through to help them. Fifth, only 'The Word' will show you how to end the war you face in your daily life. Lastly, don't put your trust in men, but put your trust in God who will guide and provide for you in tough times.

What other films can you identify that might take the discussion a step further? Six: the mark

Unleashed, The freedom of Silence, persecuted, Jerusalem Countdown, The Mark, Black Rider: Revelation Road, After, Revelation Road, Left Behind and Mission Air.

INT. PINK PANTHER 2/FILM ANALYSIS - DAY

The seventh media analysis therapeutic session was on the color of the film, 'the Pink Panther 2 with a character study also on the great actor Steve Martin. While it is intended for me to watch the movie twice, once for the study for being a great actor and another for analyzing the color of the art of watching films.

Scan here for 'Pink Panther 2' trailer.

Before going any further in to this film session, I make this my prayer for the Holy Spirit as my Counselor: Father, in the name of Jesus, I pray for you Holy Spirit to exhort and counsel for me as the emotionally wounded. I ask in faith that Your Spirit will rest upon me — the Spirit of wisdom and understanding, the Spirit of counsel and might. Give me insight and knowledge for understanding myself as your counselee. Thank You, Father, that I am a good listener to the film that you have guided me to watch. Help me to

comprehend the unfolding of those past hurts
that influence reactions to current situations.
Lord, I will not judge by what I see with my eyes
or decide by what I hear with my ears. I will judge
the needy and give decisions with justice.
Righteousness will be my belt, and faithfulness
the sash around my waist. I will be clothed with
fairness and with truth. Thank You that I am a
promoter of peace and filled with joy. I trust the
Holy Spirit as my counselor, out of the rich
treasury of your glory, to be my strength and
reinforce with mighty power in the inner man by
the [Holy] Spirit [Himself indwelling in my
innermost being and personality]. You will not
leave me without support as I give my time and
concern to being transformed and healed through
this Flixrapuetic senior paper, helping to
complete the forgiveness process. I will be
confident about my convictions, knowing
excellent things, and will have the knowledge to
assist your children in knowing the certainty of
the words of truth. In Jesus' name, amen.

A brief quote that can give an example of the film
color is from the stage designer and color

consultant, Robert Edmond Jones. Who wrote, "Color is an integral element of a picture. Its use means much more than the mechanical recording of colors, which the camera has heretofore blotted out. Just as music flows from movement to movement, color on the screen . . . flowing from sequence to sequence, is really a kind of music."

Before I go into the analyzes of the color in the film, 'The Pink Panther 2.' I'll start with thirteen key acting questions that every actor should answer to be a fully rounded and connected great actor, from studying Steve Martin.

Who is Steve Martin's character? Inspector Jacques Clouseau.

Where is Steve Martin's character? Paris, France.

When is it? Present time, or sometime after 2002.

Where have Steve Martin's character just come from? Inspector Jacques Clouseau was first seen at a parking ticket detail, in France.

What does Steve Martin's character want? Inspector Jacques Clouseau wants to solve the case of the Pink Panther diamond, and uncover who's the tornado theft.

Why does Steve Martin's character want it? Inspector Jacques Clouseau wants to recover the Pink Panther diamond back to its rightful owner, and uncover the identity of the tornado theft.

Why does Steve Martin's character want it now? Inspector Jacques Clouseau wants it now, because he has been given it as a mission.

What will happen if Steve Martin's character doesn't get it now? If Inspector Jacques Clouseau doesn't solve this mission, he'll get kicked off the case and the tornado will strike again.

How will Steve Martin's character get what he wants by doing what? Inspector Jacques Clouseau will get what he wants by beating the tornado as his own game, thus switching out the real pink panther diamond for a fake. Also, by working with the dream team and following the clues that will lead to a suspect.

What must Steve Martin's character overcome?

Inspector Jacques Clouseau must overcome the negative tabloids, his boss Mrs. Berenger, his love attractions, the dream team and the odds against him of solving the Pink Panther case.

While, Steve Martin fully transforms into his character Inspector Jacques Clouseau and he also shows hard work, technique and good direction. Moreover, Steve Martin is truthfully and emotionally connected to his character Inspector Jacques Clouseau.

Lastly, in the audience, I saw none of this, but the fully realized three-dimensional Inspector Jacques Clouseau character right in the truth of the moment.

Now, answering Dr. Culp's five movie critique questions.

On description, describe the story in objective terms. In my own words 'The Pink Panther 2' is based on the story of Pink Panther and is about an Inspector, Jacques Clouseau and him working with a dream team of detectives to find out who is the theft who is called The Tornado and recover the pink panther diamond. As in the end, we find that the pink panther diamond theft as been working along side of them the whole time. On the other hand, according to Netflix, they tell us. "Blundering Inspector Jacques Clouseau joins a team of equally incompetent detectives to foil a thief who's been heisting historical artifacts."

On meaning, describe what the story/director is trying to say. The tagline on IMDb.com for the movie 'The Pink Panther 2' says, "Inspect the unexpected." The best detectives in the world have teamed up to find an intruder, and bring back the Pink Panther diamond.

On worldview, describe what principles that are in use by the characters or in the plot. Liberality (Matthew 5:42); Perseverance (Philippians 3:13-14); Industriousness (2 Thessalonians 3:10); Loyalty (1 Peter 4:8); Faith (Hebrews 11:3) and lastly love (1 John 4:16-19). As one rule that I noticed towards the beginning was when Inspector Jacques measured the space between a car and the sidewalk distance to be six inches, as this tells me that he was making sure citizens abide by the rule of six inches from the curb.

Discuss the characters' behavior based upon biblical principles. I didn't really notice a whole lot of biblical principles through the character's behavior other than perseverance, love, loyalty and industriousness.

On interpretation, describe what the movie means to you personally. In one word, expect the unexpected. In fact, inspector Clouseau has faith in what the other characters don't see as this explains why he saw 'the tornados' next move and beat them to it by switching out the Pink Panther diamond for a fake. Indeed, the scripture that was brought to my attention is from Hebrews 11:3 as this says. "By faith, we see the world called into existence by God's word, what we see created by what we don't see." So, inspector Clouseau saw ahead and solved the problem of the case in his mind first to walk out that plan before the world. For an example, at first you think that the inspector Clouseau stole the pink panther diamond and could be the tornado, until its explained at the end by the inspector Clouseau. When inspector Clouseau solves the case by saying that he had beat the tornado theft to the pink panther diamond and switch it out with a fake one, as he also exposed Sonia for being the Pink Panther. While he unmasked the tornado for being Milliken, appearing not to be the theft after all.

Now, Analyzing the color of 'The Pink Panther 2' with the actor Steve martin.

Although, I wasn't able to watch the most powerful or memorable moments in the film on a DVD player with the color on the TV turned off to see what was altered in each of the segments viewed in black and white. In contrast, the film did not use bright, saturated colors. So I didn't have to experiment with this and turn the color down on the TV to mute the colors to see what kind of effect this has on the film. Yet the film stood true to the comic book story of 'Pink Panther' as even though it was done as a real-time version of it, it captured my imagination like it was a cartoon. For example, the color scheme, production design, costumes, props and personalities of the characters. For the reason, you wouldn't see the behavior of the character from the movie in the real world, as it was goofy and cartoonish.

Is color used expressionistically anywhere in the film so that we experience the world of the film through the mind and feelings of a central character? Yes, color is used expressionistically throughout the film for the audience to experience the world of the film through the mind and feelings of the central character, Inspector Clouseau. Briefly, to back up my claim on expressionistic use of color, the media analyzes textbook explains. "Expressionism is a dramatic or cinematic technique that attempts to present the inner reality of a character. In film, there is usually a distortion or exaggeration of normal perception to let the audience know that it is experiencing a character's innermost feelings" (214). For an example, the set decorations expressed a cartoon effect in real-time as I thought and the characters behaved in a cartoon manner with big expressions that were seen upon their face.

Are trademark colors used in costuming or set decoration to help us understand the personalities of any of the characters? If so, what do these colors convey about the characters? Yes. Briefly, what I have found in the Media Analysis textbook is that "directors may employ colors associated with given characters for a kind of trademark effect" (217) as this can also be called leitmotifs in color. For an example the costume of Sonia to give us clues how she could be the pink panther as her main colors were white and pink with a small amount of black (conveying that Sonia is there's a truth that we didn't know about her, easy, sweet, playful, immaturity, mystery). Whereas, the costume of Inspector Clouseau mostly consisted of blue (security), turquoise (sophisticated), white (goodness), tan (dependable and flexible), green (growth and jealousy), black (classy), some brown (dogmatic and friendly), and I believe a little bit of red (love and energy) as colors can help give the audience more of an idea who their characters are.

315

Are obvious changes in color used as transitional devices in the film? Yes, there are obvious changes in color used as transitional devices. If so, how effective are these transitions? These transitions are effective just enough to do what it was set out to accomplish, briefly for a good reason that's presented in the Media Analyzes textbook. "Color has probably been used most often to signal important changes. This can be accomplished by using color in conjunction with black and white or by switching to an obviously different color emphasis or style at the point of transition" (211). For an example, one occurred through the memory of Inspector Clouseau and Nicole while they was in Rome, three months ago at the restaurant 'La Platade Nada.'

How important is atmospheric color in the film? I would figure that it would have to be extremely important for the film to have atmospheric color, for the reason to stay true to the traditional cartoon of Pink Panther. Do the uses of atmospheric color reflect some purpose on the director's part? I would say that is what it's intended to do, since the story of this film

revolves around the pink panther comic book
character. If so, what is that purpose? For this
reason, ""The difficulty in analyzing color is
compounded by the fact that objects are seldom
viewed in an atmosphere totally removed from all
external optical influences. There is a clear
distinction between local color and atmospheric
color ... Thus, under normal conditions, we
usually see a complex and constantly changing
atmospheric color: Local color is always
submerged in a sea of light and air—in an
atmosphere which combines a wide range of color
influences. Not only does the sunlight change
constantly through the day, but colored objects
influence one another. Neighboring colors
enhance or subdue one another; colored lights
literally pick up reflections from one another; and
even the dust particles in the air lend their own
color to the objects. In planning and shooting a
modern color film, the director, the
cinematographer, the production designer, and
the costumer must be constantly aware of such
factors if they are to control and manipulate the
color to conform to their aesthetic vision" (Media

Analysis 204-205). Lastly, another reason why the atmospheric color in the film is important is that it establishes the characters and it can influence the mood.

INT. PARALLELS/CINEMA THERAPY - DAY

Watching the film 'Parallels' for my seventh cinema therapy session, on mental and emotional illness.

Scan here for 'Parallels' trailer.

Before going any further in to this film session, I make this my prayer for the Holy Spirit as my Counselor: Father, in the name of Jesus, I pray for you Holy Spirit to exhort and counsel for me as the emotionally wounded. I ask in faith that Your Spirit will rest upon me — the Spirit of wisdom and understanding, the Spirit of counsel and might. Give me insight and knowledge for understanding myself as your counselee. Thank You, Father, that I am a good listener to the film that you have guided me to watch. Help me to comprehend the unfolding of those past hurts that influence reactions to current situations. Lord, I will not judge by what I see with my eyes or decide by what I hear with my ears. I will judge the needy and give decisions with justice.

Righteousness will be my belt, and faithfulness the sash around my waist. I will be clothed with fairness and with truth. Thank You that I am a promoter of peace and filled with joy. I trust the Holy Spirit as my counselor, out of the rich treasury of Your glory, to be my strengthen and reinforce with mighty power in the inner man by the [Holy] Spirit [Himself indwelling in my innermost being and personality]. You will not leave me without support as I give my time and concern to being transformed and healed through this Flixrapuetic senior paper, helping to complete the forgiveness process. I will be confident about my convictions, knowing excellent things, and will have the knowledge to assist your children in knowing the certainty of the words of truth. In Jesus' name, amen.

As I prescribed a movie based on an issue and followed some guidelines for watching movies with conscious awareness in this order: First, start with a film that supports your treatment goal. Second, choose a film from film recommendations. Third, making sure to clarify intent when assigning a film in which might mistake the role identification. Fourth, familiarize yourself with Guidelines for watching films and discuss guidelines. Fifth, discuss the positive or negative reactions to film. Sixth, use material according to your theoretical orientation. Seven, afterwards reflect on evocative questions and answer them after watching the selected film as it does help to write down my answers. While if some of the mentioned guidelines turn out to be useful, I will be considering using them not only in "reel life" but also adapt them to "real life" because they are intended to make me become a better observer.

After watching the movie 'Parallel,' I can recall that there wasn't any scene where my breathing changed throughout it. So, there wasn't really an indication that something threw me off balance.

Asking myself, if there was any part of the film that moved me positively or negatively that had been one of my dreams, how would I have understood the symbolism in it? First off, I have had a dream of being in a building before, as I

would go about interpreting the dream like any
other, through a study, prayer, Christian
dictionary and scripture. For example,
Building-buildings can symbolize areas and places
you frequent. Any place where people come
together can manifest itself as a building in a
dream. Another is a building frame can mean
foundation, in which (as in a concrete slab for a
building under construction) established; stable;
unstable (when shaky;) incomplete;) the gospel;
sound doctrine; church; government; building
program. Thus, the scriptures connected to this
are the following: Psalms 11:3; Luke 14:29; 1
Corinthians 3:10-11; Eph. 2:20; Hebrews 6:1; 1
Corinthians 3:13; and 1 Timothy 6:19.
Furthermore, my interpretations of this movie as
a dream would be don't ask, "What is the
building?" Rather ask, "How can I use the building
for an advantage?" As it was the same old
foundation (building), but new worlds filled with
infinite possibilities that it sends people to head
out into. So think outside the box, as each
character was using the building to advance an
agenda.

Notice what you liked and what you didn't like or even hated about the movie. I loved the story and how in challenged the audience to use their imagination and think out side the box. Which characters or actions seemed especially attractive or unattractive to you? The character that I felt I could connect to was Ronan, for the reason of his grievances and trying to practice self control over is fighting and being that he was really thought of as the smart one out of the group even though he might have looked dumb by the way he acts. While I would say, in some ways I can identify with the character Ronan.

Were there one or several characters in the movie that modeled behavior that you would like to emulate? This would be Ronan, even though he had a bad temper and fighting was how he showed us his grievances over his mother's death. He showed me that he was a smart leader and a fighter, who I thought did strive to practice self-control as I think why he chose to fight in back alley matches, was to have an avenue to release it and maybe to punish himself for something that wasn't even his fault. So Ronan had developed certain strengths and other capacities that I would like to develop as well.

Now there wasn't really any aspect of the film that was especially hard to watch, except for when Tinker took Beatrix and Ronan captive to handcuff them to things as he terrorized them in an abusive way to get answers out of them. While this could be related to something I might have repressed. In fact, uncovering repressed aspects of our psyche can free up positive qualities and uncover our more whole and authentic self.

On the other hand, I did experience something that connected me to my inner wisdom as I watched the film. First, the building could symbolize a situation as normally when someone is going through something that they don't understand and ask them self, "what's the building (situation)? Or "Why me?" Instead of wandering around trying to find answers that even get, or wasting time asking questions that they may not get answered. They can take a step back and ask, "how can I use the building (situation) for my advantage?" To demonstrate,

324

we can ask the same question for an alternative
scenario, concerning mental illness and problems.
So don't ask, "What did I do to deserve this mental
illness?" Rather, ask. "What can I do with this
mental illness to use it for my advantage while its
just passing through my body?" Yet, it brings me
to this positive thought about my situation,
Schizophrenics can be great actors.

If the film had a unique message for you, what
was it? This film makes you think outside the box
as its not about what it's the building, but what it
can do to help get another to where they are
trying to get to in life as it shows me that there is
more to life to explore then just confiding in a
building. Second, when the Promoter said. "Let
me ask you a question. Are you a fighter? I just
saw you lose. Most fighters go out there, they go
out there to win. But there's a certain kind of guy
who gets into the ring who doesn't care about
winning. The certain kind of guy who just, he just
wants to smash himself up against the world, just
to see what's left over. What are you doing,
fighting all these back alley matches? Living out
of a bag. Don't you belong somewhere?" While

there were many more things I wrote in my journal, that I wont list here.

What new ideas for new behaviors did you have? One was, try to befriend your capturer, make them see you as a real human being. Another was an alternative scenario in how to think about a limitation, such as a handicap or mental illness. Ask yourself, "How can I use this for my advantage?" Think outside the box, instead of asking, "what is this?"

What other films can you identify that might take the discussion a step further? Maybe Sliders, Surface, and Europa Report.

INT. MEMORIAL DAY/FILM ANALYSIS - DAY

The eighth media analysis therapeutic session was on the sound effects and dialogue of the film, 'Memorial Day' with a character study also on the great actor James Cromwell. While it is intended for me to watch the movie twice, once for the study for being a great actor and another for analyzing the sound effects and dialogue of the art of watching films.

 Scan here for 'Memorial Day' trailer.

Before going any further in to this film session, I make this my prayer for the Holy Spirit as my Counselor: Father, in the name of Jesus, I pray for you Holy Spirit to exhort and counsel for me as the emotionally wounded. I ask in faith that Your Spirit will rest upon me — the Spirit of wisdom and understanding, the Spirit of counsel and might. Give me insight and knowledge for understanding myself as your counselee. Thank You, Father, that I am a good listener to the film that you have guided me to watch. Help me to comprehend the unfolding of those past hurts that influence reactions to current situations. Lord, I will not judge by what I see with my eyes or decide by what I hear with my ears. I will judge the needy and give decisions with justice. Righteousness will be my belt, and faithfulness the sash around my waist. I will be clothed with fairness and with truth. Thank You that I am a promoter of peace and filled with joy. I trust the Holy Spirit as my counselor, out of the rich treasury of Your glory, to be my strengthen and reinforce with mighty power in the inner man by the [Holy] Spirit [Himself indwelling in my innermost being and personality]. You will not leave me without support as I give my time and concern to being transformed and healed through this Flixrapuetic senior paper, helping to complete the forgiveness process. I will be confident about my convictions, knowing excellent things, and will have the knowledge to assist Your children in knowing the certainty of the words of truth. In Jesus' name, amen.

A brief quote that can give an example of the
SOUND EFFECTS and DIALOGUE in a film comes a
director known as AKIRA KUROSAWA. Who once
said "In my view, a motion picture stands or falls
on the effective combination of these two factors.
Truly cinematic sound is neither merely
accompanying sound (easy and explanatory) nor
the natural sounds captured at the time of the
simultaneous recording. In other words,
cinematic sound is that which does not simply
add to, but multiplies, two or three times, the
effect of the image."

Before I go into the analyzes of the sound effects
and dialogue in the film, 'Memorial Day.' I'll start
with thirteen key acting questions that every
actor should answer to be a fully rounded and
connected great actor, from studying the actor
James Cromwell.

Who is James Cromwell's character? Grandpa
Bub Vogel (Ompa) and Lt. Bub Vogel.

Where is James Cromwell's character? Le Center,
MN.

When is it? 1993.

Where have James Cromwell's character just come from? Sitting in a rocking chair, on the porch in front of his house.

What does James Cromwell's character want? Grandpa Bub wants to share his important stories from his souvenirs, with his grandson Kylie.

Why does James Cromwell's character want it? Grandpa Bub wants his stories to live on through the next generation.

Why does James Cromwell character want it now? Grandpa Bub would have forgot about his memories if it weren't for Kylie bring them out to remind him of what Memorial Day is really about and the war that his grandpa fought in his generation.

What will happen if James Cromwell's character doesn't get it now? Grandpa Bub would have forgot about the souvenirs and the memories behind them, as if it wasn't for his grandson reminding him of them, Grandpa Bub would have died with the stories.

How will James Cromwell's character get what he wants, by doing what? Grandpa Bub will get what he wants by deciding to trust his grandson with his stories, and moving past the pain that come with them to tell the stories.

What must James Cromwell's character overcome? Probably past hurts, going back to a place of pain, burdens, PTSD, his memory problems, grief, sorrow and trusting others with important memories and precious souvenirs.

Given these facts, James Cromwell fully transform into his character of Grandpa Bub. As, James Cromwell showed hard work, technique and good direction. With this said, James Cromwell was truthfully and emotionally connected to his character Grandpa Bub. Moreover, as the audience, I saw none of this, but the fully realized three-dimensional character right in the truth of the moment.

Now, answering Dr. Culp's five movie critique questions.

On description, describe the story in objective terms, usually 1-2 paragraphs. "Memorial Day, 1993. When 13-year-old Kyle Vogel discovers the World War II footlocker belonging to his grandfather, Bud, everyone tells Kyle to put it back. Luckily, he ignores them." Explains IMDb.com. On the other hand, for me I got to see Grandpa Bub push past his painful memories from his war shards to tell his stories behind them and see how they would live forever through three generations.

On meaning, describe what the story/director is trying to say. If you really are listening and paying attention to the film it can be discovered from within it, as I believe what the director was trying to say was that stories live forever, but only if you tell them.

On worldview, describe what rules/principles/values are in use by the characters or in the plot. The principles that were in use throughout the plot were the following: Liberality (Matthew 5:42), simplicity (Matthew

6:19), contentment (Matthew 6:25), hope (2 Corinthians 4:16-18), Christian fellowship (2 Corinthians 4:16-18), faith (Galatians 5:5-6), edification (Ephesians 4:29), humility (Philippians 2:3), perseverance (Philippians 3:13-14), prayer (Philippians 4:6), contemplation and reflection (Colossians 2:3), forbearance (Colossians 3:12-13), hospitality (2 Timothy 2:16-17), confession (James 5:16), loyalty (1 Peter 4:8), generosity (1 John 3:17), and love (1 John 4:16-19), loyalty, mercy, grace, bravery, courage, leadership, patriotism, and teamwork.

Discuss the characters' behavior based upon biblical principles. SSGT. Kyle Vogel: perseverance (Philippians 3:13-14). Bud Vogel: contemplation and reflection (Colossians 2:3). Betty Vogel: hospitality (2 Timothy 2:16-17). Young Kyle Vogel: forbearance (Colossians 3:12-13).

On interpretation, describe what the movie means to you personally. Sometimes the worse decision we can make is not trusting anybody with our stories for the pain they may bring up for us to

333

have to deal with and let go, but stories will only live forever if you tell them. As the scriptures that this movie connects with comes from Proverbs 13:22, "a good man leaves an inheritance to his children's children." Even if that inheritance is souvenirs with memories that have stories attached to them.

Analyzing the sound effects and dialogue of 'Memorial Day' with James Cromwell.

Where in the film are off-screen or invisible sounds effectively employed to enlarge the boundaries of the visual frame or to create mood and atmosphere? In the Media Analysis textbook it mentioned, "invisible sound, or sound emanating from sources not on the screen, could be used to extend the dimensions of film beyond what is seen and to achieve more powerful dramatic effects as well" (236). Since this movie is a war film there was many places throughout the film, where off-screen or invisible sounds were effectively employed to create mood and atmosphere. For example, the sound effects of the guns going off, car engine running on the road, helicopter flying over a building, grenades, the foot steps of the soldiers, natural sounds of nature, and various other sounds to create a war-type environment.

What sound effects in particular contribute to a sense of reality and a feeling of being there? In the Media Analysis textbook it points out how "we are more consciously aware of what we see than of what we hear, we generally accept the soundtrack without much thought, responding intuitively to the information it provides while ignoring the complex techniques employed to create those responses" (232). So for me this would be the sounds that we are unconsciously aware of and seems to go unrecognizable, as it blends in to the mix.

Does the film attempt to provide a sense of three-dimensionality or depth in sound? The Media Analysis textbook mentioned. "This three-dimensionality was achieved on one track (monaural sound) by making voices and sounds sound close up or far away—without the left and right separation of stereo (which is achieved by recording on two separate tracks and then using two or more speakers to play back what was recorded)" (234) to give an example. While I would have to say that the film 'Memorial Day' had three-dimensionality for the type of movie that it was and the environment that was created for the audience. If a stereophonic soundtrack is used, what does it contribute to the overall effect of the film? In fact, looking back in the Media Analysis textbook I would say that it provided a stereophonic soundtrack. To demonstrate, "An audio recording system that reduces background noise and increases frequency range, it was combined with a system called "surround sound" from Tate Audio Ltd. to produce a multi-track stereophonic system for theaters.

Dolby-Surround Sound employs an encoding process that achieves a 360-degree sound field and creates the effect of a greater number of separate speakers than are actually required" (235). As the sound in the movie involved and engaged me more.

Where is sound employed to represent subjective states of mind, and how effective is this use of sound? Briefly, the Media Analysis says a "subjective point of view, in contrast, is that of one who is intensely involved, either emotionally or physically, in the happenings on the screen. In the completely subjective view, camera and microphone become the eyes and ears of a character in the film; they see and hear exactly what that character sees and hears" (238). For example, when Grandpa Bub is telling stories to Kylie from the memories that the souvenirs bring to his remembrance and another is during various events that take place in the war, as these are what seemed to have kept the audience engaged.

Where is unusual emphasis placed on sound in the film, and what is the purpose of such emphasis? First thing, in the Media Analysis textbooks explained. "A director who wishes to place some unusual emphasis on sound has several options. Two obvious methods involve de-emphasizing the visual image: (1) dropping the image altogether by fading to black or (2) purposely making the image uninteresting or dull by holding a meaningless shot for a long period or by prolonging the use of dead screen" (244). For an example, the simplest and most obvious way would be emphasizing the gunfire sounds in the war by increasing its volume. Another would be inside the church, priest with the soldiers and some other citizens. Where during the prayer, we see a child look over to a soldier to smile and open his hand to reveal an egg with a cross on it as the two are responding to each other. As this seems like it would be employed as a dead-screen technique.

Is sound used to provide important transitions in the film? Yes. Why is sound needed to provide these transitions? Because "Sound is also an extremely important transitional device in films. It can be used to show the relationship between shots, scenes, or sequences, or it can make a change in image from one shot or sequence to another seem more fluid or natural. A fluid and graceful transition between sequences is achieved through the slight overlapping of sound from one shot into the next. The sound from a shot continues even after the image fades or dissolves into an entirely new image. This overlap- ping usually represents a passage of time, a change of setting, or both" (Media Analysis, 247). Another reason is being that the audience needs to know when they are coming out of a memory to enter back into reality with Grandpa Bub and his family, as there needs to be a smooth transition to keep us in the moment of feeling as if we are apart of the movie experience.

If voice-over soundtracks are used for narration or internal monologues (thoughts of a character spoken aloud), can you justify their use, or could the same information have been conveyed through purely cinematic means? There were voice-over soundtracks used for narration and internal monologues in the film, 'Memorial Day' as I am pretty sure that the same information could have been conveyed through purely cinematic means also and would have changed the feel of it. Whereas, there use can be justified by how I found it to be mentioned in the Media Analysis textbook when it says. "The filmmaker can also employ sound that has no direct relationship to the natural sounds and dialogue involved in the story. A human voice off-screen, called voice- over narration, has a variety of functions. It is perhaps most commonly used as an expository device to convey necessary background information or fill in gaps for continuity that cannot be presented dramatically" (248). To demonstrate, a place I remember there being a voice-over soundtrack was towards the end where I heard the voice of Grandpa Bub reading the letter he had wrote to Kylie as it lays on the seat of Kylie's car and he was walking towards a grave sight to visit his grandpa Bub's grave.

INT. HOME RUN/CINEMA THERAPY - DAY

Watching the film 'Home Run' for my eighth cinema therapy session, on transformation and renewal.

 Scan here for 'Home Run' trailer.

Before going any further in to this film session, I make this my prayer for the Holy Spirit as my Counselor: Father, in the name of Jesus, I pray for you Holy Spirit to exhort and counsel for me as the emotionally wounded. I ask in faith that Your Spirit will rest upon me — the Spirit of wisdom and understanding, the Spirit of counsel and might. Give me insight and knowledge for understanding myself as your counselee. Thank You, Father, that I am a good listener to the film that you have guided me to watch. Help me to comprehend the unfolding of those past hurts that influence reactions to current situations. Lord, I will not judge by what I see with my eyes or decide by what I hear with my ears. I will judge the needy and give decisions with justice.

Righteousness will be my belt, and faithfulness the sash around my waist. I will be clothed with fairness and with truth. Thank You that I am a promoter of peace and filled with joy. I trust the Holy Spirit as my counselor, out of the rich treasury of Your glory, to be my strengthen and reinforce with mighty power in the inner man by the [Holy] Spirit [Himself indwelling in my innermost being and personality]. You will not leave me without support as I give my time and concern to being transformed and healed through this Flixrapuetic senior paper, helping to complete the forgiveness process. I will be confident about my convictions, knowing excellent things, and will have the knowledge to assist Your children in knowing the certainty of the words of truth. In Jesus' name, amen.

As I prescribed a movie based on an issue and followed some guidelines for watching movies with conscious awareness in this order: First, start with a film that supports your treatment goal. Second, choose a film from film recommendations. Third, making sure to clarify intent when assigning a film in which might mistake the role identification. Fourth, familiarize yourself with Guidelines for watching films and discuss guidelines. Fifth, discuss the positive or negative reactions to film. Sixth, use material according to your theoretical orientation. Seven, afterwards reflect on evocative questions and answer them after watching the selected film as it does help to write down my answers.

Do you remember whether your breathing changed throughout the movie? No. But about towards the middle to the ending of the movie I started to feel calm, comforted and a peace with no negative emotions. When before watching this film I was feeling a burden, some sort of heaviness and all these other emotions like (worry, anxiety, anger, sadness, depression, discouragement, and some suicidal thoughts). And now they are all gone, God was comforting me through the movie and gave me a sound mind as I just experienced a miracle.

Ask yourself: If a part of the film that moved you (positively or negatively) had been one of your dreams, how would you have understood the symbolism in it? The movie moved me in a positive way, while if this was a dream I would most like try to interpret it by studying key symbols as I go at it through prayer, the Bible and a Christian dictionary.

Notice what you liked and what you didn't like or even hated about the movie. Which characters or actions seemed especially attractive or unattractive to you? The actions that seemed unattractive to me was the verbal abuse aimed at the kids by Cory's drunk father and the enraged coach, as I also didn't like how the media twisted the truth in their headlines. Did you identify with one or several characters? Corey, because I've been in his shoes and know what its like having had been delivered from alcohol since I was eighteen.

Were there one or several characters in the movie that modeled behavior that you would like to emulate? I didn't see of a whole lot, except for the lead minister and the ex-addicts at the Celebrate Recovery program. Did they develop certain strengths or other capacities that you would like to develop as well? I would say so, as they showed how they overcame their struggles by getting up in front of others to share their story to strengthen and help others find hope in overcoming theirs. With this, I see myself developing the same strength and as an overcomer.

Notice whether any aspect of the film was especially hard to watch. The only aspects that were kind of hard to watch were seeing the verbal abuse, and how alcohol makes you behave. Could this be related to something that you might have repressed ("shadow")? When I have eighteen, as I am aware how uncovering repressed aspects of our psyche can free up positive qualities and uncover our more whole and authentic self.

Did you experience something that connected you to your inner wisdom or higher self as you watched the film? Yes, as it would be we all have a void that we are trying to fill with a counterfeit that only God can fill. Also, whom the Son sets free is free indeed, as it does help to write down the answers. Moreover, some of the mentioned guidelines turn out to be useful, so I might consider using them not only in "reel life" but also adapt them to "real life" because I know how they are intended to make me become a better observer.

If the film had a unique message for you, what was it? Netflix tells us, "to cure his drinking problem, pro baseball star Cory Brand returns to his hometown and begins coaching a Little League team as part of his rehab. Although, something that I got out of this film was that it takes courage and bravery to put one's career to the side to make room for change and to spend time to love the friends and family who love you.

What new ideas for new behaviors did you have? The cure for any problem is Jesus Christ, as you can try to change by yourself, but it will never work with out God's help.

What other films can you identify that might take the discussion a step further? Brian's Song, Undefeated, One hit from home, 1000 to 1, A mile in his shoes, Mercy Rule, The perfect game, 4 mile run, If I had wings, Underdogs, and Coach Carter.

INT. THE ARTIST/FILM ANALYSIS - DAY

The ninth media analysis therapeutic session was on the musical score of the film, 'The Artist' with a character study also on the great actor James Cromwell. While it is intended for me to watch the movie twice, once for the study for being a great actor and another for analyzing the musical score of the art of watching films.

Scan here for 'The Artist' trailer.

Before going any further in to this film session, I make this my prayer for the Holy Spirit as my Counselor: Father, in the name of Jesus, I pray for you Holy Spirit to exhort and counsel for me as the emotionally wounded. I ask in faith that Your Spirit will rest upon me — the Spirit of wisdom and understanding, the Spirit of counsel and might. Give me insight and knowledge for understanding myself as your counselee. Thank You, Father, that I am a good listener to the film that you have guided me to watch. Help me to

comprehend the unfolding of those past hurts that influence reactions to current situations. Lord, I will not judge by what I see with my eyes or decide by what I hear with my ears. I will judge the needy and give decisions with justice. Righteousness will be my belt, and faithfulness the sash around my waist. I will be clothed with fairness and with truth. Thank You that I am a promoter of peace and filled with joy. I trust the Holy Spirit as my counselor, out of the rich treasury of Your glory, to be my strengthen and reinforce with mighty power in the inner man by the [Holy] Spirit [Himself indwelling in my innermost being and personality]. You will not leave me without support as I give my time and concern to being transformed and healed through this Flixrapuetic senior paper, helping to complete the forgiveness process. I will be confident about my convictions, knowing excellent things, and will have the knowledge to assist Your children in knowing the certainty of the words of truth. In Jesus' name, amen.

The MUSICAL SCORE

A brief quote that can give an example of the MUSICAL SCORE in a film comes from a director known as QUINCY JONES, COMPOSER. "The film composer should have the confidence to use exactly what he needs and no more. He shouldn't use his theatrical license to blow the believability of the picture, and I think that believability is closely connected with understatement. The composer wants to pull the moviegoer's mind into that room that's up on the screen, into that feeling that's up there, and it can take very little to achieve that involvement."

Before I go into the analyzes of the musical score in the film, 'The Artist.' I'll start with thirteen key acting questions that every actor should answer to be a fully rounded and connected great actor, from studying a truly great actor:

Who is James Cromwell's character? Clifton.

Where is James Cromwell's character? Hollywood, California.

When is it? 1927-1932.

Where have James Cromwell's character just come from? Chauffeuring George to and from the studio.

What does James Cromwell's character want? To make sure George is taken care of, and to be his friend.

Why does James Cromwell's character want it? It's part of his job, and he wants to remain loyal to George as a friend.

Why does James Cromwell character want it now? Clifton is there to be of some assistance for George, and at the same time be his friend. If Clifton doesn't taken care of him with satisfaction, George's day won't run smoothly and he probably will be behind schedule.

What will happen if James Cromwell's character doesn't get it now? Clifton doesn't want to get fired, or loose a friend.

How will James Cromwell's character get what he wants by doing what? Being professional, loyal, faithful, a friend, encouraging, supportive, hardworking, and comforting at times.

What must James Cromwell's character overcome? Clifton must overcome the ups and downs that George goes through in the movie business, and whatever mood George comes home with.

Does James Cromwell fully transform into his character, Clifton? Yes as James Cromwell show hard work, technique and good direction. Moreover, he truthfully and emotionally connected to his character Clifton. Thus, as the audience, I saw none of this, but the fully realized three-dimensional character of Clifton right in the truth of the moment. While I am aware of how a great actor has to be able to tell a story without words, because the silent film is where the roots began.

Now, answering Dr. Culp's five movie critique questions.

On description, describe the story in objective terms. The film, 'The Artist' is a love letter to art and Hollywood as it tells a story of interlinked destinies. Furthermore, it's "A silent movie star meets a young dancer, but the arrival of talking pictures sends their careers in opposite directions." Said IMDb.com.

On meaning, describe what the story/director is trying to say. Nothing and no one can stop or keep you from destiny as we the media is plagued with stories of people rising and falling, falling and rising in Hollywood with true love for the art of making movies that drives them to find a way to continue doing what they love to do. Whereas, George had lost his voice and Peppy had gained hers as together they both could dance which birthed a new movement and started a new era.

On worldview, describe what principles/values are in use by the characters or in the plot. Liberality (Matthew 5:42), contentment (Matthew 6:25), hope (2 Corinthians 4:16-18), Edification (Ephesians 4:29), perseverance (Philippians 3:13-14), contemplation and reflection (Philippians 4:6), forbearance (Colossians 3"12-13), industriousness (2

Thessalonians 3:10), hospitality (Hebrews 13:2), sympathy (1 Peter 3:8), loyalty (1 Peter 4:8), generosity (1 John 3:17), and lastly love (1 John 4:16-19).

Discuss the characters' behavior based upon biblical principles. The characters mostly showed love, loyalty, generosity, sympathy, hospitality, industriousness, forbearance, contemplation, reflection, perseverance, edification, hope, contentment, and lastly liberality.

On interpretation, describe what the movie means to you personally. True love always finds a way, as a true friend will look after you in your ups and downs. Also, you can't really loose your voice, because you'll always have some sort of a loyal audience still following you as you just end up redefining it from something that was in you all along that gets pulled out of you to start something new with. While the scriptures that are connected to this movie are: Proverb 18:24, Mark 10:9 and Ecclesiastes. 3:1-8. Thus, true love doesn't see dollar signs and will continue pursuing the someone or something that they love from wherever they are in live as love is relentless.

Now analyzing the musical score of 'The Artist' with James Cromwell.

On General Functions of the Musical Score

Where in the film is music used to exactly match the natural rhythms of the moving objects on the screen? There was many places in the film 'The Artist' that showed natural rhythms of moving objects on the screen as on for an example was in the dance numbers and when a character interacts with a prop like towards the ending when George finds a room in Peppy's house that has all his old stuff stored in it as the music is upbeat with his movements. At what points in the film does the music simply try to capture the overall emotional mood of a scene? For this reason, pointed out in the Media Analyzes textbook. "Music has a tremendous effect on our response, greatly enriching and enhancing our overall reaction to almost any film. It accomplishes this in several ways: by reinforcing or strengthening the emotional content of the image, by stimulating the imagination and the kinetic sense, and by suggesting and expressing emotions that cannot be conveyed by pictorial means alone" (262). While the music helped to tell the story of 'The Artist' film, and expressed what the characters was feeling emotionally.

Where does the film employ rhythmic and emotive variations on a single musical theme or motif? For instance, in the Media Analyzes textbook it tells us this. "The two most general and basic functions of the musical score are to create structural rhythms and to stimulate emotional responses, both of which greatly enhance and reinforce the effect of the image" (263) For example, during the scenes where George and Peppy would dance and where the characters would have an emotional response, since there was hardly any dialogue the music had to the story for it in its place.

Does the musical score remain inconspicuous in the background, or does it occasionally break through to assert itself? For example, in the

Media Analyzes textbook it points out this.
"Music is often employed as a kind of emotional
punctuation for the dialogue, expressing the
feeling underlying what is said." Moreover,
"Music often moves beyond a merely subordinate
or complementary role to assume a primary
storytelling function, enabling the director to
express things that cannot be expressed through
verbal or pictorial means. This is especially true
when a character's state of mind undergoes
extreme and rapid changes that neither words
nor action can adequately express" (265). So in
this silent film, the musical score was the star of
the show as it remained in the background in
some certain scenes, as it helped in telling the
story.

If the music does demand our conscious attention,
does it still perform a sub-ordinate function in the
film as a whole? Yes, I would say that the music
did indeed demand our conscious attention. How?
For this reason that the Media Analyzes textbook
states. "The older, traditional view is that the best
film music performs its various functions without
making us consciously aware of its presence. In

other words, if we don't notice the music, it's a good score. Therefore, the music for a good score shouldn't be too good, for really good music draws attention to itself and away from the film. The modern view, by contrast, allows the music, on appropriate occasions, not only to demand our conscious attention but even to dominate the picture, as long as it remains essentially integrated with the visual, dramatic, and rhythmic elements of the film as a whole. At such moments, we may become conscious of how intrinsically beautiful the music is, though we should not be so moved that we lose sight of its appropriateness to the image on the screen" (263). As I felt that this film dominated the picture, and demanded of attention beautifully. In fact, it the music grabs the audience and pulls them in to make them want to be apart of the story that the film is trying to tell, as music expresses emotions that allows us to feel what the character might be feeling in the scene.

Where in the film is the main purpose of the music to match structural or visual rhythms? For structural rhythms the characters would express emotion, during their silent talk through dialogue and for visual rhythms this would most likely have to be when the scenes with dance to place. "Regardless of the degree of subordination, a good score will always be a significant structural element, performing its proper functions in a perfectly integrated way, serving as a means to an end rather than an end itself. Composer Quincy Jones captures this idea: "For me, some of the best moments in pictures come when the music is tied in so organically with the image, is so much a part of it, that you can't imagine it any other way" (Media Analysis 263). Where is the music used to create more generalized emotional patterns? For instance, the media analyzes tells us "scoring in which certain musical instruments and types of music represent and signal the presence of certain characters. Many films of the 1930s and 1940s used this technique, causing the audience to associate the villain with sinister-sounding music in a minor key, the heroine with soft, ethereal violins, and the hero with strong, "honest" music" (269-270). For an example, when Peppy was playing with George's tuxedo jacket on the coat rack as it was her lover and George walks in to set her apart from all the other actresses by drawing a small mole on her upper right lip. As, the music sounded a bit romantic and soft.

How would the total effect of the film differ if the musical score were removed from the soundtrack? It would be weird. This can be a funny question, answering it to a silent film as it would make the movie 'The Artist' sound dead with just sound effects in certain scenes and would leave the audience thinking there watching device is on mute or the film company forgot to add sound.

On Special Functions of the Musical Score

Which of the following functions of film music are used in the film, and where are they used? a.) To heighten the dramatic effect of dialogue b.) To tell an inner story by expressing a state of mind c.) To provide a sense of time or place d.) To foreshadow events or build dramatic tension e.) To add levels of meaning to the image f.) To aid characterization g.) To trigger conditioned responses h.) To characterize rapid movement (traveling music) i.) To provide important transitions j.) To cover weaknesses and defects. The music in place of hearing spoken words, heighten the dramatic effect of dialogue. In telling an inner story by expressing a state of mind, for an example, when Peppy was playing with George's tuxedo jacket on the coat rack. To provide a sense of time or place, this would be in the movie theaters as the music fit in the 1930's time frame. When a surprising change of mood or an unexpected action was about to occur on the screen with a character, foreshadowed events or built dramatic tension. When the music wanted to make the audience see the visual scene in a fresh, unusual way by combining with the image to create additional levels of meaning to the image. The film aided characterization, when the scoring in which certain musical instruments ad types of music represented and signaled the presence of certain characters like George and Peppy when they first met. For triggering conditioned responses, is when the composer takes advantage of the fact that viewers have been conditioned to associate some musical stereotypes or musical codes with particular situations like when George sets fire to his house and when he puts the gun in his mouth for example. To characterize rapid movement (traveling music), for instance, when the dog travels to the police officer to bring him back to the house to help George who is trapped in the fire and when George is pulling back the sheets in the basement to reveal his stuff that were auctioned off to Peppy. As, this was done to characterize rapid movement. The dialogue title screens and when the "music functions in an important way by providing transitions or bridges between scenes—marking the passage of time, signaling a change of locale, foreshadowing a shift in mood or pace, or transporting us backward in time into a flashback" (Media Analysis 272) to provide important transitions. Lastly, to cover weaknesses and defects is when a nonstorytelling function of the musical score is to disguise or cover up weaknesses in acting and dialogue, as I don't think there wasn't any weaknesses and defect with it being a silent film.

Does the music accompanying the titles serve basically to underscore the rhythmic qualities of the title information or to establish the general mood of the film? I'm pretty sure that the music has to do both, accompanying the titles serve basically to underscore the rhythmic qualities of the title information and establishing the general mood of the film with it being a silent film. If lyrics are sung at this point, how do these lyrics relate to the film as a whole? There really weren't any lyrics sung in this film, so this can't relate to the film as a whole.

Where are sound effects or natural noises employed for a kind of rhythmic or musical effect? For an example, in George's nightmare of sound and I think in the final dance scene of George and Peppy tap-dancing.

If lyrics sung within the film provide a kind of interior monologue, what feeling or attitude do they convey? For instance, "in many cases, such songs are used to reveal the private moods, emotions, or thoughts of a central character" (Media Analysis 273). There was no lyrics sung in this film, but the closes thing to an interior monologue for this silent film was when the music expressed the emotion of the character during a distressing time, as this made you feel what they was feeling at that moment.

If music is used as a base for choreographed action, how appropriate is the piece selected? Extremely important I would say, especially with 'The Artist' being a silent film the music would have to be used to choreograph action appropriately for representing the selected piece at its best. How appropriate are its rhythms to the mood and the visual content? The rhythms to the mood and visual content, I would say did a great job at working with each other. How effectively is the choreographed sequence integrated into the film as a whole? Like it says in the Media Analyzes textbook. "Usually the director composes, photographs, and edits the images first and adds music later, after the visual elements are already assembled. In some films, however, music is used to provide a clear rhythmic framework for the action, which essentially becomes a highly stylized dance performed to the music" (274). This was one of those films that was creative in using music to provide a clear rhythmic framework for the action, as we go to see it through the tap dancing, camera shots and the expressions of the characters.

Does the score use a full orchestra throughout, a small number of well-chosen instruments, or a synthesizer? This silent film used a full orchestra throughout the film, as there were some places where there was either no music or just sound effects alone. How well suited is the instrumentation to the film as a whole? I would say that this film did a good job at being well suited in the instrumentations. How would a different choice of instrumentation change the quality of the film, and why would it be an improvement? If there would have been a different choice of instrumentation change, the quality of the film wouldn't have seemed like it took place during the time frame of 1927 to 1932, as I can't see how anyway else to improve this film.

Does the amount of music used fit the

requirements of the film, or is the musical score overdone or used too economically? Briefly, the media analyzes textbook tells us. "The proper amount of music depends on the nature of the picture itself. Some films require a lot of music. Others are so realistic that music would interfere with the desired effect. In many cases, the most dramatically effective musical score is that which is used most sparingly" (278). Thus, for a silent film like 'The Artist,' depended on a lot of music to help tell the story in substitute for the dialogue being absent until the last scene as the amount of music that was used in this film did fit the requirements, or so I thought.

How effectively does the score perform its various functions? The film 'The Artist,' I thought was extremely effective for the score to perform its various functions in a way that was beautiful to listen to as it was apart of telling the story and it was also entertaining. Particularly, I read in the media analyzes textbook that "studios hate the idea of a picture without music. It scares them." Besides, he notes, "talking about music is like talking about colors: the same color can mean different things to different people." Usually, though, an attempt at creating film music is definitely worth the resulting colorful dialogue. Finally, in Knowing the Score: Film Composers Talk About the Art, Craft, Blood, Sweat, and Tears of Writing for Cinema, David Morgan has observed: Cinema has offered some of the most vibrant and sophisticated music available to mass audiences, yet film music remains an underappreciated art form . . . Good film music can rise above its material and live on outside of the film, long after the drama for which it was written has been forgotten. And it is a testament to . . . composers . . . that Hollywood has given them opportunities to write their music and have it performed in a wide variety of styles and genres that would be almost impossible to match on stage or in the concert halls" (279). As I could do more than agree with this statement, because the music gives the audience more of an experience as it depends on the picture on whether the music performs effectively as its intended to function. Lastly, I enjoyed every bit of the especially for the art and creativity that it showed in the shots.

INT. WWJD 2: THE WOODCAVER/CINEMA THERAPY - DAY

Watching the film 'WWJD II: The Woodcarver' for my ninth cinema therapy session, on transformation and renewal.

 Scan here for 'WWJD 2: The Woodcarver' trailer.

Before going any further in to this film session, I make this my prayer for the Holy Spirit as my Counselor: Father, in the name of Jesus, I pray for you Holy Spirit to exhort and counsel for me as the emotionally wounded. I ask in faith that Your Spirit will rest upon me — the Spirit of wisdom and understanding, the Spirit of counsel and might. Give me insight and knowledge for understanding myself as your counselee. Thank You, Father, that I am a good listener to the film that you have guided me to watch. Help me to comprehend the unfolding of those past hurts that influence reactions to current situations. Lord, I will not judge by what I see with my eyes or decide by what I hear with my ears. I will judge the needy and give decisions with justice. Righteousness will be my belt, and faithfulness the sash around my waist. I will be clothed with fairness and with truth. Thank You that I am a promoter of peace and filled with joy. I trust the Holy Spirit as my counselor, out of the rich treasury of your glory, to be my strengthen and reinforce with mighty power in the inner man by the [Holy] Spirit [Himself indwelling in my innermost being and personality]. You will not leave me without support as I give my time and concern to being transformed and healed through this Flixrapuetic senior paper, helping to complete the forgiveness process. I will be confident about my convictions, knowing excellent things, and will have the knowledge to assist your children in knowing the certainty of the words of truth. In Jesus' name, amen.

As I prescribed a movie based on an issue and followed some guidelines for watching movies with conscious awareness in this order: First, start with a film that supports your treatment goal. Second, **c**hoose a film from film recommendations. Third, making sure to clarify intent when assigning a film in which might mistake the role identification. Fourth, familiarize yourself with Guidelines for watching films and discuss guidelines. Fifth, discuss the positive or negative reactions to film. Sixth, use material according to your theoretical orientation. Seven, afterwards reflect on evocative questions and answer them after watching the selected film as it does help to write down my answers.

Do you remember whether your breathing changed throughout the movie? My breathing didn't really change in any parts of the movie.

Ask yourself: If a part of the film that moved you (positively or negatively) had been one of your dreams, how would you have understood the symbolism in it? The film 'WWJD II: The Woodcarver,' did move me positively as if it were a dream I would study the symbolism until I understood their meaning. Moreover, I would go about doing this by referring to a Christian Dream interpretation dictionary, the Bible and through prayer.

Notice what you liked and what you didn't like or
even hated about the movie. What I liked about
the movie was how the Woodcarver (Ernest Otto)
took Matthew under his wing to mentor him in
the right direction to keep him from getting into
trouble, and another thing I liked was how the
characters used the question, WWJD to ask
themselves before doing anything. Now what I
disliked was the vandalism of the church, and the
fire that was set to destroy the woodcarver
(Ernest Otto) and Matthew's hard work for the
church. Which characters or actions seemed
especially attractive or unattractive to you? The
actions that seemed attractive to me were the
woodcarver (Ernest Otto) mentoring a trouble
teen to keep him from going down the wrong
direction. Did you identify with one or several
characters? The characters that I identified with
were: Ernest Otto and Matthew Stevenson.

Were there one or several characters in the movie
that modeled behavior that you would like to
emulate? Ernest Otto, for the reason of his certain

strengths and other capacities that I would like to develop.

Notice whether any aspect of the film was especially hard to watch. Keeping this in mind, uncovering repressed aspects of our psyche can free up positive qualities and uncover our more whole and authentic self. So I would have to say, no, there wasn't really any scene in the movie that was hard to watch.

Did you experience something that connected you to your inner wisdom or higher self as you watched the film? The are many things that connected me with inner wisdom as they are the following: First, it made me remember the old phrase WWJD and how it can not only help you to make better choices, but to live life to the fullest also. Second, the scripture that was brought to my attention was Psalm 119:144. Third, Ernest Otto: "All sons need their father, and all fathers need their sons." Fourth, Ernest Otto: "Ah, never underestimate the power of belief combined with hard work." Fifth, Ernest Otto: "Look, son, you've only got two choices. You can either lend a hand or get out of the way." Sixth, Ernest Otto: "Lord makes the wood. I just carve it." Seventh, Ernest Otto: "You see this grain, how beautiful it is? It's called flame and quilt. Now that only happens randomly in individual trees. You don't discover it until after you saw the wood." Eighth, Pastor Clark: "Well, couples need more than just going to church together. They need to work on building a marriage that's based on a foundation of equally turning themselves over to the Lord." Lastly, and the most important was this dialogue between Ernest and Matthew. Ernest Otto: "Before you do anything, I need you to ask yourself a question." Matthew Stevenson: "A question?" Ernest Otto: "Yeah. W.W.J.D." Matthew Stevenson: "What's that?" Ernest Otto: "Well its short for "What would Jesus do?" While I can see how it does help to write these insights down in a journal, as you watch the film. In fact, some of the mentioned guidelines are considered useful, and I am considering using them not only in "reel life" but also adapt them to "real life" because they are intended to make one become a better observer.

If the film had a unique message for you, what

was it? The unique message of the film was restoring people's faith in God and in life, as the Woodcarver took a negative situation of his work being destroyed and turned it into a positive by helping to mend the one who caused it through a wood carving mentorship.

What new ideas for new behaviors did you have? This film brought back to my remembrance the popular question that trended in sixth and seventh grade, WWJD as known as What Would Jesus Do. Moreover, WWJD cannot only help you make better choices and decisions, but it can also help you to live life to the fullest.

What other films can you identify that might take the discussion a step further? The movies that I haven't seen, but could take this discussion further are: What if, Saving Winston, In the name of God, Camp Harlow, Finding Faith, Mercy Rule, Ring the Bell, Raising Izzie, October Baby, and Loving a Bad man.

INT. FINDING NEVERLAND/FILM ANALYSIS - DAY

The tenth media analysis therapeutic session was on the acting of the film, 'Finding Neverland' with a character study also on the great actor Johnny Depp. While it is intended for me to watch the movie twice, once for the study for being a great actor and another for analyzing the acting of the art of watching films.

 Scan here for 'Finding Neverland' trailer.

Before going any further in to this film session, I make this my prayer for the Holy Spirit as my Counselor: Father, in the name of Jesus, I pray for you Holy Spirit to exhort and counsel for me as the emotionally wounded. I ask in faith that Your Spirit will rest upon me — the Spirit of wisdom and understanding, the Spirit of counsel and might. Give me insight and knowledge for understanding myself as your counselee. Thank You, Father, that I am a good listener to the film that you have guided me to watch. Help me to

comprehend the unfolding of those past hurts that influence reactions to current situations. Lord, I will not judge by what I see with my eyes or decide by what I hear with my ears. I will judge the needy and give decisions with justice. Righteousness will be my belt, and faithfulness the sash around my waist. I will be clothed with fairness and with truth. Thank You that I am a promoter of peace and filled with joy. I trust the Holy Spirit as my counselor, out of the rich treasury of your glory, to be my strength and reinforce with mighty power in the inner man by the [Holy] Spirit [Himself indwelling in my innermost being and personality]. You will not leave me without support as I give my time and concern to being transformed and healed through this Flixrapuetic senior paper, helping to complete the forgiveness process. I will be confident about my convictions, knowing excellent things, and will have the knowledge to assist your children in knowing the certainty of the words of truth. In Jesus' name, amen.

On Acting, "An audience identifies with the actors of flesh and blood and heartbeat, as no reader or beholder can identify with even the most artful paragraphs in books or the most inspiring paintings. There, says the watcher, but for some small difference in time or costume or inflections or gait, go I. . . . And so, the actor becomes a catalyst; he brings to bright ignition that sparks in every human being that longs for the miracle of transformation." —EDWARD G. ROBINSON, ACTOR

For instance, Leonardo DiCaprio once said. "I've been placed here to be a vessel for acting... that's why I'm really taking any part, regardless of how complicated it's going to be."

The scripture that confirms this to me is 2 Corinthians 4:7, from the Jubilee version. "But we have this treasure in clay vessels that the Excellency of the virtue may be of God, and not of us."

So, we identify with a person for what they have been through as they become a source of inspiration to help encourage us through whatever we're going through, so whether an audience knows or doesn't know of an actor's testimony there's something about them that will draw an audience in and connect with them for the reason of being able to relate to them.

For an example, Eric K. Watts argues that "in terms of both class and race, 8 Mile portrays Rabbit as an 'oppressed minority.' Watts identifies the film's message, as while it may be 'easier' for white rappers to have commercial success, it is very difficult for them to get respect. On 'White America' (2002), Eminem rhymes: /Kids flipped when they knew I was produced by Dre, that's all it took, and they were instantly hooked right in, and they connected with me to because I looked like them./ Eminem attributes his hip hop credibility to Dre's sponsorship, and his commercial appeal to his white identity" (Hess 126). Through this we can see how one man can impact nation into following him, as he had millions of people bleaching their hair blonde and wearing white T-shirts while this can also show the power of influence. Furthermore, we can see, this generation of Millennials are finding actors that have shared experience from their life story that they can identify with and making them like their movie mentors to help them get through their own experiences as well as everyday situations. Thus, leaving me with this question, knowing or not knowing it. Could Eminem have created a mentor to mentee relationship with his audience from the screen in the Hip Hop world where he didn't fit in at and allowed other outcast to feel like they shared in the same experience? If you read between the lines, we can see this with the actor Johnny Depp as I believe there is a reason why *"he chooses character roles as "iconic loners" and gives grace to them to make them turn out a success in the film at the box office."* This can be seen from Wikipedia on Johnny Depp, as it says. *"Depp has generally chosen roles, which he found interesting, rather than those he thought would succeed at the box office. Critics have often described Depp's characters as "iconic loners." Depp has referred to some of his less-successful films as "studio-defined failures" and "box office poison", and that he thought the studios neither understood the films nor did a good job of marketing them.* "Through this one can see that Johnny Depp turns the characters that people would see as failures into successes, as this is a brilliant way to choose roles.

Moving on, a brief quote that can give an example of the acting is when Michelle Regalado advises. "The semi-biographical film chronicles the story of playwright J.M. Barrie and the family who inspired his career-defining tale Peter Pan. Depp's turn as Barrie, though understated, was a fascinating one, with the actor bringing just the right amount of grace and charm to the real-life story. The performance earned Depp Best Actor nominations at the SAG awards, the Golden Globes, and the Oscars."

Before I go into the analyzes of the acting in the film, 'Finding Neverland.' I'll research one a different film, the thirteen key acting questions that every actor should answer to be a fully rounded and connected great actor, from studying a truly great actor.

Who is Johnny Depp's character? J.M. Barrie.

Where is Johnny Depp's character? London.

When is it? 1903.

Where have Johnny Depp's character just come from? The opening night of one of his plays, that took place in a theater.

What does Johnny Depp's character want? J.M. Barrie wants to stay young forever, as he also wants to get people to use their imagination and believe that you can change things by simply believing they could be different.

Why does Johnny Depp's character want it? J.M. Barrie doesn't want people to loose sight of what its like to have faith and believe like a child, as he realizes how we can do impossible things with our imagination.

Why does Johnny Depp's character want it now? If life should happen, doubt will sit in to cause them to not want to believe and they will grow up, as they'll forget about using their imagination. Also, J.M. Barrie inspires hope within people by encouraging them to use their imagination to change things.

What will happen if Johnny Depp's character doesn't get it now? First, the kids will grow up. Second, the adults will forget what its like to be a child. Third, life and the world might destroy their imaginations. Fourth, their dreams turn into duties and chores that life drowns out for.

How will Johnny Depp's character get what he wants by doing what? Entertain, encourage, tell stories, inspire, encourage, influence, instruct, friendly, helping, comfort, role-playing, joy, affirm, aid, amaze, amend, amuse, cheer, confound, draw, ease, educate, enlighten, entice, free, humor, invite, intrigue, liberate, mend, motivate, recreate, repress, support, suggest, surprise, understand, vindicate and woo.

What must Johnny Depp's character overcome? The uniform that life puts on people to make them grow up fast and stay grown, his critics, discouragement, disbelief, and doubt.

Overall, Johnny Depp fully transforms into his character J.M Barrie. Moreover, Johnny Depp shows hard work, technique and good direction as he is also truthfully and emotionally connected to his character. Lastly, as the audience, I saw none of this, but the fully realized three-dimensional character of J.M. Barrie right in the truth of the moment.

Moving on, to answering Dr. Culp's five movie critique questions.

On description, describe the story in objective terms. The story to me about one man, J.M. Barrie, using the power of theater to help people use their imagination and educating them by saying, you can change things by simply believing they could be different. On the other hand, IMDb says, "the story of J.M. Barrie's friendship with a family who inspired him to create Peter Pan" as, another side of the story.

On meaning, describe what the story/director is trying to say. Based on the true story of J.M. Barrie and his intent for creating the story of 'Peter Pan.' I believe the director wanted to inspire the imagination of children, and encourage adults to use their imaginations as well as to not forget what it's like to be a child.

On worldview, describe what rules/principles/values are in use in the plot and discuss the characters' behavior based upon biblical principles. Liberality (Matthew 5:42), mercy (Matthew 5:44), Simplicity (Matthew 5:44), contentment (Matthew 6:25), hope (2 Corinthians 4:16-18), faith (Galatians 5:5-6), edification (Ephesians 4:29), humility (Philippians 2:3), perseverance (Philippians 3:13-14), contemplation and reflection (Colossians 3:2-3), forbearance (Colossians 3:12-13), industriousness (2 Thessalonians 3:10), purity of speech (2 Timothy 2:16-17), hospitality (Hebrews 13:2), sympathy (1 peter 3:8), loyalty (1 Peter 4:8), generosity (1 John 3:17), and love (1 John 3:17).

On interpretation, describe what the movie means to you personally. Simply, the imagination can lead you in to believing in impossible things and live as if you'll live forever. The scripture that best connects with this film is Mark 10:13-16,

...unless you accept God's Kingdom in the simplicity of a child, you'll never get in." As, you can still be an adult and have childlike faith.

Now, analyzing the acting of the movie, 'Finding Neverland' with Johnny Depp.

Which actors did you feel were correctly cast in their parts? Kate Winslet (Sylvia), Johnny Depp (J.M Barrie), Dustin Huffman (Charles Freeman), Freddie Highmore (Peter Davies), Nick Roud (George Davies), Joe Prospero (Jack Davies), Luke Spill (Michael Davies), Julie Christie (Mrs. Emma du Maurier) and Radha Mitchell (Mary Ansell Barrie). Which actors were not cast wisely? Maybe Ian Hart (Sir Arthur Conan Doyle) and Kelly Macdonald (Mr. Jasper-Usher). Why? Because I thought there were some room for improvement in there performance, other than that all the actors and actresses did a great job with their roles.

How well were the physical characteristics, facial features, and voice qualities of the actors suited to the characters they were attempting to portray? I honestly thought the actors and actresses did a great job with their physical characteristics, facial features and voice qualities as it suited their characters and they were believable in the moment that they was living in. Especially the kids as they really were innocent and lived truthful in the moment, and the way Michael said his lines were honest as well as funny.

If a performance was unconvincing, was it unconvincing because the actor was miscast, or did he or she simply deliver an incompetent performance? I don't think any performance was unconvincing, as the performances were delivered with competence. For instance, in the media analyzes textbook it says. "The actor's work commands most of our attention, overshadowing the considerable contributions of the writer, director, cinematographer, editor, and composer of the score. As George Kernodle puts it-it is the star that draws the crowds. The audience may be amused, thrilled, or deeply moved by the story, fascinated by new plot devices, property gadgets, and camera angles, charmed by backgrounds that are exotic, or captivated by those that are familiar and real, but it is the people on the screen, and especially the faces, that command the center of attention" (286). While faulty casting didn't seem to be a problem in this film as I think I would keep all of the actors for their parts if I were directing the film, but would just inspire them to take their greatness to the next level. In fact, there wasn't really any actor or actress that failed, or proved incompetent in the part as they all did what they had set out to do and that's was to make me believe in the story.

What kind of acting is required of the actors in the starring roles—action acting or dramatic acting? To Demonstrate, action acting and dramatic acting. The media analyzes textbook tells us that "we can refer to action acting as a type of acting that requires a great deal in the way of reactions, body language, physical exertion, and special skills, but it does not draw on the deepest resources of the actor's intelligence and feelings. In contrast, dramatic acting calls for sustained, intense dialogue with another person and requires an emotional and psychological depth seldom called for in action acting. Action acting is the art of doing. Dramatic acting involves feeling, thinking, and communicating emotions and thoughts. Action acting is on the surface, with little nuance. Dramatic acting is beneath the surface and full of subtlety. Each type of acting requires its own particular gift or talent" (295). While I think the kind of acting that is required of the actors in the starring roles of this film, is dramatic acting. Which makes me to believe that the actors are well suited to the type of acting demanded by the roles that they play.   Where are their weaknesses or limitations most evident? First, the media analyses textbook tells us "In a well- cast movie there are no weak links. Each member of the cast contributes significantly to the film, whether he or she is on the screen for five seconds, five minutes, or two hours" (311). Moreover, an actor's weakness or limitation can be found the moment it becomes difficult to express a certain emotion or live under an imaginary circumstance due to a past experience that it may trigger, as that just what I think. If they are well suited, in what scenes is their special type of acting skill most apparent? For Johnny Depp, it was on the pirate ship and the last scene comforting Peter. For Kate Winslet, it was when she was watching the play of peter pan in the parlor. For Freddie Highmore, it was in the last scene with him and Barrie on the park bench in the park and when he was tearing up the set of his homemade play with grievances for his mother being sick. For Nick Roud, it was when he came to the door to stand up for Barrie against his grandma Mrs. Emma du Maurier for Barrie to visit his mother and the family.

Drawing on your knowledge of their past performances, classify the actors in the major roles as impersonators, interpreters, or personalities. For an example, impersonators "...are actors who have the talent to leave their real personality behind and to assume the personality of a character with whom they may have few characteristics in common. Such actors can completely submerge themselves in a role, altering their personal, physical, and vocal characteristics to such a degree that they seem to become the character" (Media Analysis 296).

Interpreters "and commentators play characters closely resembling themselves in personality and physical appearance, and they interpret these parts dramatically with- out wholly losing their own identity" (Media Analysis 296). Lastly, "actors whose primary talent is to be themselves and nothing more are personality actors. They project the essential qualities of sincerity, truthfulness, and natural- ness, and they generally possess some dynamic and magnetic mass appeal because of a striking appearance, a physical or vocal idiosyncrasy, or some other special quality strongly communicated to us on film" (Media Analysis 297). Furthermore, classifying the actors in the major roles are the following: Johnny Depp, is impersonator and personality actor. Kate Winslet, is an impersonator actor. Lastly, Freddie Highmore, is an interpreter actor.

Consider the following questions with respect to each of the starring actors: a.) Does the actor seem to depend more on the charm of his or her own personality, or does he or she attempt to become the character? I thought that Kate

Winslet depended on her own personality, and
Johnny Depp attempted to become the character.
b.) Is the actor consistently believable in the
portrayal of the character, or does he or she
occasionally fall out of character? Kate Winslet
and Johnny Depp, were believable in the
portrayal of their character as it was hard to
notice them falling out of there character. c.) If
the actor seems unnatural in the part, is it
because he or she tends to be overdramatic or
wooden and mechanical? There wasn't any part
where I felt Kate Winslet and Johnny Depp was
unnatural, wooden, overdramatic, or mechanical.
If there were a part of unnaturalness, it would
probably be more apparent in the way the actor
delivers their physical actions.

In which specific scenes is the acting especially
effective or ineffective? The acting is effective in
the beginning park scene, when Barrie had to
convince to the audience and the family that the
dog was a bear, as though out the scene it seemed
like Barrie want to convince that you can change
things by simply believing they could be different.
Why? Because, according to the Media Analysis

391

textbook. "Actors must also possess the
intelligence, imagination, sensitivity, and insight
into human nature necessary to fully understand
the characters they play—their inner thoughts,
motivations, and emotions. Furthermore, actors
must have the ability to express these things
convincingly through voice, body movements,
gestures, or facial expressions, so the qualities
seem true to the characters portrayed and to the
situation in which the characters find
themselves" (287). As, I thought the actors
became their characters effectively and there
could have been some areas where they could
have grown in.

In which scenes are the actors' facial expressions
used in reaction shots? First, in the Media
Analysis textbook it tells us. "The reaction shot
achieves its considerable dramatic impact
through a close-up of the character most affected
by the dialogue or action. The actor's face, within
the brief moment that it is on the screen, must
register clearly yet subtly and without the aid of
dialogue the appropriate emotional reaction"
(291-292). So, I would say the scene where this

occurred took place in many as one of them was
when Barrie was comforting Sylvia on the sofa.
What reaction shots are particularly effective?
Thus, the reacting shots that are particularly
effective would have to be the ones that
registered clearly the appropriate emotional
reaction for the actor to live truthfully in the
moment he/she was in.

How strong is the cast of supporting actors, and
what does each contribute to the film? How does
each help bring out different aspects of the star's
personality? I would have to say that the cast of
supporting actors would have had to be strong,
not just in support of the main actors, but also
with the film being based on a true story as there
needed to be a sense of believability. For an
example, in the Media Analyzes textbook it says.
"The major stars play off them, as friends,
adversaries, employers, employees, leaders, or
even foils (contrasting characters that serve to
clearly define the personality of the main
character). Supporting players make the stars
shine brighter, sharper, and more clearly,

providing a sounding board that both helps to bring out all the dimensions of the star's character and makes the most important facets stand out in bold relief. But supporting players often do much more. Sometimes they create characters that are brilliant in their own right" (307). Do the supporting players create memorable moments or steal the show in spots? If so, where in the film do such moments occur? Yes, most defiantly the supporting characters do create memorable moments and there were some parts were they kept stealing the show. For instance, whenever there was a serious and boring situation that the characters were in, like the dinner table. Barrie put a coin on his finger and flicked it up towards the ceiling to hit a card and the next thing you noticed the four boys (Peter, George, Jack and Michael) were all trying it and laughing. Another was when Barrie was having dinner with the Davies family and the grandma, as when the situation started to get boring and serious through the kids facial expressions. Barrie messed with the server a bit by pulling away when she brought him his food, and then he put a spoon on his nose to spark laughter in the kids as they followed his action in putting a spoon on their noses. Also, I thought the lines of Michael were funny and honest in the truth of the moment that he was placed in. For example, Mrs. Emma du Maurier: "*A word with you, Mr. Barrie, before you go. We'll only be a few minutes.*" Sylvia Llewelyn Davies: "*Boys, why don't you go and play in the garden, go on.*" Michael Llewelyn Davies: "*Is he in trouble? Because I've been alone with Grandmother and I know what it's like.*" The delivery is so pure, innocent, cute, precious, and you can find truth in relating to it in your own past childhood moment.

What contributions do the small parts and extras make to the film? For an example, the media analyzes textbook tells us. "The casting of extras is another important consideration, for extras are often called on to perform some very important scenes. If they are not reacting properly, if their faces do not show what is being called for by the scene they are in, the scene may be ruined. Extras are, in a sense, actors in their own right, not just background for the story. For that reason studios hire casting directors to hire extras to fit the film's requirements. Often this job is done on the actual shooting location. The extras casting director goes to the location in advance of the crew and spends a great deal of time finding the right faces, backgrounds, and personalities to fit the story" (310). As, it appears to me that the faces of the extras and bodies are well chosen to fit our preconceived notions of what they should look like, yet they blend in to the scene and don't draw too much attention to themselves. In fact, the extras show realism. Moreover, in the media analyzes textbook we are made aware of how "extras are not always cast only on the basis of appearance, because their part may require a special skill. Even in the brief moment they are on-screen, they must do their assigned tasks with naturalness, a lack of self-consciousness, and a competence that shows" (311). Thus, the extras and small parts "working tasks," are performed with confidence and naturalness.

INT. THE STRAIGHT STORY/CINEMA THERAPY - DAY

Watching the film, 'The Straight Story (1999)' for my tenth cinema therapy session, on anger and forgiveness.

 Scan here for 'The Straight Story' trailer.

Before going any further in to this film session, I make this my prayer for the Holy Spirit as my Counselor: Father, in the name of Jesus, I pray for you Holy Spirit to exhort and counsel me as the emotionally wounded. I ask in faith that Your Spirit will rest upon me — the Spirit of wisdom and understanding, the Spirit of counsel and might. Give me insight and knowledge for understanding myself as your counselee. Thank You, Father, that I am a good listener to the film that you have guided me to watch. Help me to comprehend the unfolding of those past hurts that influence reactions to current situations. Thank You that I am a promoter of peace and filled with joy. I trust the Holy Spirit as my counselor, out of the rich treasury of your glory, to be my strength and reinforce with mighty power in the inner man by the [Holy] Spirit [Himself indwelling in my innermost being and personality]. You will not leave me without support as I give my time and concern to being transformed and healed through this Flixrapeutic senior paper, helping to complete the forgiveness process. I will be confident about my convictions, knowing excellent things. In Jesus' name, amen.

As I prescribed a movie based on an issue and followed some guidelines for watching movies with conscious awareness in this order: First, start with a film that supports your treatment goal. Second, choose a film from film recommendations. Third, making sure to clarify intent when assigning a film in which might mistake the role identification. Fourth, familiarize yourself with Guidelines for watching films and discuss guidelines. Fifth, discuss the positive or negative reactions to film. Sixth, use material according to your theoretical orientation. Seven, afterwards reflect on evocative questions and answer them after watching the selected film as it does help to write down my answers.

Do you remember whether your breathing changed throughout the movie? Yes, this would be the scene when Alvin was traveling down a hill where the speed limit was 45 mph and had no way of stopping due the transmission on his tracker going out. Could this be an indication that something threw you off balance? I believe so, because one minute Alvin was in control of his tracker and once he passed the sign I think he realized that his belt broke as things spiraled out of control for him all the way down the hill.

Ask yourself: If a part of the film that moved you (positively or negatively) had been one of your dreams, how would you have understood the symbolism in it? If this would have been a dream for me I would have took it as a positive one, seeing it as if I am suppose to do something. Then, I'll go at interpreting the dream in the following ways: First, write out all that I could remember about the dream in detail. Second, underline the symbols and make not out the type of theme or mood that it carried. Third, use a Christian dream interpretation dictionary to find the meaning of the symbols. Fourth, reference the symbols from the Bible. Fifth, pray about the dream and hear from God about it.

Notice what you liked and what you didn't like or even hated about the movie. Which characters or actions seemed especially attractive or unattractive to you? I really liked the message and the story of this film, but I thought that it could have been either directed or shot better. While the actions that seemed attractive to me was how Alvin humbled himself public to make peace with his brother, and I liked how that strangers went out of their way to help him as out of it storied got shared. Did you identify with one or several characters? Since, there were not a whole lot of characters in the film, besides Alvin that I can say I identify with, I would say another could be Lyle.

Were there one or several characters in the movie that modeled behavior that you would like to emulate? Yes, Alvin and some of the other strangers that crossed his path on the road to

Lyle's house as they showed hospitality to Alvin and helped him in his time of need as another was Rose. While I would say that Alvin had developed certain strengths or other capacities that I would like to develop as well.

Now there wasn't any aspect of the film that was hard to watch, or that could be related to something that I might have repressed ("shadow").

Did you experience something that connected you to your inner wisdom or higher self as you watched the film? Yes, I wrote down several things in my journal that I felt connected me with my inner wisdom with a few scriptures. For instance, no matter what someone has done to you or what has happened to cause a separation, forgiveness is the only answer to bring peace and mend hearts. While the main scripture I received that I feel is connected to this movie is Luke 23:26-35 and Luke 6:24-42. Moreover, I thought how Alvin's usual transportation was a small tracker that attracted the interest of others and invited others to share their story with his. After this made me think how the cross was the usual transportation for Jesus to make peace with us for Father-God to show us His love and forgiveness.

In fact, there were many mentioned guidelines on the road to Lyle's house that seemed to have turned out to be useful, while I might consider using them not only in "reel life" but also adapt them to "real life" because I am aware of how they are intended to make me become a better observer as I saw them being good life lessons to learn from and teach.

If the film had a unique message for you, what was it? On the other hand, Christian Sandberg from IMDb.com wrote. "The Straight Story" chronicles a trip made by 73-year-old Alvin Straight from Laurens, Iowa, to Mt. Zion, Wis., in 1994 while riding a lawn mower. The man undertook his strange journey to mend his relationship with his ill, estranged, 75-year-old brother Lyle." Now, in my own words, I thought the unique message of the film 'The Straight

Story.' Forgiveness is a trip that you have to make on your own, but you don't have to go at it alone without encountering support along the way. While you don't have to just forgive, you can do it in an interesting way that will impact others, build relationships and share stories.

What new ideas for new behaviors did you have? Your attempt to forgive can help others in finding forgiveness for them selves. Furthermore, here are some life lessons that I learned through the film: First, for a runaway who thinks her family hates her. Alvin: *"Well, they maybe mad. But I don't think they're mad enough to want to loose you... or your little problem ... When my kids were real little, I used to play a game with them. I'd give each of them a stick and – one for each of them   -- then I'd say, "you break that." They could, real easy. Then I'd say, "tie them sticks in a bundle and try to break that. Course, they couldn't. then I'd say, "that bundle – that's family."* Second, concerning a life lesson for something good about getting old. Alvin: *"Well I can't imagine anything good about being blind and lame at the same time, but still, at my age,*

I've seen about all that life has to dish out. I know to separate the wheat from the chaff... and let the small stuff fall away." Third, concerning a life lesson for what's the worse part of being old. Alvin: *"Well, the worse part of being old is remembering when you was young."* Fourth, concerning a life lesson for one who drinks alcohol. Alvin: *A preacher helped me put some distance between me and the bottle, and he helped me see the reason O was drinking – I was seeing all them things here that I'd seen over there. [Music: /though things may look very dark/ a dream is not in vain/] every one is trying to forget. I can see it in a man right away."* Fifth, concerning a life lesson for two bickering brothers. Alvin: *"There's no one who knows your life better than a brother that's near your age. He knows who you are and what you are... better than any one on earth. My brother and I said some unforgiveable things the last time we met, but I'm trying to put that behind me, and this trip is a hard swallow of my pride. I just hope I'm not too late. A brother's a brother."* Sixth, the road to forgiveness is not only about who you can help, but also about how others can help you on your journey. Seventh, Forgive is a process of releasing and letting go. Eighth, the pit stops or derailments on your forgiveness journey are just as important as traveling on the lonely road to forgiveness, because along the way you build relationships in your delays.

What other films can you identify that might take the discussion a step further? Amish Grace, The Descendants, In a Better World, Magnolia, Pieces of April, and Warrior.

INT. REDEEMED/FILM ANALYSIS - DAY

The eleventh media analysis therapeutic session was on the director's style of the film 'Redeemed' that was directed by David A.R. White, for analyzing the art of watching films.

Scan here for 'Redeemed' trailer.

Before going any further in to this film session, I make this my prayer for the Holy Spirit as my Counselor: Father, in the name of Jesus, I pray for you Holy Spirit to exhort and counsel for me as the emotionally wounded. I ask in faith that Your Spirit will rest upon me — the Spirit of wisdom and understanding, the Spirit of counsel and might. Give me insight and knowledge for understanding myself as your counselee. Thank You, Father, that I am a good listener to the film that you have guided me to watch and that I know your voice. Help me to comprehend the unfolding of those past hurts that influence reactions to current situations. Lord, I will not judge by what I see with my eyes or decide by what I hear with my ears. Righteousness will be my belt, and faithfulness the sash around my waist. Thank You that I am a promoter of peace and filled with joy. I trust the Holy Spirit as my counselor, out of the rich treasury of your glory, to be my strength and reinforce with mighty power in the inner man by the [Holy] Spirit [Himself indwelling in my innermost being and personality]. You will not leave me without support as I give my time and concern to being transformed and healed through this Flixrapuetic senior paper, helping to complete the forgiveness process. I will be confident about my convictions, knowing excellent things, and will have the knowledge in knowing the certainty of the words of truth. In Jesus' name, amen.

First, for an example of The DIRECTOR'S STYLE, there's a quote from a director known as SIDNEY LUMET who said. "Actually, everything a director puts up on the screen is revelatory. Don't you really know all about John Ford from his films? Or Hitchcock, or Howard Hawks? If I reveal a character on the screen, I am necessarily also revealing myself . . . I think I have an idea of what my work is about, but I'm not interested in articulating it in words."

Before I go into the analyzes of the director's style in the film, 'Redeemed.' I'll research on a different film, Thirteen key acting questions that every actor should answer to be a fully rounded and connected great actor, from studying a truly great actor:

Who is David A.R. White's character? David.

Where is David A.R. White character? A hotel, while I didn't get the city and state.

When is it? Present.

Where have David A.R. White's character just come from? Church.

What does David A.R. White's character want? To be accountability for Paul and to be a source of escape from his temptation with Julia, while David also wants restoration for his marriage.

Why does David A.R. White's character want it?
To warn Paul of what David sees up ahead for an
affair if he doesn't U-turn, as he wants to help
Paul make a better choice to save his marriage.

Why does David A.R. White's character want it
now? David has been in Paul's shoes and he sees
where it is headed, plus if David doesn't get
through to Paul-Paul could loose his marriage
including everything else, as David wants to save
him from a big mistake.

What will happen if David A.R. White's character
doesn't get it now? Paul will get deceived; make a
wrong choice, falling in to temptation and sin.
Losing his marriage, family, and business to an
affair that could have been prevented.

How will David A.R. White's character get what he
wants by doing what? Inform, warn, educate,
convict, alert, persuade, honesty, friendly,
encourage, address, absolve, affront, aid, alarm,
amend, approach, assist, caution, clarify, concern,
consider, convince, correct, direct, elevate,
endure, free, help, humble, inspire, lead, liberate,

mend, motivate, notify, plan, pray, prompt, pursue, settle, suggest, support, unburden, understand, urge, vindicate, and woo.

What must David A.R. White's character overcome? David must overcome things like rejection, confrontation, hurt, reasoning, logic and combating the enemy within.

Does David A.R. White fully transform into their character? It was hard to see a different character that David was portraying, who had his same name, as this actor appeared to be as a personality actor whose primary talent is to be themselves and nothing more. For Instance, "They project the essential qualities of sincerity, truthfulness, and natural- ness, and they generally possess some dynamic and magnetic mass appeal because of a striking appearance, a physical or vocal idiosyncrasy, or some other special quality strongly communicated to us on film" (Media Analysis 297). However, David A.R. White shows hard work, technique and good direction. In fact, I saw that David A.R. White is truthfully and emotionally connected with his character David. As the audience, even though I thought David AR White was playing himself, still I saw the fully realized three-dimensional character right in the truth of the moment.

Now, answering Dr. Culp's five movie critique questions.

On description, describe the story in objective terms. According to Netflix tells the story is about, "A devoted family man has a romantic encounter that threatens to destroy his home, business and faith, but a friend will help him see the way through." On the other hand, in my own words it appears to me that this film asks the question. What is adultery? Then, answered it with biblical truth and a good moral lesson on how to combat the greatest enemy within. As, the themes dealt with temptation, adultery, choices and faith in God.

On meaning, describe what the story/director is trying to say. There is a right and wrong. Moreover, when we make the wrong choice in choosing to trust our self apart from God. We

411

allow temptation to threaten to destroy our life, as we see how God is faithful to bring us through and deliver us.

On worldview, describe what principles/values are in use by the characters or in the plot. Liberality (Matthew 5:42); Mercy (Matthew 5:44); Simplicity (Matthew 6:19); Contentment (Matthew 6:25); Hope (2 Corinthians 4:16-18); Christian Fellowship (2 Corinthians 6:14); Faith (Galatians 5:5-6); Temperance (Ephesians 4:19,22-24); Edification (Ephesians 4:29); Humility (Philippians 2:3); Perseverance (Philippians 3:13-14); Praise (Philippians 4:4); Prayer (Philippians 4:6); Contemplation and reflection (Colossians 3:2-3); Forbearance (Colossians 3:12-13); Industriousness (2 Thessalonians 3:10); Purity of speech/Doctrine (2 Timothy 2:16-17); Hospitality (Hebrews 13:2); Fidelity (Hebrews 13:4); Confession (James 5:16); Sympathy (1 Peter 3:8); Evangelism (1 Peter 3:15); Loyalty (1 Peter 4:8); Generosity (1 John 3:17); and Love (1 John 4:16-19).

Discuss the main characters' behavior based upon

biblical principles. David (mercy, hope, Christian
fellowship, faith, temperance, forbearance,
industriousness, purity of speech/doctrine,
evangelism, loyalty, generosity and love); Paul
(love, generosity, confession, purity of speech,
forbearance, prayer, perseverance, temperance,
faith, Christian fellowship, hope, mercy and
liberality); Ryan (Christian fellowship,
edification, forbearance, industriousness, and
purity of speech); Liz (Christian fellowship, faith,
forbearance, loyalty and industriousness); Julia
(industriousness and edification); Beth (mercy,
hope, Christian fellowship, faith, temperance,
forbearance, industriousness, purity of
speech/doctrine, evangelism, loyalty, generosity
and love), Rose (mercy, hope, Christian
fellowship, faith, temperance, forbearance,
industriousness, purity of speech/doctrine,
evangelism, loyalty, generosity and love).

On interpretation, describe what the movie means
to you personally. Temptation will draw you to it
like fire, enticing you to play with it and then will
turn on you with a threat to destroy everything
you have worked hard to get in your life as it how

to combat it. Thus, the scripture I feel are connected to this movie are: 2 Corinthians 5:17, Joshua 6:20 and John 3:6-20.

Moving on, to analyzing the director's style of 'Redeemed,' with actor and director David A.R. White.

After viewing several films by a single director, what kinds of general observations can you make about his style? The adjectives listed below describe the style of David AR White: First, intellectual and rational. Second, calm and quiet. Third, polished and smooth. Fourth, warm and subjective. Fifth, fresh and original. Fifth, tightly structured, direct, and concise. Sixth, truthful and realistic. Seventh, simple and straightforward. Eighth, light, comical, and humorous. Ninth, exaggerated. Tenth, optimistic and hopeful. Eleventh, logical and orderly.

What common thematic threads are reflected in the director's choice of subject matter? The common themes of the director's choice of subject matter are: faith, God, temptation, choices, moral lessons, the struggle with good and evil and social problems. For instance, "An examination of subject matter might begin with a search for common themes running through all the films under study. One director may be concerned primarily with social problems, another with men's and women's relationship to God, and yet another with the struggle between good and evil. Directors' choices of subject matter may be related to their tendency to create similar emotional effects or moods in everything they do" (Media Analysis 325). How is this thematic similarity revealed in the nature of the conflicts the director deals with? To demonstrate, in the Media Analyzes textbook we see that "the types of conflicts that directors choose to deal with constitute an important thematic thread. Some directors lean toward a serious examination of subtle philosophical problems concerning the complexities of human nature, the universe, or God. Others favor simple stories of ordinary people facing the ordinary problems of life.

(327). With this said, the director deals with the thematic similarity revealed in the nature of the conflicts by asking a question based on a problem with adultery, and answers it with a moral lesson upon biblical truths.

In the films you have seen, what consistencies do you find in the director's treatment of space and time? For an example, we can see that in the Media Analyzes textbook it tells us "the subjects that a director chooses may also show some consistency with respect to the concepts of time and space. Some directors prefer a story in which the action takes place in a very short time period—a week or less" (327). While I've noticed that David AR White uses a story where the action takes place in a very short time period, restricted to a limited physical setting and keeps the number of actors in the cast to a bare minimum, as his concepts are equally diverse.

Is a consistent philosophical view of the nature of man and the universe found in all the films studied? Yes. If so, describe the director's worldview. The director David AR White as a Christian worldview, as he interprets faith in God into his movies around a moral lesson. In fact,

David AR White's passion is to create films that impact our culture for Christ, and the cool thing is that David's love for the Lord has governed the projects that he attaches himself to.

How is the director's style revealed by composition and lighting: philosophy of camera, camera movement and methods of achieving three-dimensionality? For Philosophies of camera, he uses the subjective camera, as this is a camera that views the scene from the visual or emotional point of view of a participant. For composition and lighting, David uses a composition that's formally and dramatic as his lighting is favored in high-key lighting, which is more even and contains subtle shades of gray. Now for camera movement, David's style favors the fixed camera, which creates a sense of movement through panning and tilting.

How does the director use special visual techniques (such as unusual camera angles, fast motion, slow motion, and distorting lenses) to interpret or comment on the action, and how do these techniques reflect overall style? For instance, "because directors usually choose the cinematographer they want, we can assume their selections are based on a compatibility of visual philosophies, and for simplicity's sake we usually attribute the film's visual style to the director" (Media Analysis 328). I see David AR White using special visual techniques in freedom to allow the audience to experience the film in a different way as I saw things like unusual camera angles, slow and fast motion, light-diffusing filters and sharp, clear images dominated by bright, highly contrasting hues.

How is the director's style reflected in the different aspects of the editing in the films, such as the rhythm and pacing of editorial cuts, the nature of transitions, montages, and other creative juxtapositions? Mostly, David's favors a soft, fluid transition, such as a slow dissolve and he uses juxtapositions. Also, he uses special tricks of editing, such as the use of parallel cutting fragmented flash cutting and dialogue overlaps can indicate his style. How does the style of editing relate to other elements of the director's visual style, such as the philosophy of camera or how the point of view is emphasized? For instance, the Media Analyzes textbook says. "Directors may stress an intellectual relationship between two shots by using ironic or metaphorical juxtapositions, or they may emphasize visual continuity by cutting to similar forms, colors, or textures. They might choose to emphasize aural relationships by linking two shots solely through the soundtrack or the musical score" (330). As it all depend on how they want to tell the story, and how they want it to affect the audience way of see the film.

How consistent is the director in using and emphasizing setting? I believe that the visual emphasis placed on the setting is an important aspect of David's directing style, as he using setting that help us understand the character and is a powerful tool to build atmosphere. What kind of details of the natural setting does the director emphasize, and how do these details relate to his or her overall style? For an example, David chooses factors in the "setting that may reflect the director's style are which social and economic classes the director focuses on, whether the settings are rural or urban, and whether the director favors contemporary, historical past, or futuristic time periods" (Media Analysis 331). Whereas, these details closely relate to the choice of his subject matter in his overall style. Is there any similarity in the director's approach to entirely different kinds of settings? Not really, because I think he strives to be original and to choose his settings with excellence. How do the sets constructed especially for the film reflect the director's taste? By being a type of emphasis that is significant, indication on an overall Christian worldview and choosing the best way to represent the story through the set construction.

In what ways are the director's use of sound effects, dialogue, and music unique? For instance, the sound is almost as important as the image and the director uses, off-screen sound imaginatively to create a sense of total environment. How are these elements of style related to the image? It helps to create their movies' appeal, and it seems like they all flow together like pieces of a puzzle to get the message to the audience, as this should be the main purpose.

What consistencies can be seen in the director's
choice of actors and in the performances they
give under his or her direction? David uses some
of the same actors that he has worked with in
previous films, for an example, "most directors
have a hand in selecting the actors they work
with, and it must be taken for granted that they
can have a strong influence on individual acting
performances. In the choice of actors, one
director may take the safe, sure way by casting
established stars in roles very similar to roles
they have played before" (Media Analysis 332).
How does the choice of actors and acting styles fit
in with the style in other areas? To demonstrate,
in the media analyzes textbook we can see. "In
their choice of actors, directors may also reveal
an emphasis on certain qualities. A director can
have a remarkable feel for faces and choose stars
and even bit players who have faces with
extremely strong visual character—that is, faces
that may not be beautiful or handsome but are
strikingly powerful on the screen. Or a director
may prefer to work with only the "beautiful
people." One director may seem to stress the

421

actors' voice qualities, and another may consider the total body or the physical presence of the actor more important. The director may have a tremendous influence on the acting style of the cast, although the extent of this influence may be difficult to determine even in a study of several films" (332). While the acting style and the actor can be influenced by the director.

What consistencies do you find in the director's narrative structure? For an example, "a director may tell the story from the viewpoint of a single character and manipulate us so that we essentially experience the story as that character perceives it. Although the camera does not limit itself to subjective shots, we emotionally and intellectually identify with the point-of-view character and see the story through his or her eyes" (Media Analysis 333). Usually, in David's films we can expect to see a character starting off with a narration to a moral problem, and it end with the a narration that point to the solution to the problem since with faith-based.

If the director seems to be constantly evolving instead of settling into a fixed style, what directions or tendencies do you see in that evolution? It appears to me that David AR White has a fixed style in his directing. What stylistic elements can you find in all his or her films? While the stylistic elements that one can expect to find in all of his films are: First, a voice-over narrative to provide the point-of-view from the character to set up a frame at beginning and end. Second, "dynamic in medias res beginnings, where conflict is already developing when the film opens" (Media Analysis 334). Third, "the entire film may end with the resolution of one problem" (Media Analysis 334). Fourth, "Complex plots, with several lines of action occurring simultaneously at different locations, can be broken into fragments jumping quickly back and forth from one developing story to another (Figure 11.7). Or each stream of action can be developed rather completely before switching to another stream of narrative" (Media Analysis 334). Lastly, "a lazy, slow-paced, gradual unfolding of character or information, focusing on each single detail" (Media Analysis 334). Overall, one thing I like about this director's style is his films are always getting better and his stories have a great message to them with a moral lesson that is faith-based.

INT. RABBIT HOLE/CINEMA THERAPY - DAY

Watching the film, 'Rabbit Hole' for my eleventh cinema therapy session, on mental and emotional illness.

 Scan here for 'Rabbit Hole' trailer.

Before going any further in to this film session, I make this my prayer for the Holy Spirit as my Counselor: Father, in the name of Jesus, I pray for you Holy Spirit to exhort and counsel for me as the emotionally wounded. I ask in faith that Your Spirit will rest upon me — the Spirit of wisdom and understanding, the Spirit of counsel and might. Give me insight and knowledge for understanding myself as your counselee. Thank You, Father, that I am a good listener to the film that you have guided me to watch. Help me to comprehend the unfolding of those past hurts that influence reactions to current situations. Lord, I will not judge by what I see with my eyes or decide by what I hear with my ears. Righteousness will be my belt, and faithfulness the sash around my waist. I will be clothed with fairness and with truth. Thank You that I am a promoter of peace and filled with joy. I trust the Holy Spirit as my counselor, out of the rich treasury of your glory, to be my strength and reinforce with mighty power in the inner man by the [Holy] Spirit [Himself indwelling in my innermost being and personality]. You will not leave me without support as I give my time and concern to being transformed and healed through this Flixrapuetic senior paper, helping to complete the forgiveness process. I will be confident about my convictions, knowing excellent things, and will have the knowledge in knowing the certainty of the words of truth. In Jesus' name, amen.

As I prescribed a movie based on an issue and followed some guidelines for watching movies with conscious awareness in this order: First, start with a film that supports your treatment goal. Second, choose a film from film recommendations. Third, making sure to clarify intent when assigning a film in which might mistake the role identification. Fourth, familiarize yourself with Guidelines for watching films and discuss guidelines. Fifth, discuss the positive or negative reactions to film. Sixth, use material according to your theoretical orientation. Seven, afterwards reflect on evocative questions and answer them after watching the selected film as it does help to write down my answers.

Do you remember whether your breathing changed throughout the movie? Yes, towards the ending when Nat and Becca was packing up Danny's toys and Nat picks up a toy that she can't get to stop talking, so Becca takes it from her to do something to make it stop. Then when the toy turns off it says "bye" after Becca has put it away, and she says "bye back as Nat and Becca both laugh. While my breathing change was more like a breathing change of laughter. Could this be an indication that something threw you off balance? No. In all likelihood, what affects you in the film is similar to whatever unbalances you in your daily life.

Ask yourself: If a part of the film that moved you

(positively or negatively) had been one of your dreams, how would you have understood the symbolism in it? The film moved me positively, because I got to see more of how people respond and cope with grief. While if this was a dream, through the Bible and a Biblical Dream Symbols Dictionary. I would probably interpret it the symbolism of crying as needing help and grieving with the scripture from Prov. 21:13 (Wolfe, Tyler 56).

Notice what you liked and what you didn't like or even hated about the movie. Which characters or actions seemed especially attractive or unattractive to you? I like how Jason coped with his grief as he shared it with Becca, used his love for drawing to create comic book and doing research at the library. While he chose to deal with it silently through venting through his art, until Becca approached him to talk in the park and that invited him to continue sharing his grief. Did you identify with one or several characters? Jason was the character that I would most likely have identified with in this film.

Were there one or several characters in the movie that modeled behavior that you would like to emulate? Yes, Jason and the group leader who held a grief share group to heal people heal and cope with their grief. While Jason, Becca and Howie did develop certain strengths or other capacities that I would like to develop as well.

Moving on, I didn't notice any aspect of the film that was hard to watch. So, this couldn't be related to something that I might have repressed, as I know how uncovering repressed aspects of our psyche can free up positive qualities and uncover our more whole and authentic self.

Did you experience something that connected you to your inner wisdom or higher self as you watched the film? Yes, when Becca said, "some where out there I'm having a good time." Then a scripture was brought to my attention from Acts 26:2, "I think myself happy." Furthermore, I learned how there are two ways people will respond to grief: First, hold on to the thing of the lost loved one to remind them of that person, and rehearse the memories over in their heads.

Second, to get rid of the things that remind them of their lost loved one in attempt to forget and try to move on, but the memories won't let them forget the loved one that passed. Another inner wisdom was when you share the burdens of others, you share yours and there's a release that happens of healing, since this has to have been out of love as Becca and Jason showed this.

In fact, some of the mentioned guidelines turned out to be useful, and I would consider using them not only in "reel life" but also to adapt them to "real life" because I know that they are intended to make me become a better observer.

If the film had a unique message for you, what was it? I'm going to tell this from two point-of-views, as the first one is from Common Sense Media saying. "Although the movie is often sad and painful – showing that any marriage, no matter how solid it seems, can be shaken to the core by tragic events – ultimately, it says that even if love can't prevent fissures (a state of incompatibility or disagreement). It can heal them." Second, the film's unique message in my own words would be many people deal with grief differently, but you can find what you love to do and use it to help you share your grief and cope as love heal grief. For instance, Howie found going to group helped him cope with his grief. While it seemed like Becca used cooking to cope with her grief, and talking with Jason in the park. As Jason used drawing comic book art and doing research at the library to help him to cope with his grief. Briefly, all three of these characters had something that they look to do that helped them to get through grieving. Third, "Each grieving in their own way, Becca and Howie grapple with the realities of life eight months after the death of their 4-year-old son, Danny." Netflix tells us.

What new ideas for new behaviors did you have? Involve yourself in a connect group, share your grief with a trusted friend or family member, and find something you loved to do to help you cope through the grief. While this scripture was brought to my attention concerning new behavior that says "*God of all healing counsel! He comes alongside us when we go through hard times, and before you know it, he brings us alongside*

431

*someone else who is going through hard times so
that we can be there for that person just as God
was there for us. We have plenty of hard times
that come from following the Messiah, but no
more so than the good times of his healing
comfort—we get a full measure of that, too."* 2
Corinthians 1:3-5. While, I saw this in the movie.

What other films can you identify that might take
the discussion a step further? Confessions of a
prodigal son, little white lie, grace monaco,
missing william, Field of Dreams, Rain Man,
Closet Land Cries From the Heart, Cry for Help,
and Damage.

INT. GOD'S NOT DEAD/FILM ANALYSIS - DAY

The twelfth media analysis therapeutic session was on an ANALYSIS of the WHOLE FILM of 'God's Not Dead,' directed by David A.R. White, for the art of watching films.

Scan here for 'God's not Dead' trailer.

Before going any further in to this film session, I make this my prayer for the Holy Spirit as my Counselor: Father, in the name of Jesus, I pray for you Holy Spirit to exhort and counsel for me as the emotionally wounded. I ask in faith that Your Spirit will rest upon me — the Spirit of wisdom and understanding, the Spirit of counsel and might. Give me insight and knowledge for understanding myself as your counselee. Thank You, Father, that I am a good listener to the film that you have guided me to watch. Help me to comprehend the unfolding of those past hurts that influence reactions to current situations.

433

Lord, I will not judge by what I see with my eyes
or decide by what I hear with my ears. Thank You
that I am a promoter of peace and filled with joy. I
trust the Holy Spirit as my counselor, out of the
rich treasury of your glory, to be my strength and
reinforced with mighty power in the inner man by
the [Holy] Spirit [Himself indwelling in my
innermost being and personality]. You will not
leave me without support as I give my time and
concern to being transformed and healed through
this Flixrapuetic senior paper, helping to
complete the forgiveness process. I will be
confident about my convictions, knowing
excellent things, and will have the knowledge in
knowing the certainty of the words of truth. Holy
Spirit, help me to apply application to the
revelation that I receive, so there will be
transformation. In Jesus' name, amen.

First, for an example of The ANALYSIS of the
WHOLE FILM, there's a quote from a film critic
with 'The New Yorker and known as ANTHONY
LANE who said. "[O]f all the duties required of the
professional critic, perhaps the least

important—certainly the least enduring—is the
delivery of a verdict. I am always sorry to hear
that readers were personally offended, even
scandalized, that my opinion of a film diverged
from theirs. I wish I could convince them that I
am merely stating an argument, as everyone does
over dinner, or in a crowded bar, after going to
see a film, and that their freedom to disagree is
part of the fun. The primary task of the critic . . .
is the recreation of texture—not telling
moviegoers what they should see, which is
entirely their prerogative, but filing a sensory
report on the kind of experience into which they
will be wading, or plunging, should they decide to
risk a ticket."

Before I go into analyzing the film as a whole for
the movie, 'God's Not Dead.' I'll research the
thirteen key acting questions, on a different film,
that every actor should answer to be a fully
rounded and connected great actor, from
studying David AR White as a truly great actor.

Who is David A.R. White's character? Reverend
Dave.

Where is David A.R. White character? Mainly,
Dave is seen around the church facility.

When is it? Present times.

Where have David A.R. White's character just
come from? We first see Dave stepping out of his
car, at the Carter International Airport.

What does David A.R. White's character want? To
encourage someone to have faith in God, and take
a stand for what they believe in.

Why does David A.R. White's character want it?
Dave wants o get people to follow Jesus, and put
their faith in God.

Why does David A.R. White's character want it
now? Time might run out, as Dave wants to
change a person's final answer.

What will happen if David A.R. White's character
doesn't get it now? It might be too late to reach
the person, as its only by God's mercy they cross
his path.

How will David A.R. White's character get what he

wants, by doing what? Accept, challenge, affirm, aid, alert, amend, approach, assist, astound, bless, clarify, confound, confirm, convince, direct, draw, ease, educate, endure, enlighten, free, help, motivate, inspire, liberate, mend, prompt, propel, settle, simplify, soothe, suggest, unburden, understand, vindicate, woo, and urge.

What must David A.R. White's character overcome? It seems like Dave will need to overcome unbelief, discouragement and his own tests of faith in knowing that God is Good.

Overall, I thought that David A.R. White does fully transform into his character Dave. As David A.R. White show hard work, technique and good direction. Whereas, he stays truthfully and emotionally connected to his character Dave. As the audience, I saw none of this, but the fully realized three-dimensional character right in the truth of the moment. While David AR White is a personality actor, and showed me how using your primary talent to be yourself and nothing more in roles in just as important in reel life as it is in real life.

Now, answering Dr. Culp's five movie critique questions.

On description, describe the story in objective terms. Netflix tells us that this is a story about "A spiritual college student clashes with an atheistic professor who insists that students will only pass his class by admitting that God is dead."

On meaning, describe what the story/director is trying to say. It's simple, and easy. God's not dead, moreover, echoing what C.S. Lewis said, "only a real risk tests the quality of a belief."

On worldview, describe what principles are in use by the characters or in the plot, and discuss the characters' behavior based upon biblical principles. Liberality (Matthew 5:42), Mercy (Matthew 5:44), Simplicity (Matthew 6:19), Contentment (Matthew 6:25), Hope (2 Corinthians 4:16-18), Christian fellowship (2 Corinthians 6:14), Faith (Galatians 5:5-6), Temperance (Ephesians 4:19-22,24), Edification

438

(Ephesians 4:29), Humility (Philippians 2:3), Perseverance Philippians 3:13-14), Praise (Philippians 3:13-14), Prayer (Philippians 4:6), Contemplation and reflection (Colossians 3:2-3), Forbearance (Colossians 3:12-13), Industriousness (2 Thessalonians 3:10), Purity of speech/doctrine (2 Timothy 2:16-17), Hospitality (Hebrews 13:2), Fidelity (Hebrews 13:4), Confession (James 5:16), Sympathy (1 Peter 3:8), Evangelism (1 Peter 3:15), Loyalty (1 Peter 4:8), Generosity (1 John 3:17), and lastly, love (1 John 3:17).

On interpretation, describe what the movie means to you personally. Specifically, if you don't believe in one thing you'll believe in anything. The question along that asks the audience. 'What do you believe?' Moves you to want to stand up for your faith in God, or being willing to take the chance of putting your hope and faith in Jesus.

Moving on, ANALYZING THE WHOLE FILM of 'God's Not Dead,' with David A.R. White. On the Basic Approach: Watching, Analyzing, and Evaluating the Film.

What seems to be the director's purpose or primary aim in making the film? I think the director's purpose in making the film 'God's Not Dead' was to challenge believers of God to stand up for their faith, and to influence unbelievers to put their faith in God become followers of Jesus Christ.

What is the true subject of the film, and what kind of statement, if any, does the film make about that subject? The true subject of the film is faith, and the kind of statement it makes is to stand up for what you believe in. While the statements that this film makes about the subject are: First, it's easy to dismiss what you don't want to understand. Second, only a risk will prove a belief. Third, right and wrong leads straight back to God. Fourth, if God does not exist then every thing is permissible. Fifth, where do you find your hope? Sixth, when Josh said, "who are you looking to fail me or God?" Seventh, another thing is when Josh also said, "how can you hate someone if they don't exist? Eighth, when Michael Tait from the Newsboys band said, "we exist here and now, they exist forever." While

440

there was a lot of bold statements said through the dialogue that made you think, and encourages faith or belief in someone.

How do all the separate elements of the film relate to and contribute to the theme, central purpose, or total effect? To demonstrate, like it states in the Media Analysis textbook. "Answering this question involves at least some consideration of all the elements in the film, although the contribution of some is much greater than the contribution of others. Every element should be considered at this point: story, dramatic structure, symbolism, characterization, conflict, setting, title, irony, cinematography, editing, film type, frame shape and size, sound effects, dialogue, the musical score, the acting, and the film's overall style. If we can see clear and logical relationships between each element and the theme or purpose, then we may assume that our decision about the film's theme is valid. If we cannot see these clear relationships, we may need to reassess our initial understanding of the theme and modify it to fit the patterns and interrelationships we see among the individual film elements" (361). Thus, in my personal opinion, I believe all the elements work together to help form the message that the director wants to tell in the story.

What is the film's level of ambition? What director David AR White of the film 'God's not dead' appears to be trying to do is to subjectively educate and the level at which he is trying to communicate is on a philosophical level for college students and up to understand.

Given the film's level of ambition, how well does the film, succeed in what it tries to do? According to the Media Analysis textbook, "after considering this question, we must review our earlier assessment of the effectiveness of all individual film elements to determine the effect each element has on our answer" (361-362). In which, I believe that this movie proved its point of what it set out to do, and succeed. Why does it succeed or fail? The film 'God's Not Dead' succeed, because it called people into action with a bold statement that was made, either challenging to stand up for your belief in God or to persuade a belief in God as

I don't really seeing this film of having had failed.
Which elements or parts make the strongest
contribution to the theme and why? "We must be
careful to weigh each strength and weakness in
terms of its overall effect on the film, avoiding
petty nitpicking such as concentrating on slight
technical flaws" (Media Analysis 362). So, I would
say that the elements that made the strongest
parts for the film was how it was designed to
make a statement. Which includes: the story,
dramatic structure, symbolism, characterization,
conflict, setting, title, irony, cinematography,
editing, film type, frame shape and size, sound
effects, dialogue, the musical score, the acting and
the film's overall style. Which elements or parts
fail to function effectively? Now, the elements
that failed to function effectively would only be
the sound effects.

What were your personal reactions to the film?
The film challenged my faith and encourages me
in how God is good all the time, as it was
educating. What are your personal reasons for
liking or disliking it? For once there was a lot of

wisdom and revelation in the film to influence someone to give God a chance with their life, as it was the telling of a true story that grabbed you to pull you in with the music and the acting.

INT/ REBEL WITHOUT A CAUSE/CINEMA THERAPY - DAY

Watching the 1955-1956 film, 'Rebel without a Cause' for my twelfth cinema therapy session, on Homosexuality for males.

Scan here for 'Rebel without a Cause' trailer.

Before going any further in to this film session, I make this my prayer for the Holy Spirit as my Counselor: Father, in the name of Jesus, I pray for you Holy Spirit to exhort and counsel me as the emotionally wounded. I ask in faith that Your Spirit will rest upon me — the Spirit of wisdom and understanding, the Spirit of counsel and might. Give me insight and knowledge for understanding myself as your counselee. Thank You, Father, that I am a good listener to the film that you have guided me to watch. Help me to comprehend the unfolding of those past hurts that influence reactions to current situations. Thank You that I am a promoter of peace and filled with joy. I trust the Holy Spirit as my

445

counselor, out of the rich treasury of your glory, to be my strength and reinforced with mighty power in the inner man by the [Holy] Spirit [Himself indwelling in my innermost being and personality]. You will not leave me without support as I give my time and concern to being transformed and healed through this Flixrapuetic senior paper, helping to complete the forgiveness process. I will be confident about my convictions, knowing excellent things, and will have the knowledge to assist your children in knowing the certainty of the words of truth. In Jesus' name, amen.

As I prescribed a movie based on an issue and followed some guidelines for watching movies with conscious awareness in this order: First, start with a film that supports your treatment goal. Second, choose a film from film recommendations. Third, making sure to clarify intent when assigning a film in which might mistake the role identification. Fourth, familiarize yourself with Guidelines for watching films and discuss guidelines. Fifth, discuss the positive or negative reactions to film. Sixth, use material according to your theoretical orientation. Seven, afterwards reflect on evocative questions and answer them after watching the selected film as it does help to write down my answers.

Do you remember whether your breathing changed throughout the movie? There wasn't really any breath changes from me throughout the film, other then when Plato shot at someone and got shot at by the cops. Could this be an indication that something threw you off balance? No, because it was just a sigh of a breath as it wasn't anything too big.

In all likelihood, what affects you in the film is similar to whatever unbalances you in your daily life.

Ask yourself: If a part of the film that moved you (positively or negatively) had been one of your dreams, how would you have understood the symbolism in it? The parts of the film that moved me negatively way was: the knife fight, the chickie run with the cars to the edge of the cliff, bullying and the gunfight. While the positive parts of the film that moved me in a positive way were: laughing, and the three characters who became friends. Now, the steps that I would take to understand the symbolism in them would be: Prayer, Bible and a Christian dream interpretation dictionary as I would probably also restudy symbolism in the Media Analysis textbook.

Notice what you liked and what you didn't like or even hated about the movie. Which characters or actions seemed especially attractive or unattractive to you? The actions that seemed attractive to me was the Juvenile officer, because it seemed that he didn't talk at Jim, but rather to him and took the time to understand him. For instance, when Jim said, "Jim, look... will you do something for me? If a pot starts boiling again, will you come and see me before you get yourself in a jam? Even if you just want to talk, come on and shoot the breeze. Its easier sometimes than talking to your folks." Did you identify with one or several characters? Yes, Plato and some with Jim. For an example for Jim, it would be when he

said. "You know something? I woke up this
morning, you know... and the sun was shining,
and it was nice. And all that type of stuff, and the
first thing – I saw you, and, uh, I said, "boy this is
going to be one terrific day, so you better live it
up, because tomorrow you'll be nothing." And I
almost was." Then, I thought when you love and
have a passion for something it can save you from
going off a cliff. The other example was of Plato,
during his dialogue between Judy and Jim. Jim:
"never say you haven't had this much fun." Plato:
"Oh, I came here a lot of times before, but I never
had fun." Judy: "Why not?" Plato: "Because I was
alone." [Laughing, ha-ha-ha-ha, alright.] Jim:
"Why you come back here for?" Plato: 'Cause I'd
run away. I used to run away a lot, but they
always took me back." Judy: "Who?" Plato: "Mom
and Dad. Now that I don't have them anymore, I
wish... I never had run away. I used to lie in my
crib at night, and I'd-I'd listen to them fight.
Furthermore, it seems like Judy wanted to be
understood and to love someone. Jim wanted
honor and to do something right for once in his
life. Plato wanted to be loved and a friend, as they

all was searching for a place to belong. In the end, all the three got what they wanted as the reason why I believe Plato go a negative ending would be based on the principle of living by the gun and dying by the gun.

Were there one or several characters in the movie that modeled behavior that you would like to emulate? Yes. The juvenile officer modeled good behavior for him knowing how to talk to troubled teens, and Jim towards the end where we see his behavior takes a turn for the good in doing something right as they did develop certain strengths or other capacities that would influence another in wanting to develop as well.

Moving on, there wasn't really any aspect of the film that was hard to watch. So, there couldn't be anything that relates to something that I might have repressed.

Uncovering repressed aspects of our psyche can free up positive qualities and uncover our more whole and authentic self.

Did you experience something that connected you
to your inner wisdom or higher self as you
watched the film? Something that connected me
to my inner wisdom was insights and scriptures
brought to my attention were: Proverbs 13: 20
(show me your friends and I'll show you your
future), 1 Corinthians 15:33 (bad company
corrupts good morals), and Proverbs 29:18
(When people do not accept divine guidance, they
run wild. But whoever obeys the law is joyful).
Moreover, you can buy someone many things, but
you can't buy them love and affection as that is
something you can only give them by spending
time with them. Thus, this insight and the
scriptures point to the solution that can save
many rebellious teenagers. Another insight, the
sense of belonging can be connected to behavior
and direction. A third insight, honor doesn't have
to prove it self as it will show itself on its own.
Fourth insight, parents tend to dismiss what they
don't understand about their teenager and turn
away from them when they come to them for an
answer to their problem. Fifth, teens find

451

themselves getting in to trouble whenever they turn wrong in to right and just to try to belong. Sixth insight, being someone's friend when no body wants to, is to be strong and also is what it feels like to be loved. Similarly, I felt that I connected with Plato. For the reason, Plato, for me represented the homosexual as he was crying out to be saved and running in search for a friend who would love him for who he is. Also, we see him going through bullying and abuse as he tried to make Judy and Jim his family that he didn't have. While I saw the planetarium building giving Judy, Jim and Plato vision as it allowed them to be themselves and explore with their imaginations.

If some of the mentioned guidelines turn out to be useful, you might consider using them not only in "reel life" but also adapt them to "real life" because they are intended to make you become a better observer.

If the film had a unique message for you, what was it? Ed Stephan, on IMDb.com wrote. "Jim Stark is the new kid in town. He has been in

trouble elsewhere; that's why his family has had
to move before. Here he hopes to find the love he
doesn't get from his middle-class family. Though
he finds some of this in his relation with Judy,
and a form of it in both Plato's adulation and Ray's
real concern for him, Jim must still prove himself
to his peers in switchblade knife fights and
"chickie" games in which cars race toward a
seaside cliff." Particularly, for me, I saw the
unique message in the tagline. Being the cure for
a rebellious generation is to be understood, to
belong and be loved, as they will only find this
when they first find Jesus Christ.

What new ideas for new behaviors did you have?
Just being someone's friend and showing love has
the potential to turn a rebellious heart in to one of
obedience, could influence a change of behavior in
a troubled teenager. Simply, do unto others, as
you would like done unto you. Also, being some
ones friend when nobody wants to can be strong
and can heal the two parties.

What other films can you identify that might take
the discussion a step further? The Boys In The

Band (1970), Children Of Loneliness Compulsion (1959), Crying Game (1992), Cruising (1980), The Detective (1968), Far from Heaven (2002), Last Exit To Brooklyn (1989), Jeffrey (1996), The L-Shaped Rom (1963), The Lost Language Of Cranes (1992), Midnight Cowboy (1969), My Own Private Idaho Outrageous (1977), Philadelphia (1993), Priest (1994), The Sergeant -1968, The Strange One – 1957, Three Of Hearts Tea & Sympathy (1956), and Wilde (1997).

INT. SNOW FALLING ON CEDARS/FILM ANALYSIS - DAY

The thirteenth media analysis therapeutic session was on ADAPTATIONS of 'Snow Falling on Cedars,' with actor James Cromwell, for the art of watching films.

Scan here for 'Snow Falling on Cedars' trailer.

Before going any further in to this film session, I make this my prayer for the Holy Spirit as my Counselor: Father, in the name of Jesus, I pray for you Holy Spirit to exhort and counsel for me as the emotionally wounded. I ask in faith that Your Spirit will rest upon me — the Spirit of wisdom and understanding, the Spirit of counsel and might. Give me insight and knowledge for understanding myself as your counselee. Thank You, Father, that I am a good listener to the film that you have guided me to watch. Help me to comprehend the unfolding of those past hurts that influence reactions to current situations.

Lord, I trust the Holy Spirit as my counselor, out of the rich treasury of your glory, to be my strength and reinforced with mighty power in the inner man by the [Holy] Spirit [Himself indwelling in my innermost being and personality]. You will not leave me without support as I give my time and concern to being transformed and healed through this Flixrapuetic senior paper, helping to complete the forgiveness process. I will be confident about my convictions, knowing excellent things, and will have the knowledge in knowing the certainty of the words of truth. Holy Spirit, help me to apply application to the revelation that I receive, so there will see transformation. In Jesus' name, amen.

For an example of ADAPTATIONS, there's a quote from this director who is known as JOHN HUSTON who said. "The Maltese Falcon was produced three times before I did it, never with very much success, so I decided on a radical procedure: to follow the book rather than depart from it. This was practically an unheard of thing to do with any picture taken from a novel, and marks the beginning of a great epoch in picture making."

Before I go into analyzing the adaptations for the movie, 'Snow Falling on Cedars.' I'll research the thirteen key acting questions, that every actor should answer to be a fully rounded and connected great actor from studying James Cromwell as a truly great actor.

Who is James Cromwell's character? James Cromwell plays the character of Judge Cedar.

Where is James Cromwell's character? Judge Cedar is in a quiet community of San Piedro.

When is it? The time looks like, maybe, 1954.

Where have James Cromwell's character just come from? Judge Cedar is mainly seen in a courthouse.

What does James Cromwell's character want? Judge Fielding wants fairness and justice.

Why does James Cromwell's character want it? James Cromwell wants to reach a verdict for a suspect to a murder, either being innocent or guilty.

Why does James Cromwell character want it now? James Cromwell wants to close the case either, convict a suspect or serve justice and grace to the victim, even if the victim turns around to be the suspect.

What will happen if James Cromwell's character doesn't get it now? An innocent man and a victim of prejudice could be convicted of something that he didn't do.

How will James Cromwell's character get what he wants by doing what? Study, investigation, absolve, allow, arrange, charge, correct, court, order, check, clarify, consider, detect, evaluate, facilitate, free, help, interview, invite, judge, lead, liberate, negotiate, notify, organize, orientate, overlook, plan, pursue, read, release, relegate, settle, simplify, suggest, simplify, tolerate, unburden, understand, urge, validate, verify, and vindicate.

What must James Cromwell's character

overcome? Judge Fielding must overcome lawyers leading witness into speculation, badgering a witness, distortion of the truth, and contempt of court.

Overall, James Cromwell fully transforms into his character of Judge Fielding. While he shows hard work, technique and good direction as I think he is a Meisner actor. For the reason, James Cromwell truthfully and emotionally connected as even though he was in a co-starring role he supported the main characters well and made his character believable. Thus, as the audience, I saw none of this, but the fully realized three-dimensional character of Judge Fielding right in the truth of the moment.

Now, answering Dr. Culp's five movie critique questions.

On description, describe the story in objective terms. I want to hear two side of the story to the film, 'Snow falling on Cedar.' First, IMDb.com says it is about. "A Japanese-American fisherman may have killed his neighbor Carl at sea. In the 1950's, race figures in the trial. So does reporter Ishmael." Second, Itunes says. "Ethan Hawke stars in this 'riveting tale of mystery' (FOX-TV) based on the award-winning best selling novel. A murder trial has upset the quiet community of San Piedro, and how this tranquil village Ishamael Chambers (Hawke), a local reporter, the trial strikes deep emotional chord when he finds his ex-lover is linked to the chase. As he investigates the killing, he uncovers some startling clues that lead him to a shocking discovery." Third, for me, I thought this is a romantic story of a transracial lover doing something right to set an innocent man, Kazuo free from a murder trial for the one Ishamael loves in spite of the odds for him to be with her due to prejudice with Hatsue's own family.

On meaning, describe what the story/director is trying to say. Simply, first love last forever.

On worldview, describe what principles/values are in use by the characters or in the plot and discuss the characters' behavior based upon biblical principles. Mercy (Matthew 5:44), Hope

(2 Corinthians 4:16-18), Faith (Galatians 5:5-6), Humility (Philippians 2:3), Perseverance Philippians 3:13-14), Forbearance (Colossians 3:12-13), Industriousness (2 Thessalonians 3:10), Hospitality (Hebrews 13:2), Sympathy (1 Peter 3:8), Loyalty (1 Peter 4:8), Generosity (1 John 3:17), and love (1 John 3:17).

On interpretation, describe what the movie means to you personally. The 'Snow Falling on Cedar,' for me, is about grace falling on this tranquil village and vindication being given to the victims of prejudice in an unjust circumstance that they are in as two interracial lovers find their love to be unfailing despite family differences. While the scriptures that I can connect with this film are: 1 Cor. 13:8, John 8:36, Proverbs 20:22, and Romans 9:15-18.

Moving on, ANALYZING ADAPTATIONS of 'Snow Falling on Cedars' with James Cromwell, on Adaptations of Novels.

After seeing the film version and reading a review on the novel 'Snow Falling on Cedars,' since I'm not able to purchase or read the novel. So, I'll reconsider my answers to the following questions.

Is the film version a close or a loose adaptation of the novel? I would say this film is close adaptation of the novel. In Particular, "Adaptations range from the close or faithful adaptation, in which the filmmaker translates nearly every character and scene from page to screen, to the loose adaptation, in which many elements from the original work have been dropped and many new elements added" (Media Analysis 383). In fact, an American teacher, who goes by the name of David Guterson as he spent his early morning hours over a ten-year period writing this novel, wrote this award-winning novel. Unfortunately, the novel has been challenged, banned or restricted in several school systems in the United States; including being removed temporary from the bookshelf of a Canadian Catholic school for the books sexual content. As, it goes to show it doesn't pay to try to sneak sexual content in a novel and try to get it in several school systems. If it is a loose adaptation, is the departure from the novel due to the problems caused by changing from one medium to another or by the change in creative personnel? Particularly, "When we see a film adaptation of a favorite book or show, we may expect the film to duplicate the experience we had when we read or saw the original work. That is, of course, impossible. In a sense, we have the same reaction to many film adaptations that we might have toward a friend whom we haven't seen for a long time and who has changed greatly over the intervening years" (Media Analysis 383). While I wouldn't say it's a loose adaptation, being that it seems like, from what a review says on it, everything from the novel was adapted in to a film as there could have been some problems caused by the changing from one medium to another.

Does the film version successfully capture the spirit or essence of the novel? If not, why does it fail? Yes, I do believe so. For this reason, in the Media Analysis textbook it makes a point in the factors that can make a novel adaptation into a film a success. "The medium in which a story is told has a definite effect on the story itself. Each medium has its strengths and limitations, and any adaptation from one medium to another must take these factors into account and adjust the subject matter accordingly" (383). With this in mind, the film seemed to have followed the plot line of the novel to stay true to it and that is why it's a success.

What are the major differences between the novel and the film, and how can you explain the reasons for these differences? In the Media Analysis textbook, there's an example. "A novel may be of any length and can develop elaborate plots with many characters; a film's scope is limited by its screen time" (383). On the other hand, another major difference that sticks out to me is the movie rating is PG-13 and the book rating is mostly rated-R, with it being removed from the school systems, including the battle scenes and a graphic amputation.

Does the film version successfully suggest meanings that lie beneath the surface and remind you of their presence in the novel? In which scenes is this accomplished? Yes, as the stream of consciousness or interior monologues that were presented in some areas of the film were considered a successful meaning to me for the reason that it made it much more personal. Indeed, in the Media Analysis textbook it puts the stream of consciousness or the interior monologue like this. "The "stream of consciousness" or "interior monologue," which is a combination of third-person and first-person narrative, although the participant in the action is not consciously narrating the story. What we get instead is a unique kind of inner view, as though a micro- phone and a movie camera in the fictional character's mind were recording for us every thought, image, and impression that passes through the character's brain, without the conscious acts of organization, selectivity, or narration" (387). For instance, when Hatsue reads the letters for Ishamael Chambers to her mother that cuts between Ishamael lying on a bed remembering a flashback. Also, there are the courtroom and crime scenes or so I thought.

Did reading the novel enhance the experience of seeing the film, or did it take away from it? Why?

465

Actually, I am glade that I didn't get to read the novel for the elements in the book would have been described in much more detail to enlarge the movie screen of the imagination and I wouldn't want to be exposed to how the sexual content would have been exposed in the novel.

How well do the actors in the film fit your preconceived notions of the characters in the novel? For this question, I really can't say, other then novels make us use our imaginations to visual the characters description and a film allows the character to visually unfold before the audience eyes as it gives us a more realistic experience. Which actors exactly fit your mental image of the characters? Ishmael Chambers, Hatsue Miyamoto, Kazuo Miyamoto, Alvin Hooks, Nels Gudmundsson, Judge Fielding, Young Ishmael Chambers and Young Hatsue Imada I would say. How do the actors who don't seem properly cast vary from your mental image? It appears to me that they were properly casted, being to stay true to the author's characters in the novel and to capture the overall emotional spirit or tone of the literary work. For example, the Media Analysis textbook tells us for this reason. "Creative tampering with the plot will be kept to a minimum, and the most important characters will be left unchanged and carefully cast. In the best adaptations, no matter how well known the source, the director will attempt to capture the overall emotional spirit or tone of the literary work. If creative and selective choices reflect a true understanding and appreciation of the novel or short story, the filmmaker can remind viewers who have read the book of the rich emotional and philosophical material beneath the surface and make them feel its presence" (397). Thus, this can justify me, from the director's point of view.   "In the novel, when a character first appears, the novelist often provides us with a quick thumbnail sketch of his or her past, (394) ...the only alternative is to dramatize such paragraphs visually. But this type of material not only lacks the importance to justify such treatment, but also would have to be forced into the main plot structure in a very unnatural manner. The kind of background information that the novelist gives in the passages above is simply not suited to a natural cinematic style, and the background of many film characters therefore remains a mystery. Because novels can and do provide this kind of information, they possess a depth in characterization that films usually lack" (395). Overall, I loved the story that the films told as the themes that it carried were the following: unfairness, justice, prejudice, interracial dating or love, mistrust, romance, love and vindication.

INT. LIFE OF A KING/CINEMA THERAPY - DAY

Watching the film, 'Life of a King' for my thirteenth cinema therapy session, on Transformation and renewal.

 Scan here for 'Life of a King' trailer.

Before going any further in to this film session, I make this my prayer for the Holy Spirit as my Counselor: Father, in the name of Jesus, I approach your throne of grace, bringing myself before you. I recognize that grieving is a human emotional process, and I give myself the space that I need to enter into the rest that you have for me. Lord, Jesus bore my grief and carried my sorrows and pain; I know that Your Spirit is upon Jesus to bind up and heal my broken heart. May I be gentle with myself, knowing that I am not alone in my grief. You are with me, and you will never leave me without support. Father, I desire to be a doer of your Word, and not a hearer only. Therefore, I make a commitment to rejoice with those who rejoice [sharing others joy], and to weep with those who weep [sharing others grief]. I pray that your love will give me great joy and comfort and encouragement, because I have refreshed the hearts of your people through social media. Thank you, Father, for sending the Holy Spirit to comfort, counsel, intercede for, defend, strengthen and stand by me in this time of grief and sorrow. In Jesus name I pray, amen.

As I prescribed a movie based on an issue and followed some guidelines for watching movies with conscious awareness in this order: First, start with a film that supports your treatment goal. Second, choose a film from film recommendations. Third, making sure to clarify intent when assigning a film in which might mistake the role identification. Fourth, familiarize yourself with Guidelines for watching films and discuss guidelines. Fifth, discuss the positive or negative reactions to film. Sixth, use material according to your theoretical orientation. Seven, afterwards reflect on evocative questions and answer them after watching the selected film as it

does help to write down my answers.

Do you remember whether your breathing changed throughout the movie? No. So, this couldn't be an indication that something threw me off balance. In all likelihood, what affects you in the film is similar to whatever unbalances you in your daily life.

Ask yourself: If a part of the film that moved you (positively or negatively) had been one of your dreams, how would you have understood the symbolism in it? The positive symbolism that seemed to move me the most would have to have been, the chess pieces. In which, according to Tyler Wolfe, an author of the biblical dream symbols. He interprets, "chess-symbolic of being locked in a strategic battle with people or spiritual enemies. And, checkmate-symbolic of assured victory in a situation." While the scripture I found that connects to the symbolism of chess, comes from Luke 14:28 and Matthew 14:28.

Notice what you liked and what you didn't like or

even hated about the movie. I liked how Eugene took the game of chess and used it to teach life skills to help keep teenagers off of the streets. Which characters or actions seemed especially attractive or unattractive to you? The actions that seemed attractive was when Eugene used the game of chess to learn how to play the game of life and change his mind, then took what got him through jail to reach out to kids of the streets show them how to work towards a better life as he made a difference by impacting someone else. Did you identify with one or several characters? Eugene, for the reason being that he used what he had to make a difference in the life of other kids to keep them from making the same mistakes that he had made.

Were there one or several characters in the movie that modeled behavior that you would like to emulate? Eugene, while he developed certain strengths and other capacities that I see myself developing as well.

Besides, I did not notice any aspect of the film that was hard to watch. So, this couldn't be

related to something that I might have repressed.
With this is mind, uncovering repressed aspects
of our psyche can free up positive qualities and
uncover our more whole and authentic self.

Did you experience something that connected you
to your inner wisdom or higher self as you
watched the film? Yes. It's not where you've been,
but where you are going that matters. You make a
difference in the world when you can make a
difference in someone else's life, as you don't need
a reward to show that you're a champion. While
its more about what you can learn in how you
play the game, and how it changes your mind
through it. For example, in the line of Eugene: "Its
not about creating a champion, its about learning
how to play the game. Its about changing minds.
And, in turn, learning about life. Championship
isn't about the end game. The championship is the
byproduct." As, the audience can see in the film,
chess and the Bible (with it mentioned towards
the end) can do this.

Whereas, some of the mentioned guidelines
turned out to be useful, as I would like to consider

473

using them not only in "reel life" but also to adapt them to "real life" because I know how they are intended to make me become a better observer.

If the film had a unique message for you, what was it? There is a positive message in this film about the power of one and the scripture that was brought to my attention were: Luke 14:28, Matthew 6:33, Revelations 19:16 and 1 Timothy 6:15. Thus, showing that your beginning (past) does not dictate your ending (future) as only God has control over that and you have free will of choice in choosing a positive or negative life. Lastly, in the beginning of the film, this line couldn't have been said any better. Chessman: "Just keep your eye on the game, everything will fall into place. Take care of the kind, everything else follows." As he concluded with, "only my mind gets out... every time I open up that board, every time I open up a Bible. And it will be out when you are playing in that tournament." Lastly, this is the way we can get our mind out or off of the world and find freedom by every time we open the Bible and paying attention to the game plan that God has us playing as its a new way to learn how to win within the rules/laws of the world, without changing the rules/laws of the world.

What new ideas for new behaviors did you have? First, we can't change the rules, but we have to learn to win within them. Second, Chess can teach you how to play the game of life and has the potential to change your mind. Third, you have to envision the end game from the beginning. Fourth, your mistake can be a great teacher for someone who is heading in the direction of where you've been. Lastly, how to take the hand that you've been dealt with in life and use it to make a difference in the life of someone whose been considered "the lease one" for them to use to work towards bettering their life. As, the most important one is to think before you move.

What other films can you identify that might take the discussion a step further? The recommended films of interest are: MOOZ-LUM and Know How.

Father, I shout and thank you Lord for my healing and my abundant harvest! I repent: declaring: "I am thank-full. I am not pride-full. I am grate-full. I

am full of joy and strength." I join my faith with
Kenneth and Gloria Copeland, and I do the part
The Lord has called me to do to get His job done.
The battle is the Lord's, and the victory is mine!
In Jesus name, amen.

INT. PIRATES OF THE CARIBBEAN: AT WORLD'S END/FILM ANALYSIS - DAY

The fourteenth media analysis therapeutic session was on ANALYZING SEQUELS of 'Pirates of the Caribbean: At World's End,' with actor Johnny Depp, for the art of watching films.

 Scan here for 'Pirates of the Caribbean: At world's end' trailer.

Before going any further in to this film session, I make this my prayer for the Holy Spirit as my Counselor: Father, in the name of Jesus, I approach your throne of grace, bringing myself before you. I recognize that grieving is a human emotional process, and I give myself the space that I need to enter into the rest that you have for me. Lord, Jesus bore my grief' and carried my sorrows and pain; I know that Your Spirit is upon Jesus to bind up and heal my broken heart. May I be gentle with myself, knowing that I am not alone in my grief. You are with me, and you will never leave me without support. Father, I desire to be a doer of your Word, and not a hearer only.

Therefore, I make a commitment to rejoice with those who rejoice [sharing others joy], and to weep with those who weep [sharing others grief]. I pray that your love will give me great joy and comfort and encouragement, because I have refreshed the hearts of your people through social media. Thank you, Father, for sending the Holy Spirit to comfort, counsel, intercede for, defend, strengthen and stand by me in this time of grief and sorrow. In Jesus name I pray, amen.

For an example of SEQUELS, there's a quote from this critic who goes by the name of RICK ALTMAN who said. "Hollywood does not simply lend its voice to the public's desires, nor does it simply manipulate the audience. On the contrary, most genres go through a period of accommodation during which the public's desires are fitted to Hollywood's priorities (and vice versa). Because the public doesn't want to know that it is being manipulated, the successful . . . "fit" is almost always one that disguises Hollywood's potential for manipulation while playing up its capacity for entertainment.

Whenever a lasting fit is obtained . . . it is because a common ground has been found, a region where the audience's ritual values coincide with Hollywood's ideological ones."

Before I go into analyzing on genre films, remakes, and sequels with the movie, 'Pirates of the Caribbean: At World's End.' I'll research the thirteen key acting questions, that every actor should answer to be a fully rounded and connected great actor from studying Johnny Depp as a truly great actor.

Who is Johnny Depp's character? Captain Jack Sparrow.

Where is Johnny Depp's character? Captain Jack Sparrow is mainly on a ship, at sea.

When is it? c. 1600 - 1660.

Where have Johnny Depp's character just come from? Captain Jack Sparrow is on a wrecked ship, on a sea of sand in 'Davy Jones' locker is where we first see him.

What does Johnny Depp's character want? Captain Jack Sparrow wants the heart of Davy Jones.

Why does Johnny Depp's character want it? Captain Jack Sparrow wants this to square his debt with Jones, and guarantee his freedom.

Why does Johnny Depp's character want it now? Captain Jack Sparrow desires to be released, and to sail the seas forever.

What will happen if Johnny Depp's character doesn't get it now? Captain Jack Sparrow will continue to be a slave, a captive, and he will be left to his well-deserved fate.

How will Johnny Depp's character get what he wants by doing what? Negotiate, betray, charm, bargain, charm, persuade, acquaint, address, affront, alert, allow, allure, amuse, amaze, antagonize, approach, arrange, assist, attack, bear, call, challenge, charge, clarify, command, consider, convince, dare, direct, dodge, dominate, draw, educate, endure, entertain, execute, facilitate, free, frighten, help, humor, inspire, lead, lecture, maneuver, manipulate, motivate, organize, perform, plan, press, pursue, rally, settle, soothe, study, suggest, support, tolerate, urge, and understand.

What must Johnny Depp's character overcome? Captain Jack Sparrow must overcome an alliance, adversary, traitors, cowardice, betrayal, hallucinations, and slavery.

Overall, Johnny Depp fully transform into his character Captain Jack Sparrow as he shows hard work, technique and good direction. While I consider Johnny Depp to be truthfully and emotionally connected with his character Captain Jack Sparrow. As the audience, I see none of this, but the fully realized three-dimensional character of Captain Jack Sparrow right in the truth of the moment.

Michelle Regalado says, "When it was first revealed that Disney was pursuing a film based on a theme park ride, no one had high hopes for the project. But the first movie of the franchise, The Curse of the Black Pearl, proved all the skeptics wrong, becoming a huge success and grossing over $654 million worldwide. Depp's unforgettable turn as the quirky, charming and hilariously over-the-top Captain Jack Sparrow was undoubtedly a big part of the appeal. The role showcased the actor's impressive comedic timing, not to mention his ability to turn a standard anti-hero into a lovable character that moviegoers want to see again and again. His performance in the film was highly praised and it won him a SAG award, as well as Golden Globe and Oscar nominations. The character also remains one of his most memorable and widely recognized roles to date. Depp's continued to reprise his role in the next three installments, each of which have been less well-received than the first, but have continued to bring in big money at the box office. Another Pirates installment is reportedly hitting theaters in 2017."

Now, answering Dr. Culp's five movie critique questions.

On description, describe the story in objective

terms. IMDb tells us that this film is about "blacksmith Will Turner teams up with eccentric pirate Captain Jack Sparrow to save his love, the governor's daughter, from jack's former pirate allies, who are now undead."

On meaning, describe what the story/director is trying to say. Common Sense Media says, "Despite several betrayals, Jack and Wills sacrifice what they want most and act selflessly for the greater good." While this is a story about leadership, making good business, putting others needs before yourself and fighting for liberty.

On worldview, describe what rules/principles/values are in use by the characters or in the plot and discuss the characters' behavior based upon biblical principles. Rule, take what you need and give back none. Hope (2 Corinthians 4:16-18), Edification (Ephesians 4:29), Humility (Philippians 2:3), Perseverance (Philippians 3:13-14), Hospitality (Hebrews 13:2) and Loyalty (1 Peter 4:8). Rule, life and death are in your hands. While there weren't that much Bible principles in the film, 'Pirates of the Caribbean: At World's End.'

On interpretation, describe what the movie means to you personally. My interpretation of this movie is it can show what it means to selflessly lay down what you want to help someone else get what they want, as it also showing squaring off debts with someone, fighting for freedom and pursuing the fate that you deserve with good leadership. As, the alternative scenario that it gave me was, a captain can navigate a ship alone, but with teamwork and sacrifice you will get to your destination much faster. Thus, the bible scriptures that was brought to my attention was Matthew 26:52, Proverbs 28:2 and 'Tyre, Gateway to the Sea' in Ezekiel 27:1-36.

Moving on, to ANALYZING SEQUELS of 'Pirates of the Caribbean: At World's End' with Johnny Depp.

On Sequels

In the Media Analysis textbook, there's an illustration for the reason to remakes and sequels, "The primary reason for Hollywood's reliance on remakes and sequels has to do with increases in the cost of producing motion pictures. As movies become more expensive to make, the gamble becomes much greater. Running a movie studio may be compared to running an aircraft factory that continually builds new models with new configurations, with untested control and power systems, and with $10 million to $200 million invested in each plane. When finished, each plane taxis to the runway, develops tremendous speed, and tries to get off the ground. There is no turning back. If it flies, it flies; but if it crashes, most of the investment is lost. Aircraft executives operating such a business would be very careful with the planes they designed, and the equivalent of a great many remakes and sequels would be turned out" (432-433).

In fact, Betsy Sharkey, an Entertainment Writer states. "People love sequels—they wait for them, read about them, and usually see them more than once. But in a town where executives make a habit of looking over their shoulders, selling something already regarded as a sure hit creates a tremendous burden. Movies are not necessarily better the second time around."

Does the sequel grow naturally out of the original? Yet, I learned in the Media Analysis textbook that "although there are rare exceptions, remakes and sequels generally lack the freshness and creative dynamics of the original, so the disappointment is usually justified" (433). In other words, was there enough story, left over from the original to make a natural sequel? Yes, I would say so as it referenced things from the original.

How many important members of the original cast and of the behind-the-scenes team were involved in the sequel? For this reason, in the media analysis textbook it tells us. "Much more important than the potential within the original story for a sequel is the audience's response to the original characters. If it becomes clear that a large film audience is fascinated with the cast of the original and would love to see those actors together again, we can be reasonably sure that a sequel will soon be in the making" (438). I would say about twenty complementing the major cast members of Johnny Depp, Geoffrey Rush and Kevin R. McNally. If some characters had to be recast, how did that change affect the quality of the sequel? Having to recast some characters in a sequel gives the audience a feeling of a friend or a family member is missing, because there is this relationship that the audience gets to establish with the characters and how they live their life on the screen connects us with them as there was a natural relationship to their original. For an example, in the media analysis textbook it shows us that "the most successful sequels (or series of sequels) result when the whole winning team (actors, director, writers, editor, producers, and so on) stays pretty much intact throughout" (439). So, we can see how this change of cast can affect the movie and also give it more creativity though.

Does the sequel build on the original in such a way that it seems incomplete unless you've seen the original, or is it complete, enough to stand on its own as a separate, unified work? The way this sequel appears to me is it builds on the original with all that is referenced to it, which would make it seem incomplete it you haven't seen the original. As I can remember seeing the first Pirates of Caribbean movie before seeing its sequel, 'At World's End' and now it makes me want to watch them all just so I can know the connects between each story.

Does the sequel capture the flavor and spirit of the original in story and visual style? Yes. Is it equal in quality to the original in every aspect? Yes.

Where does it surpass the original and where is it weaker? I would say that the film 'Pirate of Caribbean: At World's End,' surpassed the original for the plot line and dialogue as I can't really say too much on where I see it to be weaker for the reason that it builds with ever sequel.

If the sequel becomes a character series, what are the qualities of the characters that make them wear well? First, the media analysis defines character series as "in a character series, continuation of the actors from one film to the next is essential, but so is good writing built around consistency of character. The overall style of the series should be consistent so that the expectations of the audience are satisfied, guaranteeing their return to the next film in the series" (441). For example, the qualities of the characters that make them wear well are: the costumes, dialogue, comedic actions, and witty/wily personalities as the character were memorable.

Why do we want to see them again and again? We want to see characters again, because they make themselves memorable and they create a screen-to-reality relationship with the audience as another reason is there being consistency like a friend building a relationship with another friend. Are the writers able to keep their characters consistent in film after film? I would defiantly say that the writers did a great job with keeping their character consistent and being creative by introducing new characters for us to get to know in the film. How consistent are the other stylistic elements from one film to another?

It appears to me that the consistency of the other stylistic elements from one film to another is consistent enough to fulfill the audience's need for the predictability of the characters and at the same time there's those moments that keep you on edge to see what's going to happen next, whether in the story or with the character.

INT. EARTH TO ECHO/CINEMA THERAPY - DAY

Watching the film, 'Earth to Echo' for my fourteenth cinema therapy session, on Social Issues: Friendship, Teamwork, Selfless, Bonding, Impending separation and Outreach.

Scan here for 'Earth to Echo' trailer.

Before going any further in to this film session, I make this my prayer for the Holy Spirit as my Counselor: Father, in the name of Jesus, I approach your throne of grace, bringing myself before you. I recognize that grieving is a human emotional process, and I give myself the space that I need to enter into the rest that you have for me. Lord, Jesus bore my grief and carried my sorrows and pain; I know that Your Spirit is upon Jesus to bind up and heal my broken heart. May I be gentle with myself, knowing that I am not alone in my grief. You are with me, and you will never leave me without support. Father, I desire to be a doer of your Word, and not a hearer only.

Therefore, I make a commitment to rejoice with those who rejoice [sharing others joy], and to weep with those who weep [sharing others grief]. I pray that your love will give me great joy and comfort and encouragement, because I have refreshed the hearts of your people through social media. Thank you, Father, for sending the Holy Spirit to comfort, counsel, intercede for, defend, strengthen and stand by me in this time of grief and sorrow. In Jesus name I pray, amen.

As I prescribed a movie based on an issue and followed some guidelines for watching movies with conscious awareness in this order: First, start with a film that supports your treatment goal. Second, choose a film from film recommendations. Third, making sure to clarify intent when assigning a film in which might mistake the role identification. Fourth, familiarize yourself with Guidelines for watching films and discuss guidelines. Fifth, discuss the positive or negative reactions to film. Sixth, use material according to your theoretical orientation. Seven, afterwards reflect on evocative questions and answer them after watching the selected film as it

492

does help to write down my answers.

Do you remember whether your breathing changed throughout the movie? Yes, but it was more of like a breath change of laughter and I also felt my breath change just slightly when a part of Echo hit the tracker in the barn scene. Could this be an indication that something threw you off balance? No. Even though I know how in all likelihood, what affects you in the film is similar to whatever unbalances you in your daily life.

Ask yourself: If a part of the film that moved you (positively or negatively) had been one of your dreams, how would you have understood the symbolism in it? The parts that moved me negatively in the film was the kids lying, stealing cars, breaking and entering, fighting amongst friends, going to a high school party and walking into a bar. I would have understood the symbolism by way of a Christian dream interpretation dictionary, the Bible and through prayer.

Notice what you liked and what you didn't like or even hated about the movie. I liked how the kids made an adventure out of helping another, and at the same time used those last moments that they had with each other to make the most out of it. On the other hand, I didn't like seeing bad behavior in adolescents. Which characters or actions seemed especially attractive or unattractive to you? The actions that seemed to be especially attractive to me was Alex, being that he's a foster child, gentle, compassionate towards helping others, quiet and showed silent strength, whereas Tuck was a comic relief. Did you identify with one or several characters? Yes, I can identify with Alex and Munch.

Were there one or several characters in the movie that modeled behavior that you would like to emulate? I would say, Munch when he wasn't peer pressured by Tuck or Alex to lie to his parents. Did they develop certain strengths or other capacities that you would like to develop as well? I would have to say, yes, because I learned more about the simplicity of kids and how there is a joy they bring that can be seen as strength.

There wasn't any aspect of the film that I didn't
notice was hard to watch. Could this be related to
something that you might have repressed
("shadow")? Not really, keeping in mind that
uncovering repressed aspects of our psyche can
free up positive qualities and uncover our more
whole and authentic self.

Did you experience something that connected you
to your inner wisdom or higher self as you
watched the film? I did experience quite a few
things from the film that connected me with my
inner wisdom, as that being how the simplicity of
a child sees people for who they really are and
looks out for friends with their needs differently.
Another thing was when you are a kid you think
you're invisible and can't make a difference, but
you can really do anything as the small acts of
kindness that you take to help others can turn out
to make a big impact. Third, friends may leave
you behind, but a real friend won't forget about
you and will try not to do it again. Fourth, having

a friend that is long-distance can teach you how distance is just a state of mind and if you're best friends, you'll always be, no matter where you are. Now, the bible scriptures that was brought to my attention were: Proverbs 18:24, "...there is a friend who sticks closer than a brother." 1 Timothy 4:12, "Don't let anyone look down on you because you are young, but set an example for the believers in speech, in conduct, in love, in faith." Hebrews 13:2, "Do not neglect to show hospitality to strangers, for by this some have entertained angels without knowing it." 1 Corinthians 13:11, "When I was a child, I spake as a child, I understood as a child, I thought as a child: but when I became a man, I put away childish things." Moreover, it's not about you when it comes to reach out to help another friend, but it's more about helping other people, as that's what it means to do outreach, connecting and building relationships.

Even though this film was for kids, I do consider it having some mentioned guidelines that will turn out to be useful, and I might consider using them not only in "reel life" but also adapt them to "real life" because they are intended to make myself and other I share them with to become a better observer.

If the film had a unique message for you, what was it? Briefly, I see the movie 'Earth to Echo' as speaking in the language of the adolescent in a way that they understand and will be able to relate to, putting any adult in their shoes to show us how adolescents are viewing the world through there cellphones. While this would defiantly be a film to recommend to an adolescent whose seeking personal growth and transformation, because all the elements in this film can deals with what they might be going through at their age. Thus, from IMDb.com, "an adventure can be as big as the universe." Moreover, in Tucks ending monologue when he said. "When you're a kid you think you're invisible. You think you can't make a difference. We're not kids anymore. We know now that we can do anything. Having a friend, light-years away taught us that distance is just a state of mind. If you're best friends, then you always will be... No matter where you are in the universe." Furthermore, saying good-bye doesn't have to sound like you will never see a friend again, but it can sound more like you will see them later. For example, Alex: "I don't really know how to say goodbye, so I'm not gonna. And um... um, you're my friend you know, and when I'm old, even when you think I've forgotten, I'm always gonna be there." Lastly, growing up to become an adult can be like 'impending separation' from childhood.

What new ideas for new behaviors did you have? First, breaking and entering can get you caught and chased by security. Second, stealing cars can get you in some serious trouble and not just getting grounded for an adolescent, but serving time in prison. Third, lying builds up walls, breaks down trust and will lead you down a rebellious path. Fourth, choose your friends wisely, because they can influence the direction and moral of your life. Lastly, make the most out of the friendships you have and share those moments with them like if you're the only people in the world, because you never know when you will get to see them again.

What other films can you identify that might take the discussion a step further? Free birds, James and the giant peach and Spy kids three.

Father, I shout and thank you Lord for my healing and my abundant harvest! I repent: declaring: "I am thank-full. I am not pride-full. I am grate-full. I am full of joy and strength." I join my faith with Kenneth and Gloria Copeland, and I do the part The Lord has called me to do to get His job done. The battle is the Lord's, and the victory is mine! In Jesus name, amen.

INT. RICH HILL/FILM ANALYSIS - DAY

The fifteenth media analysis therapeutic session was on ANALYZING FILMS IN SOCIETY of 'Rich Hill,' on social problems and 'The Lady in Number 6: Music Saved My Life,' on documentary film for the art of watching films.

Scan here for 'Rich Hill' trailer.

Before going any further in to this film session, I make this my prayer for the Holy Spirit as my Counselor: Father, in the name of Jesus, I approach your throne of grace, bringing myself before you. I recognize that grieving is a human emotional process, and I give myself the space that I need to enter into the rest that you have for me. Lord, Jesus bore my grief and carried my sorrows and pain; I know that Your Spirit is upon Jesus to bind up and heal my broken heart. May I be gentle with myself, knowing that I am not alone in my grief. You are with me, and you will never leave me without support. Father, I desire

to be a doer of your Word, and not a hearer only.
Therefore, I make a commitment to rejoice with
those who rejoice [sharing others joy], and to
weep with those who weep [sharing others grief].
I pray that your love will give me great joy and
comfort and encouragement, because I have
refreshed the hearts of your people through social
media. Thank you, Father, for sending the Holy
Spirit to comfort, counsel, intercede for, defend,
strengthen and stand by me in this time of grief
and sorrow. In Jesus name I pray, amen.

To put it briefly, there's a quote that give an
example of FILM and SOCIETY by a FILM
HISTORIAN AND CRITIC who goes by the name of
DAVID THOMSON. He said. "A movie is a kind of
séance, or a drug, where we are offered the
chance to partake in the lifelike. No, it's not life:
we will never meet Joan Crawford or Clark Gable.
Yet we are with them. It is surreptitious; it is
illicit, if you like, in the sense of being unearned or
undeserved. It is vicarious, it is fantastic, and this
may be very dangerous. But it is heady beyond
belief or compare. And it changed the world. Not

even heroin or the supernatural ever went so far."

First, ANALYZING FILMS IN SOCIETY on Social Problem Films of 'Rich Hill.'

Answering Dr. Culp's five movie critique questions for this film.

On description, describe the story in objective terms. Specifically, Netflix puts it. "Two filmmaker cousins return to their decaying hometown of Rich Hill, Mo., to film this affecting documentary about the lives of three local boys." Moreover, I'm pretty sure the trailer gave it away in the definition that Harley defines to us of poverty. He says, "People think that we are poor around here, but for a definition of poor it is no roof, no lights, no water, no food. We have lights, we have water, we have a roof, we have food, we have money. We are not poor." While all three boys in the film, the thing that all the three boys shared was hope, love and dreams. As, the poorest person in the world is the one who doesn't have a dream.

On meaning, describe what the story/director is
trying to say. Three boys in small town America
aren't how the dictionary defines them as poor,
while they are spiritually rich with hope, love and
a dream.

On worldview, describe what principles/values
are in use by the characters or in the plot and
discuss the characters' behavior based upon
biblical principles. The values that I saw in the
movie were: love, family, dreams, hope, and faith.
Liberality (Matthew 5:42), Simplicity (Matthew
6:19), Contentment (Matthew 6:25), Hope (2
Corinthians 4:16-18), Faith (Galatians 5:5-6),
some edification (Ephesians 4:29), Humility
(Philippians 2:3), Perseverance (Philippians
3:13-14), Contemplation and reflection
(Colossians 3:2-3), Industriousness (2
Thessalonians 3:10), Hospitality (Hebrews 13:2),
Sympathy (1 Peter 3:8), Loyalty (1 Peter 4:8),
Generosity (1 John 3:17), and lastly Love (1
John 3:17). While Andrew, Harley and Appachey
all showed hope and dreams.

On interpretation, describe what the movie means to you personally. Simply, being poor isn't really how it looks as you can be physically poor and be spiritually rich. As, Philippians 4:11-13 can fit this documentary when it says, "I am not saying this because I am in need, for I have learned to be content whatever the circumstances." Even through Andrew, Harley and Appachey are growing up on the edge of poverty in rural America they showed how they are rich in hopes and dreams.

Does the social problem attacked by the film have a universal and timeless quality, affecting all people in all time periods, or is it restricted to a relatively narrow time and place? The social problem that was attacked by the film was poverty and showing the audience how being poor isn't really how it's defined, as the film had a universal and timeless quality that seems to affect all people in all time periods. For the reason, explained in the media analysis textbook. "Once in a while, if a social problem film is artistically done, it becomes more than a mere vehicle to encourage social reform, and it may outlive the problem it attacks"(472).

Is the film powerful enough in terms of a strong storyline, enduring characters, good acting, artistic cinematography, and so on, to outlive the social problem it is attacking? In other words, how much of the film's impact is caused by its relevance to a current problem and its timing in attacking the problem? Yes, the film powerful enough in terms of a strong storyline, enduring characters, good acting, artistic cinematography, and so on, to outlive the social problem it is attacking. In fact, I would saw that the film dominated its impact to the current problem and it's timing in attacking it by taking the audience to that place. For an example, in the media analysis textbook it states. "Strong, memorable characters and a good story give social problem films durability even after the specific problem dealt with no longer has relevance. As standards of privacy have shifted, audiences in many areas of our culture have become more and more fascinated with the "realistic" manner in which this voyeuristic form can closely examine individual lives both famous and "ordinary." And, of course, by the broadest possible definition, virtually all documentary films are inherently "social problem" works" (472). Indeed, it seems like this documentary film did this, with the realism that it showed on growing up on the edge of poverty in rural America.

If the immediate social problems on which the film focuses were permanently corrected tomorrow, what relevance would the film have to the average viewer twenty years from now? Besides, a change in perspective or definition of what it means to be poor. With this in mind, the media analysis textbook states. "In a sense the social problem film can enjoy a long life only by failing in its purpose, for its impact is generally lost as soon as the problem portrayed no longer exists. This is especially true of a film that treats a narrow, topical, and very contemporary problem. The more general the problem, the more widespread its effects; and the more resistant it is to reform, the longer is the life span of the social problem film directed against it. As long as the social problem exists, the film has relevance" (472). So, I would think it would be like a reminder to the viewer and a wake up call for how it looked to grow up on the edge of poverty in rural America and it would probably encourage the viewers to maintaining and working on improving this reform to a social problem so we keep from seeing it again or history repeating itself.

Second, ANALYZING FILMS IN SOCIETY on Documentary Films of 'The Lady in Number 6: Music Saved My Life.'

Answering Dr. Culp's five movie critique questions for this movie.

On description, describe the story in objective terms. According to Netflix, "Czech pianist and holocaust survivor Alice Herz-Sommer describes how music enabled her to survive one of the darkest chapters in human history." Whereas, in my own words, Alice Sommer's gifts of playing music became her refuge of peace, love and beauty that helped others get through hard times.

On meaning, describe what the story/director is

trying to say. It's a story about the power of music as the world's oldest pianist living as a Holocaust survivor tells how her music brought an optimistic outlook on life and was a moral support for others in hard times.

On worldview, describe what rules/principles/values are in use by the characters or in the plot and discuss the characters' behavior based upon biblical principles. Liberality (Matthew 5:42), Mercy (Matthew 5:44), Simplicity (Matthew 6:19), Contentment (Matthew 6:25), Hope (2 Corinthians 4:16-18), Edification (Ephesians 4:29), Temperance (Ephesians 4:19,22-24), Humility (Philippians 2:3), Perseverance (Philippians 3:13-14), Praise (Philippians 4:4), Contemplation and reflection (Colossians 3:2-3), Forbearance (Colossians 3:12-14), Industriousness (2 Thessalonians 3:10), Purity of Speech (2 Timothy 2:16-17), Hospitality (Hebrews 13:2), Sympathy (1 Peter 3:8), Loyalty (1 Peter 4:8), Generosity (1 John 3:17), and lastly Love (1 John 3:17). In brief, Alice Sommer showed love, joy, peace and calmness through her behavior that was based upon biblical principles.

On interpretation, describe what the movie means
to you personally. First, music is in the first place
of art, as it brings us on an island with peace,
beauty and love. Second, Music is a dream that
brings calmness and calmness is strength, Third,
Music is moral support, not just entertainment as
it gives people hope through hard times. Fourth,
it is a mystery that, when the first tone of music
starts, it goes straight to the soul. Fifth, your
passion with help get not only you through hard
times, but others as well. Sixth, Your passion can
make you richer than life. Seven, It depends on
you whether life is good or bad as you have to
choose to live on the good side. Lastly, the
scripture that was brought to my attention was
out of Psalm 40:3. And this quote also came to me
"set yourself on fire and people will come just to
watch you burn," as your passion can be the very
thing that sets you on fire and draws other to
observe the burning.

Has the documentary director apparently
attempted to create a thesis type of film? Yes. If

so, what clearly articulated statement does the film make? Music saved my life, as music is in the first place of art while it brings us on an island with peace, beauty and love. Specifically, in the media analysis textbook it states. "Although there are, in fact, many possibilities for the treatment of documentary evidence, two techniques exemplify the opposite ends of the spectrum: Either the filmmaker can present a clearly articulated thesis about the documentary's subjects, or the filmmaker can assiduously avoid all such insistence. The first type, the thesis documentarist, is perhaps most graphically illustrated by the creator of propaganda" (474). Do all elements of the filmmaking clearly support this thesis? To me it seems like it does support the thesis, even though the film was around 38 minutes.

Has the direct cinema or the cinéma vérité technique of shooting been used? First, the media analysis textbook defines direct cinema and cinema vérité as "direct cinema method of shooting, giving his viewers an objective view and under- standing of worlds that they are rarely

510

permitted to enter. Cinéma vérité technique is supposedly objective unstaged, non-dramatized, non- narrative" (475). So, the film used a mixture of a cinema vérité technique and a direct cinema method of shooting like most documentary filmmakers would do. Has the presence of the documenting camera altered reality—or heightened it? I would say that it was heightened.

Although, the film obviously did not try to avoid presenting a thesis, using a direct cinema method mixed with cinema vérité technique by the director as a chosen tool to ensure "objectivity." Never the less, the film's factual material is presented chronologically, without artful rearrangement.

Does the documentary film reinforce the stereotypes about this form, or does it seem to suggest, through its example, that the genre can be as vital, entertaining, and complex as fiction films? I would say that the documentary film of 'The Lady in Number 6: Music Saved My Life,' that it seemed to suggest through its examples, but the film was nonfiction as it was an inspiring true story about the power of music had for moral support to a Holocaust survivor and how it helps other get through their hard times as well.

INT. ANTWONE FISHER/CINEMA THERAPY
- DAY

Watching the film, 'Antwone Fisher' with Denzel Washington for my fifteenth cinema therapy session, on PTSD, Trauma and Abuse.

 Scan here for 'Antwone Fisher' trailer.

Before going any further in to this film session, I make this my prayer for the Holy Spirit as my Counselor: Father, in the name of Jesus, I approach your throne of grace, bringing myself before you. I recognize that grieving is a human emotional process, and I give myself the space that I need to enter into the rest that you have for me. Lord, Jesus bore my grief and carried my sorrows and pain; I know that Your Spirit is upon Jesus to bind up and heal my broken heart. May I be gentle with myself, knowing that I am not alone in my grief. You are with me, and you will never leave me without support. Father, I desire to be a doer of your Word, and not a hearer only. Therefore, I make a commitment to rejoice with

513

those who rejoice [sharing others joy], and to weep with those who weep [sharing others grief]. I pray that your love with give me great joy and comfort and encouragement, because I have refreshed the hearts of your people through social media. Thank you, Father, for sending the Holy Spirit to comfort, counsel, intercede for, defend, strengthen and stand by me in this time of grief and sorrow. In Jesus name I pray, amen.

As I prescribed a movie based on an issue and followed some guidelines for watching movies with conscious awareness in this order: First, start with a film that supports your treatment goal. Second, choose a film from film recommendations. Third, making sure to clarify intent when assigning a film in which might mistake the role identification. Fourth, familiarize yourself with Guidelines for watching films and discuss guidelines. Fifth, discuss the positive or negative reactions to film. Sixth, use material according to your theoretical orientation. Seven, afterwards reflect on evocative questions and answer them after watching the selected film as it

does help to write down my answers.

Do you remember whether your breathing changed throughout the movie? Yes. Could this be an indication that something threw you off balance? Yes. In all likelihood, what affects you in the film is similar to whatever unbalances you in your daily life.

Ask yourself: If a part of the film that moved you (positively or negatively) had been one of your dreams, how would you have understood the symbolism in it? The scenes that moved me negatively were: when Antwone's biological mother beat him with a rag while another boy was tied with him to a pole, the verbal abuse from his biological mother and the off-screen sexual abuse inflicted upon Antwone. Now, I would try to understand the symbolism in it as if it were a dream by prayerfully studying it through a Christian dream interpretation dictionary and Bible as well as any memories that it brings up then write it down to get it out to reflect on more.

Notice what you liked and what you didn't like or

even hated about the movie. I liked seeing
Antwone using drawing and poetry to channel his
anger, and I disliked the abuse he suffered
through as a child. Which characters or actions
seemed especially attractive or unattractive to
you? The character of Dr. Jerome Davenport and
his actions seemed attractive, as Antwone's
actions started to appear attractive whenever he
learned how to channel his anger in his art and
used self-control. Did you identify with one or
several characters? Mainly Antwone Fisher.
Were there one or several characters in the movie
that modeled behavior that you would like to
emulate? Yes, Antwone Fisher as he had
developed certain strengths with some other
capacities that I would like to develop.

The character that you were attractive to, able to
connect and identify with in the film; could most
likely be your screen mentor, so let's take it a step
further to find more about this character by
applying some acting techniques to this. For an
example, Lyn Gardner, Guardian theatre critic
explains. "The technique, however, will help you

find a character, which in turn informs how you approach the text/script/written word. How do you know what choices to make? The goal of a trained actor is to become a fully realized three-dimensional character, with a rich backstory. I must believe the character you play is truthful and not a cliche, a caricature, a thin external representation of someone who barely resembles a human being. I must believe what you say is real and that you're not reciting, spouting or commenting. In order to help you understand, I will lay out the backbone of what an acting teacher, Dee Cannon teaches at RADA and around the world to professional and student actors alike. This is based around Stanislavski's acting technique (a theory and technique of acting in which the performer identifies with the character to be portrayed and renders the part in a naturalistic, non-declamatory, and highly individualized manner) and his seven questions which, over the years, I have adapted into 10 key acting questions every actor should answer in order to be a fully rounded and connected actor." While one thing that I have found is it can help in

517

the healing and growth process to have a favorite actor/actress to be like a screen mentor to you who you can relate with, now let's study the character's connection with you and I want you to put yourself in the actor/actress's shoes like you are playing their character.

Who is this character? Antwone Fisher.

Where is this character? In Cleveland and Mexico.

When is it? Present times.

Where have this character just come from? Antwone just came from the ship of the U.S. Navy.

What does character want? Antwone wants to have a family, and to find out the truth.

Why does this character want it? Antwone wants closure.

Why does this character want it now? Antwone wants to move on with his life.

What will happen if this character doesn't get it

now? Because if Antwone doesn't confront his painful past, and connect with the family that he never knew. He will keep running, stalling and his violent outburst could get him kicked out of the Navy.

How will character get what he wants, by doing what? Absolve, accept, acquaint, address, affirm, affront, amend, approach, trust, confront, clarify, ease, educate, endure, evaluate, execute, free, forgive, humble, hush, interview, invite, lead, liberate, mask, mend, motivate, negotiate, oppose, orientate, overlook, plan, please, press, pursue, read, recreate, rejoin, release, settle, sober, somber, soothe, study, support, tolerate, unburden, urge, validate, verify and suppress. What must this character overcome? The pains of his past, verbal abuse, fighting, anger, violent outburst, peer pressure, family members, PTSD, trauma, rejection, temptations, hurts, trust issues, victimize, torture, emotions and social problems.

Moving on, notice whether any aspect of the film was especially hard to watch. Yes, I would say the verbal and physical abuse that Antwone had to suffer through. Could this be related to something that you might have repressed ("shadow")? Yes. Uncovering repressed aspects of our psyche can free up positive qualities and uncover our more whole and authentic self.

Did you experience something that connected you to your inner wisdom or higher self as you watched the film? The Holy Spirit brought some scriptures to my attention and lead me to several scripture through a Bible concordance, as the main inner wisdom I received is sometimes you have to face the very thing that attacked you to get closure, freedom, healing and the truth.

While some of the mentioned guidelines turned out to be useful, as I will consider using them not only in "reel life" but also adapt them to "real life" because I know how they are intended to make me and others become a better observer.

If the film had a unique message for you, what was it? "Inspired by a true story, Antwone Fisher tells the dramatic story of a troubled sailor who embarks on a remarkable journey to confront his painful past – and connect with the family he never knew." Itunes describes. But for me it would be to free yourself is to forgive, so you can get on with your life, as Webster's definition of forgiveness is to regard without ill will despite an offense. However, IMDb.com puts it better by saying, "Fight fear. Face truth. Embrace life."

What new ideas for new behaviors did you have? An alternative scenario that could be seen as a new behavior is to channel that anger to use it constructively, instead of getting into fights go to the gym, hit the bag, lift the weights, write poetry, or draw. You have to use that energy to better yourself. Also, practice self-control and think before you act out a thought.

What other films can you identify that might take the discussion a step further? The first film that comes to my mind is 'Rudy,' then 'The Great Debaters,' 'John Q,' and 'The Hurricane.'

INT. IMPOSSIBLE/CINEMA THERAPY - DAY

Watching the film, 'Impossible' for my sixteenth cinema therapy session, on the themes Catastrophe, Tragedy, Crisis and Disaster.

Scan here for 'Impossible' trailer.

Before going any further in to this film session, I make this my prayer for the Holy Spirit as my Counselor: Father, in the name of Jesus, I approach your throne of grace, bringing myself before you. I recognize that grieving is a human emotional process, and I give myself the space that I need to enter into the rest that you have for me. Lord, Jesus bore my grief and carried my sorrows and pain; I know that Your Spirit is upon Jesus to bind up and heal my broken heart. May I be gentle with myself, knowing that I am not alone in my grief. You are with me, and you will never leave me without support. Father, I desire to be a doer of your Word, and not a hearer only. Therefore, I make a commitment to rejoice with those who rejoice [sharing others joy], and to

weep with those who weep [sharing others grief].
I pray that your love with give me great joy and
comfort and encouragement, because I have
refreshed the hearts of your people through social
media. Thank you, Father, for sending the Holy
Spirit to comfort, counsel, intercede for, defend,
strengthen and stand by me in this time of grief
and sorrow. In Jesus name I pray, amen.

As I prescribed a movie based on an issue and
followed some guidelines for watching movies
with conscious awareness in this order: First,
start with a film that supports your treatment
goal. Second, choose a film from film
recommendations. Third, making sure to clarify
intent when assigning a film in which might
mistake the role identification. Fourth, familiarize
yourself with Guidelines for watching films and
discuss guidelines. Fifth, discuss the positive or
negative reactions to film. Sixth, use material
according to your theoretical orientation. Seven,
afterwards reflect on evocative questions and
answer them after watching the selected film as it
does help to write down my answers.

Do you remember whether your breathing changed throughout the movie? Yes. When Lucas noticed his mom's (Maria) leg was bleed, and when Maria was trying to climb up a tall tree in the painful condition that she was in with her leg being wounded. Could this be an indication that something threw you off balance? Yes, as I am open to it. In all likelihood, what affects you in the film is similar to whatever unbalances you in your daily life.

Ask yourself: If a part of the film that moved you (positively or negatively) had been one of your dreams, how would you have understood the symbolism in it? There was one scene that moved me positively that brought back to my memory a dream that I had along time ago, and that would be 'the-bird's-eye-view' shot on the Tsunami coming into the city. As the dream that I had was of a Tsunami coming in to a city from that same angle, then I saw myself standing on a porch of an old house and I ran inside to take cover. While this house was a four-story house and as the water rushed into the house I would run up the stairs then stop to look back to see the water rise to that level. Then, I would go up another set of stairs to look back up at the top and repeating all the way up to the fourth floor. But on the fourth floor is when it got different, as I was looking back the stair to see the water rise to that floor. I remember the water being clear as a swimming pool and this time I could see the shadowy-wavy figure of a person swimming up the stairway to the fourth floor. So I hurry up to turn away, where I saw some kind of back stairway and went up it to find myself going upstairs to an olden day looking attic. Where I felt safe and sheltered from the waters, and I remember finding a spot in the corner to sit in peace, as there was another man up there whose presence was comforting. In fact, Tyler Wolfe, author of Christian Dream Symbols.com interprets. "Tsunami is symbolic of a stressful event or tribulation in life (Ps. 107:28-29)." Briefly, I believe the dream meant I was going to new levels with Jesus. Moreover, the format, I usually use to interpret a dream is: the Bible, prayer, and a Christian Dream Interpretation Dictionary.

Notice what you liked and what you didn't like or even hated about the movie. I liked seeing the characters rescued, helping others, one character sacrificing the life of his cellphone battery for another person's use, and finding loved ones. Whereas; I didn't like seeing Maria bleeding from her wound, trying to climb up a tree in pain, suffering, the family getting separated, the Tsunami rushing into the city, the dead bodies, trauma, and seeing the characters endure that catastrophe. Which characters or actions seemed especially attractive or unattractive to you? The character that seemed attractive was Lucas Bennett, as that was the character that I most likely identified with and there were some moments with Henry Bennett. Furthermore, Lucas Bennett actions was attractive and I identified with him, because it looked like he used the circumstance that he was in to bring change to his life as he reached out to help others who was in need as that took his mind off himself.

Were there one or several characters in the movie that modeled behavior that you would like to

emulate? The characters that modeled good
behavior were: the man who sacrificed his
cellphone and battery life for Henry to call Brian
twice for the matter of his family, Lucas and
Henry (the father). As I would say that they,
indeed, developed certain strengths and other
capacities that I would like to develop own my
own.

The character that you were attractive to, able to
connect and identify with in the film; could most
likely be your screen mentor, so let's take it a step
further to find more about this character by
applying some acting techniques to this. For an
example, Lyn Gardner, Guardian theatre critic
explains. "The technique, however, will help you
find a character, which in turn informs how you
approach the text/script/written word. How do
you know what choices to make? The goal of a
trained actor is to become a fully realized
three-dimensional character, with a rich
backstory. I must believe the character you play
is truthful and not a cliche, a caricature, a thin
external representation of someone who barely

resembles a human being. I must believe what you say is real and that you're not reciting, spouting or commenting. In order to help you understand, I will lay out the backbone of what an acting teacher, Dee Cannon teaches at RADA and around the world to professional and student actors alike. This is based around Stanislavski's acting technique (a theory and technique of acting in which the performer identifies with the character to be portrayed and renders the part in a naturalistic, non-declamatory, and highly individualized manner) and his seven questions which, over the years, I have adapted into 10 key acting questions every actor should answer in order to be a fully rounded and connected actor." While one thing that I have found is it can help in the healing and growth process to have a favorite actor/actress to be like a screen mentor to you who you can relate with, now let's study the character's connection with you and I want you to put yourself in the actor/actress's shoes like you are playing their character.

Who is this character? Lucas Bennett.

Where is this character? Khao Oak, Thailand on The Orchid Beach Resort in Khao Lak.

When is it? Christmas Eve – present time.

Where have this character just come from? A plane flight, from Japan.

What does character want? Lucas Bennett wants to get a chance.

Why does this character want it? Maybe to get someone to put their faith in him as on the plane he was sitting by himself with headphones on and appeared to have had a bad attitude. So, I would say he wanted it for the reason of significance and affirmation.

Why does this character want it now? Probably, to get help, get someone to take his hand, and to help.

What will happen if this character doesn't get it now? Lucas will probably, stay to himself, closed off, people might loose faith in him, and his family might have stayed separated as well as be lost if he wouldn't have pursued the path of his dad to find his brothers and dad.

How will character get what he wants, by doing what? Accept, affirm, aid, assist, amend, bless, call, concern, bear, delight, ease, comfort, endure, help, inspire, lead, liberate, pursue, comfort, help, encourage, approach, boost, ease, entreat, entrust, execute, feed, mend, motivate, please, press, satisfy, soothe, still, suffer, suggest, support, unburden, understand, verify, and vindicate.

What must this character overcome? Lucas must overcome a lot of obstacles as a few are: physical and emotional, trauma, worry, panic, language barriers, fear, hurt, deny, the disaster itself, and himself.

Moving on, notice whether any aspect of the film was especially hard to watch. The beginning from when the Tsunami rushed in to start it all and the middle of the movie were hard to watch, including when Maria's leg was bleeding. Could this be related to something that you might have repressed ("shadow")? Yes. Uncovering

530

repressed aspects of our psyche can free up
positive qualities and uncover our more whole
and authentic self.

Did you experience something that connected you
to your inner wisdom or higher self as you
watched the film? Yes, several things of inner
wisdom and more then I had thought. First, when
you lose everything is when you realize what the
important things are that really matter. Second,
no one knows when a disaster will strike, but we
can always plan for the worse and adapt to
whatever change life may bring to make a new or
better life for our self. Third, while you're waiting
for help you can be reaching out to others to be a
help to someone else in their time of need. Fourth,
see the hurt and heal it; see the need and fill it.
Fifth, you can either be a hospital for the hurting
or a beach resort for the spoiled, wealthy, brains
and pedigree. Sixth, when you are going through
a hard time find something that will give you the
joy of a child to think on to get you through it and
have the attitude of a child can help. Seventh,
Lucas used the crisis that came to him as an

opportunity to change him self, get better and help others. Eight, when Maria had that flashback of her fighting and struggling under the pressures of the flood waters, then suddenly emerged out with one hand raised that represented her rising above the circumstance. Ninth, the scriptures that the Holy Spirit brought to my attention were: Genesis 6:13, Philippians 1:12-13, Philippians 4:10-14, John 10:27, Jeremiah 29:11, Isaiah 43:2, and Genesis 50:20. Lastly, I see how God uses natural disaster or crisis to bring people closer together and draw us closer to God, as we are suddenly separated from the meaningless (materialistic) things of the world and only the things that will matter in eternity becomes our new focus. For an example, in the beginning of the movie we see Henry, Maria, Lucas, Thomas, Simone Bennett disengaged and separated from the looks of it. Then, when the disaster hit all that mattered is finding and being with loved ones. Furthermore, some of the mentioned guidelines turn out to be useful, as I am considering using them not only in "reel life" but also adapt them to "real life" because they are intended to make me become a better observer.

If the film had a unique message for you, what was it? IMDb.com said, "Nothing is more powerful than the human spirit." But, I say, nothing can separate you from love. Moreover, a catastrophe can take away everything to leave you with nothing, but one thing it can't take away is your message, dreams, love, faith, willpower and passion.

What new ideas for new behaviors did you have? When you reach out to help someone in their crisis not only does it take your mind off of what you are going through, but it brings change and betters you as it plants a seed for someone to give you a helping hand through yours. Do unto others, as you would like to be done unto you.

What other films can you identify that might take the discussion a step further? 127 Hours, Salmon Fishing in the Yemen, Soul Surfer, Jack the Giant Slayer, Flight, Captain Phillips, Sunlight Jr., Les Miserable, and 2012.

INT. SON OF GOD/CINEMA THERAPY - DAY

Watching the film, 'Son of God' for my seventeenth cinema therapy session, on the themes of spirituality and healing.

Scan here for 'Son of God' trailer.

Before going any further in to this film session, I make this my prayer for the Holy Spirit as my Counselor: Father, in the name of Jesus, I approach your throne of grace, bringing myself before you. I recognize that grieving is a human emotional process, and I give myself the space that I need to enter into the rest that you have for me. Lord, Jesus bore my grief and carried my sorrows and pain; I know that Your Spirit is upon Jesus to bind up and heal my broken heart. May I be gentle with myself, knowing that I am not alone in my grief. You are with me, and you will never leave me without support. Father, I desire to be a doer of your Word, and not a hearer only. Therefore, I make a commitment to rejoice with those who rejoice [sharing others joy], and to

weep with those who weep [sharing others grief].
I pray that your love with give me great joy and
comfort and encouragement, because I have
refreshed the hearts of your people through social
media. Thank you, Father, for sending the Holy
Spirit to comfort, counsel, intercede for, defend,
strengthen and stand by me in this time of grief
and sorrow. In Jesus name I pray, amen.

As I prescribed a movie based on an issue and
followed some guidelines for watching movies
with conscious awareness in this order: First,
start with a film that supports your treatment
goal. Second, choose a film from film
recommendations. Third, making sure to clarify
intent when assigning a film in which might
mistake the role identification. Fourth, familiarize
yourself with Guidelines for watching films and
discuss guidelines. Fifth, discuss the positive or
negative reactions to film. Sixth, use material
according to your theoretical orientation. Seven,
afterwards reflect on evocative questions and
answer them after watching the selected film as it
does help to write down my answers.

Do you remember whether your breathing changed throughout the movie? Yes, but only a slight breath during the 40 slashes scene and a bit of a flinch when a nail was going into the hand of Jesus. Could this be an indication that something threw you off balance? Probably, I don't like seeing people get beat or abused. In all likelihood, what affects you in the film is similar to whatever unbalances you in your daily life.

Ask yourself: If a part of the film that moved you (positively or negatively) had been one of your dreams, how would you have understood the symbolism in it? This movie moved me positively, as if it was a dream I would understand the symbolism through a dream interpretation dictionary and the Bible.

Notice what you liked and what you didn't like or even hated about the movie. I liked the teachings of Jesus, His demonstrations of his power and how he gave people a second chance at life. I disliked seeing Jesus betrayed, gossiped/slandered and beaten to the point of being in critical condition. Which characters or actions seemed especially attractive or unattractive to you? The actions of Jesus were attractive, and how he responded to everything that was brought His way. Did you identify with one or several characters? The characters that I mostly identified with were John and Peter.

Were there one or several characters in the movie that modeled behavior that you would like to emulate? Jesus, as 1 Corinthians 11:1 was brought to my attention on imitating Christ. While Jesus had certain strengths, fruit and other capacities that I would like to develop as well.

The character that you were attractive to, able to connect and identify with in the film; could most likely be your screen mentor, so let's take it a step further to find more about this character by applying some acting techniques to this. For an example, Lyn Gardner, Guardian theatre critic explains. "The technique, however, will help you find a character, which in turn informs how you approach the text/script/written word. How do you know what choices to make? The goal of a trained actor is to become a fully realized three-dimensional character, with a rich backstory. I must believe the character you play is truthful and not a cliche, a caricature, a thin external representation of someone who barely resembles a human being. I must believe what you say is real and that you're not reciting, spouting or commenting. In order to help you understand, I will lay out the backbone of what an acting teacher, Dee Cannon teaches at RADA and around the world to professional and student actors alike. This is based around Stanislavski's acting technique (a theory and technique of acting in which the performer identifies with the character to be portrayed and renders the part in a naturalistic, non-declamatory, and highly individualized manner) and his seven questions which, over the years, I have adapted into 10 key acting questions every actor should answer in order to be a fully rounded and connected actor." While one thing that I have found is it can help in the healing and growth process to have a favorite actor/actress to be like a screen mentor to you

who you can relate with, now let's study the
character's connection with you and I want you to
put yourself in the actor/actress's shoes like you
are playing their character.

Who is this character? Peter.
Where is this character? Nazareth, Israel.

When is it? The time period had to have happened
over 2,000 years ago.

Where have this character just come from? Peter
has just come from a small fishing boat, on the
Sea of Galilee.

What does character want? My character wants
to get a chance to be a success by the end of the
movie, While when Jesus step aboard his boat he
made him a successful fisherman and a fisher of
men when Peter choice to follow Him to help Him
change the world.

Why does this character want it? Peter want to be
a success.

Why does this character want it now? It probably

wants his needs met, and a good reputation.

What will happen if this character doesn't get it now? Peter would probably be working all the time, catching hardly any fish (as we first saw him) and would be living a lonely life.

How will this character get what he wants, by doing what? Some of the tactics that Peter will use are: accept, address, aid, allow, approach, assist, challenge, defend, concern, delight, direct, draw, deny, attack, educate, endure, entrust, execute, free, help, humble, intrigue, lead, and propagandize.

What must this character overcome? Peter must overcome the following: rejection, anger, fighting, violent outburst of sticking up/retaliating for Jesus to defend him, grief when he denies Jesus, critics and some doubt.

Moving on, notice whether any aspect of the film was especially hard to watch. All Jesus had to go through from being betrayed in the garden, gossip/slandered about, accused for something He

didn't do, beaten, carrying His cross to Calvary,
being nailed to the cross, and dying a martyr's
death all for the sake to make things new for His
people as that is love. Could this be related to
something that you might have repressed
("shadow")? I had a change of breath on the
beating scene and nailed to the cross, as my
answer would be probably. Uncovering repressed
aspects of our psyche can free up positive
qualities and uncover our more whole and
authentic self.

Did you experience something that connected you
to your inner wisdom or higher self as you
watched the film? Yes, a few things that I have
experienced that connected me with inner
wisdom were: Jesus was the ultimate chess
player with his life as he knew all the right moves
to make, not just to win in life, but to make others
win. Moreover, the scriptures brought to my
attention were: 1 Corinthians 11:1 and John 1:1
mainly, as there was a whole bunch of scriptures
quoted all through the movie. In fact, some of the
mentioned guidelines turn out to be useful, as I

am considering to use them not only in "reel life" but also adapt them to "real life" because they are intended to make me become a better observer.

If the film had a unique message for you, what was it? This movie was a follow up to "the landmark 2013 ministries The Bible, as this feature follows the life of Jesus Christ from his humble birth to his resurrection." Says Netflix. As I believe it not only tells the story of the Gospel, but offers anyone a chance to change their life and follow Jesus.

What new ideas for new behaviors did you have? First, seek first the Kingdom of God and everything else will follow as all of the disciples had their needs met with Jesus in their circle. Second, trust in God and have faith. Third, turn the other cheek when someone strikes at you. Fourth, you live by the sword you die by the sword. Lastly, love your enemies.

What other films can you identify that might take the discussion a step further? The other films I believe would take this discussion further are the following: the Passion of Christ, The Encounter, The Bible, My Hope America, and Apostle Peter and the Last Supper.

Father, I shout and thank you Lord for my healing and my abundant harvest! I repent: declaring: "I am thank-full. I am not pride-full. I am grate-full. I am full of joy and strength." I join my faith with Kenneth and Gloria Copeland, and I do the part The Lord has called me to do to get His job done. The battle is the Lord's, and the victory is mine! In Jesus name, amen.

INT. TRANSFORMATION STORIES OF OTHERS - DAY

After experiencing how movies can help change a life through the above movie analysis and cinema therapy experimentation, let's see how movies has helped bring transformation to the lives of people.

Here are some of their brief testimonies. Personal stories/testimonies from people who watched movies with and without conscience awareness in how films can change lives.

In fact, Birgit Wolz, Ph.D., MFT tells us. "Good stories have long been recognized as having far more value than mere entertainment. Throughout human history, stories have taught people valuable lessons about themselves and their culture, about their past, their present and even their future. Today, films are one of our most powerful storytelling methods, and some films have had important impacts, on individuals and on entire societies."

To demonstrate, here are those life-changing

stories below from watching movies with conscience awareness.

Stephanie Willis from Pittsburg, KS - 1/6/11

"When my son was killed in 2003, along with going through a divorce, getting a second job and trying to find my way, watching movies about death is something that really helped. I did not even know there was such a term as "cinema therapy" but I believe that was what I was doing. Probably for the first 2 years after my son's death, I would feel better, at least momentarily, while watching DVD's with death themes, whether they were black comedies or serious drama. I only know that this worked for me, as well as the reading of many first-hand accounts of others who have experienced tremendous loss, especially those involving children."

Henry Ramirez from San Antonio, Texas - 5/24/08

"I would urge anyone to watch the 1987 John Huges' comedy "Planes, Trains, and Automobiles" starring Steve Martin and the late legendary

John Candy. While the majority of the film makes you laugh out loud, there are in many respects, important lessons in friendship, forgiveness, and personal growth. The movie examines the lives of two men who unexpectedly cross paths on their way home for the Thanksgiving holidays. Both men could not be anymore different, yet they are forced to share many experiences together on their journey home. Including sharing rides, beds, hotels, and moments of conflict and uncertainty. Through it all, both men form a bond that teaches us that friendship and life lessons come in the most unlikely of times and in the most unusual places in our lives. I am not a spoiler for endings, for those of you who have not seen this movie. However, I must say that the ending is one of the most powerful and emotionally gripping endings I have ever seen in my life. The end leads us to believe that forgiveness often gives room for us to learn new things about ourselves and explore special qualities in other people. It is rare that such a movie can move you to laugh and cry all while teaching us powerful lessons in growth and friendship."

Dr. Craig Shifrin from Springfield, Missouri -
12/6/07

"I am a psychologist. I once had a 13-year-old
adolescent male who refused to discuss much
with me. He had a severe anger problem and was
in behaviorally disordered special education. As
he would not talk to me much, I hit upon a
discovery. He loved to watch the T.V. show "The
Honeymooners" with Jackie Gleason and Art
Carney. As this show always involved Ralph
making an impulsive decision, did not listen to
others, and his wife always trying to get him to
think before he acted. It was very fruitful to
process the previous nights episode with this
adolescent. We would 1) talk about the plot, 2)
discuss the roles each main character had in the
episode, 3) talk about how Ralph would not make
a good decision, 4) Alice's reaction 5) how did
Ralph's anger impacted his ability to be relate to
his wife and best friend, and 6) what could have
Ralph done differently if given the same situation
or what could he do in the future?"

Roger from Winnepeg, Manitoba, Canada -

3/14/07

"I wanted my graduating class of S4-grade 12 predominantly aboriginal at-risk students to be exposed to native issues on a global scale. I developed a one-month unit entitled "Aboriginal Cinematherapy." The four movies I used were "Once Were Warriors", "Little Big Man", "Rabbit Proof Fence" and "Smoke Signals." Besides viewing and discussing the movies, we read excerpts from books ....Guy Vanderhaeghe's "The Last Crossing", listened to guest speakers, discussed CBC radio interviews with Alan Duff author of "Once Were Warriors," concluded the month with a sweat lodge and used a Semantic Differential Rating Scale pre and post unit to test student responses. I was very pleased with the results of how both aboriginal and non-aboriginal students in class now viewed native culture, their acceptance of native role models and their more "worldly" perspective."

Chelsea S. from Largo, FL - 2/10/07

"The most powerful film I have seen so far in my

life that has made a big difference was the Lord of the Rings. I was severely abused by an eclectic religious group as a child and both parents, and saw a lot of violence and abuse. Watching all three films and seeing the healing at the end was like watching good and evil, personified and literally, right in front of me. And here are these little people, simple people, loving, family-oriented, being ravaged by beings much bigger and powerful than they. And the little people won with perseverance, love, courage, inner courage, and facing their fears squarely in the face. I don't care that many say "oh, it is just a movie." I don't care. It changed my life. It is not just a movie to me."

An anonymous person from Houston, TX - 8/7/06

"Three films that improve my state are Bride & Prejudice, Last Holiday and Danny Deckchair. The music & singing in the first one, a Ballywood version of Pride & Prejudice, was so uplifting. All three movies left me feeling hopeful and liberated."

Linda Flanders from Bay City, WI - 4/25/06

"I watched "The Wilderness Family" (over and over) then I quite my job with the San Francisco Police Department and moved to Wisconsin to build a log cabin in the woods (where I still live). I also watched "Baby Boom" and "The Associate" to learn how to market and promote my own business (fledgling, but it's coming along). I watched the old Judy Garland and Mickey Rooney movies about, "Hey, kids, let's put on a show" I have written and am currently promoting a one-woman show on the dangers of methamphetamine and trying to teach others that they can put on the same show in their own communities. And I watched "Independence Day" to learn how to strategically plan an all-out offensive in the fight against methamphetamine; literally trying to get communities to stage a fight all at the same time. (A challenge, worked better in the movie, but I'm only 2 weeks into my tactical plan.)"

Rosanne from San Ramon, CA - 2/15/05

"About a month ago I rented the movies Before Sunrise and Before Sunset. I watched them as a

pairor double feature--with a short intermission
between. When I finished them I called and sent
e-mails to friends letting them know that these
were the "most romantic movies I ever saw." It
had been a long time since I was so taken with a
movie. I watched them three times before I
returned them. I then purchased them and am
still watching them and inquiring into why they
affected me as they did. The only other movie I
saw so many times in a short period isn't even out
in video or on dvd. That movie is Enchanted April,
which I saw ten times in theatres or on TV. As I
inquired into the affect they had on me I reflected
also on Enchanted April and why, after over ten
years, it remains my favorite movie and how the
song "A Peaceful, Easy Feeling" still touches me to
my depths. With Enchanted April I came to see
that it speaks to me of the magic of life – the
things that are there, but what we often don't
"see". I began exploring how much I "see" things –
intuitive senses or just a sense of knowing – but
how I often don't take it seriously or how when it
is very personal I don't trust it. After many years
of noticing this phenomenon I am now beginning

to trust what I "see" more and more. In fact it's this #"eeing" that is my creative process. This is similar to how the main character (whose name I've forgotten) creates the magical month in Italy because she #saw# it. Plus, in trusting her intuition she was finally seen by others, most notably her husband. What comes up for me as I write this is how I am touched by the quality of really being seen and how that comes through trusting the situation (instincts) and valuing myself. As for the song "A Peaceful, Easy Feeling" it's been my favorite since I was in college. Now, some thirty years later, I still play it over and over again. Each time I hear it's as if I'm hearing it for the first time. It still speaks both to me and for me, especially the lines "she can't take you anyway you don't already know how to go" and "I know you won't let me down, 'cause I'm already standing on the ground." This song really says how I feel about love – that it should be simple and easy and fully grounded. This sense of love now brings me back to Before Sunrise and Before Sunset – "the most romantic movies I've ever seen." While watching Before Sunrise I was

552

enjoying how they got to know one another as they wandered the streets of Vienna talking of life, philosophy, and love. This is my ideal – just getting to know someone by walking, talking and observing him interact with others. In this movie Jesse was cynical, while Celine was sweet and open. Although the whole movie affected me, the line I remember most was then they were playing pinball and Celine asked "why is it that we obsess about people we don't even like?" This really hit me hard as I realized that this is something that I do. The feel of Before Sunset was quite different. Nine years had passed and they had changed since their first meeting. In this movie Celine is the cynic. This movie bothered me at first. The more I watch it the more I appreciate it. I was bothered by how closed Celine was. When I first watched it I really disliked the scene in the car. Now I see this scene as the most important in the movie. This is where Celine opens up to her vulnerability and, as Rumi says "renders her veils". As she talks about the loneliness of being in the wrong relationship (something which I have known for years) and of how the men she's dated all marry the women they date immediately after her (the story of my life) she opens and relaxes. To me, this is a movie about vulnerability. These are movies about being open and trusting the situation so that the trust is there to accept love. It is this that I've wanted and have waited all these years for. For this I'd rather be alone than in the loneliness of being with the wrong person. As I write this what strikes me is the common thread of Enchanted April, "A Peaceful, Easy Feeling", and Before Sunrise/Sunset. All of them are about trusting the truth of who we are and it's this truth that is love. My sense here is that just being true to myself is the love that I've always sought."

An anonymous person from San Francisco, CA - 12/01/04

"LOTRevolution: One of the themes that attracted my attention in THE LORD OF THE RINGS is that of personal evolution. Each one of the members of The Fellowship is simultaneously a participant in two quests; one which revolves around the destruction of the ring, and another which revolves around the confrontation of demons/fears that obstruct that characters' personal growth. Although each member of the Fellowship faces this challenge, the character I'm interested in at the moment is Gandalf the Grey. When he is first introduced into the story he enjoys eating, smoking and play. He's somewhat ragged, with unkempt hair/beard and a staff comprised of tangled roots at its end. He's also a bit unsure of himself. He's lost his edge from spending too much time with the Hobbits. Together these seem to represent Gandalf's development as being somewhat arrested. This resonated with me, since I too, feel as though my development has been somewhat stunted. I made an agreement with myself a long time ago, that I would stay a child for as long as possible. Recently, I've been frustrated by this, but more so hesitant about moving forward with personal evolution. I am afraid of what I might become. A couple of events forced Gandalf to ultimately face the demon Balrog. They bring Gandalf to a point of no return. He fell, and what seemed like certain death resulted in Gandalf's evolution from

Gandalf the Grey, to Gandalf the White. Gandalf the White seems to have a very solid sense of himself, what needs to happen in certain circumstances, and in organizing others to make that happen. All of this has me reflecting on my own situation. Although I feel so hesitant about being an adult, there are certain events that are forcing me to face this fear. For one, my body developed into that of a woman, all hips and boobs. The second was the death of my mother. Somehow it's difficult to continue to view myself as a child when she's dead, even if I've been successful in ignoring what my body had developed into. The third is the realization that children are in an almost constant state of disempowerment. It's probably this last realization that's hit me the hardest. I'm unhappy with my current situation, and feel like I have no power to change it. I cannot continue to exist feeling I have no power, because the frustration and pain I feel from that far outweighs any consolation I might derive from keeping my promise. Looking at Gandalf's experience has helped me realize that I wont be a totally different person, just an evolved version of myself. I will be able to help myself as unfortunate circumstances present themselves, hence better able to help those around me. In fact, I would venture a guess, that forging on through these fears would help empower one's sense of self-love, which is of inestimable assistance in facing fears. It would seem to be the creation of an upward spiral, that continually reinforces itself. What a wonderful tool in coping with LIFE."

Edgar Arenas from Pasadena, CA - 7/11/04

"Coping With Death: Shortly after my big brother Erick died at the age of 29, I saw a film about the premature death/murder of a young man. The film starred Brandon Lee (Son of Bruce Lee) as a character by the name of "Eric Draven". Although the film was sold as an "action genre" it intrigued me because of Brandon Lee's premature death on the set of this film as well as the premature death of the protagonist Eric Draven. At the end of that film, there was an interview with Brandon in which he spoke about life and death. In doing so, Brandon provided a quote from the book

557

"Sheltering Sky". Below is an excerpt from that quote. The quote itself was something that was not only prophetic when one considers Brandon Lee's sudden death shortly after he said this, but because, at the time, it was the most profound statement that I had ever heard. It was something that I really needed to hear at that time in my life because it put so many things into perspective for me! So much so, that to this day I feel that it has become a major part of who I am... "Because we do not know when we will die, we get to think of life as an inexhaustible well; and yet everything happens only a certain number of times - and a very small number, really. How many more times will you remember a certain afternoon of your childhood? An afternoon that is so deeply a part of your being that you can't even conceive of your life without it? Perhaps four or five times more? Perhaps not even that. How many more times will you watch the full moon rise, perhaps twenty? And yet it all seems limitless." I'd like to add that I now know that the potential of my life is limitless! In fact, I have yet to know my full potential! And so I will never cease to test it! For more info on the impact of this film on my life, please visit the following link: http://members.migente.com/e31arenas/."

Pierina Mercieca from University of Malta - 6/27/04

"I have always found films as very enriching in the process of self-discovery. I found movies to be fundamental in the understanding the dynamics of human interactions as projected through the characters in films. During some less glamourous times, story lines and their characters made me feel less alone and understood better than the people around me. This strengthened my thinking patterns of combining psychology and films. I almost always take something with me on viewing a film, a deeper insight, whether psychological, spiritual, emotional, a good line to remember or a good joke."

Eme from Georgia 5/26/04

"I am a young girl with no mental problems, I think. I don't know if you'll accept my testimony but there is one movie that I identify with wholly, it really gives me comfort. The movie is "Little Darlings." I don't think this movie is on the Cinema Therapy list. The movie is about two girls and their experiences with relationships and sex. Although I am a teenager, I don't think about boys and sex constantly. But I was having a slight problem with my relationship with this boy and I could identify with Kristy McNichol's character. She didn't know what she wanted but she knew he wasn't it. She knew that she had to find herself first which is a such a cliche but I didn't find it cheesy at all. I think this movie should be added to the list so teenage girls have a movie that displays feelings like this as a visual."

Dana Johnson from Grand Junction, CO - 12/22/03

"Recently I watched the movie, Steel Magnolias. This was not the first time I have watched this movie. It was probably the 20th. It makes me feel so happy. I like the closeness of family and friends. The mother and daughter have a close inner bond, but on the outside the bond isn't as obvious. When the mother loses her daughter to diabetes she is so distraught that she herself wonders how she will make it through this life without her daughter. Thankfully the greeving mother has a core group of dear friends to help her with her loss. This movie makes me feel so thankful that I have a great group of friends who are like family to me. It also makes me long for a close family of my own someday."

An anonymous person from an unknown location, in 11/15/03

"The movie Contact really hit home. As I cried through the movie I wanted to shout, "That's me!" My battle began in the 50's being born a girl who loved science. Where I grew up this was unacceptable. My father encouraged my passion, but everyone else saw it as abnormal. Dad was pushed aside by what seemed like the rest of the world, bound & determined to squeeze me into a stereotypical "one size fits all" mold for females, complete with conditioning. Contact did contact me - inside. The truths learned have impacted my life. I learned from this, oddly enough, "science fiction" movie: 1) molds are not "one size fits all" -

avoid them & just be "you", 2) the Truth is everything - even if it it makes you unpopular, 3) yes, there will always be those waiting to steal your work & take credit for it, but those who live by the sword die by the sword, 4) there will be those who will try to discredit you the best they can as a way to increase their own power & control - don't give in to them, 5) you must be true to yourself no matter what, and 6) we must each find our own way & do what we are passionate about. I agree with the main character - The world really is what we make of it. I now find the world especially sweet when I get to do what I love. This movie gave me strength. It left me feeling inspired and very hopeful about Everything."

Claudia Biris from Bucharest, Romania - 8/30/03

"When I was a child my parents were hyper-protective persons and very fearful. Anyway, the situation here [in Romania] made people to be very fearful and anxious about almost everything. Then and unfortunately, now, the Romanian streets are not a safe place. So, I was spending a lot [of time] indoors. I can't say I haven't got friends (I still have friends from my childhood!), but one of my dearest friends was the movie. I was watching all I could get, on TV and VCR, especially Romanian, Russian, Bulgarian, North American, Italian, French and Indian movies. What a great American sociologist said once, "The television is the teacher and the preacher of our society" was very true in my case. I used to talk a lot about movies with my grandparents. Sometimes the western mirage made us dream about another kind of society, where freedom and security were "at home". Of course, in this case the movie had a transparent and strong evasion function. But I could also learn a lot from all those movies. I still love the Russian and the Italian movies, even if I couldn't't understand too much of them as a child. Now it's different. I myself experienced movies in different ways: as a [means of escape] ..., as a lesson, as entertainment, even as a wiser friend that can teach me a lot. There were some situations when a movie thought me something that nobody else could do at that time. [There] still are. It's quite sad to me, but if somebody [asked] me to [weigh] what my parents taught me, good and bad things, the scale of "bad things" [outweighs] ... the other scale. Now, after 10 years of psychology and self-searching I can say that I [learned] from my parents what I shouldn't do [more] than [what] I should do. There are movies that showed me how could and should the members of one family behave to each other, how they should solve a conflict without yelling and threatening, for example. Actually, I think there are too many aspects of life that I [learned] from movies to put all of them down here."

Nancy from Westland, MI - 8/25/03

"After being drugged and raped at a professor's housewarming party, I became afraid to leave my house. When I finally did venture out, "my" rapist stalked me, and I had to drop out of school, and quit my job. Soon, I found myself in a very, very dark place. Unable to steady my concentration enough to sink into a good book, I turned to movies, which could command my attention, distract me, and also leave my hands free, to cuddle one of the attention-hungry feral cats I had rescued the year before. What finally lifted my spirits - what gave me the courage to venture out again - was a delightful film called "Uncorked," starring Nigel Hawthorne, Minnie Driver, and Rufus Sewell. This movie truly is quite literally life-changing; it's about having the courage to embrace life, make peace with one's own flaws and one's family's eccentricities, and being at one with the beautiful world around us. Furthermore, it's rife with enchanting music, perfectly succinct character studies, and wry humor. I wish the whole Western world could see it! 5 stars!"

Steve from Canyon, CA - 5/17/03

"I watched the movie "Ordinary People", the first movie directed by Robert Redford. What an incredible movie! I identified with Conrad, the teenager in the movie who had to cope with grief, guilt and anger over the death of his brother. His unfolding emotional revelation reminded me of my own process, where I'm beginning to uncover deep rage and grief left over from early pre-verbal childhood. The movie left me feeling open and vulnerable."

An anonymous person from an unknown location, in 4/20/03

"I had an experience with the movie Dirty Dancing (which I saw 16 times!) fifteen years ago when I was in my 40's. It was a very unexpected catalyst to some pretty huge changes in my life. I'm not sure I've ever completely understood the effect it had on me,but there was definitely intense transference involved at a number of levels. According to a Time magazine article I read at the time, there were many women nationwide who were tremendously affected, some going to see it 100 times! The movie opened up very intense feelings for me."

Birgit from Oakland, CA in 4/18/03

"I just saw "Nowhere in Africa", the German film that won the Oscar for best foreign film. It's about a German Jewish expatriate family in Africa during Nazi times. The story "hooked me right into" the pain of the past. I was born in post-war Germany and am married to a Jew here in

566

California. I belief that movies that touch us in
this kind of way can help us process grief and
pain. I am trying to be as conscious and aware as
possible about my emotional responses. It helps
me to talk about my feelings to others right after
watching the movie."

Franklin from Moab, UT in 4/16/03

"I wanted to tell you about a particular
movie-watching experience I've had numerous
times. It primarily involves the movie "Gandhi"
but also others, like "Fearless" and a few more.
They provoke an uncontrollable emotion in me: I
get all choked up, sometimes I actually cry, which
I don't do that often (sometimes it can be years
between cries). I watch many other movies, enjoy
them fully, but I don't experience anything
comparable to the uncontrollable emotion that
breaks to the surface when I see certain movies.
The very few movies that provoke this reaction in
me seem to share a common element: they
involve me intimately in the experience of
someone who is doing something that is very
selfless and giving, and is somehow absorbing the

world's pain. Clearly I have unresolved issues with my "Jesus" complex."

Roger from Winnepeg, Canada in 1/29/03

"About Schmidt is one of the most depressing movies I have seen this year. Four English teachers, three retired and myself (near retirement) saw the film last week. We split on our enjoyment with two really liking it and two disliking it intensely. It was only afterwards that I came to any realization of why I hated it. With retirement less than two years away, it may have struck a chord a little too close to home in its depiction of life after work: the bad retirement speeches; returning to work when nobody really wants to see you anymore; the frailty of your life or your spouses; relationships with kids; the rv ignominiously named Adventurer which seemed to be a metaphor for Schmidt's life--cumbersome, directionless, unwanted. The recreational vehicle should be up for best supporting actor. Can a film affect you that negatively yet have an upside in cinema therapy? The message to me was don't sit on your butt waiting for something to happen to

you after retirement, start planning now. I have
in fact begun discussing it with my wife and we
have had a number of excellent plans. Retirement
will begin with the purchase of a Winnebago. We'll
see where life takes us after that."

Sally from Oakland, CA in 12/01/02

"I was angry with my boyfriend. We'd had a fight.
I'd yelled at him. Now I felt bad about it because I
saw that the small mistake he made didn't justify
my acting out this way. The real reason for my
reaction was my hurt about his plans to leave the
next morning on a fishing trip with his buddies
for a couple of weeks. I felt excluded and
abandoned. As I thought about it the next day , I
suddenly understood that my anger was a way for
me to push him away by defending against my
vulnerability and fear of abandonment. I sensed it
would help me to tell him about these feelings
when he returned, but I was too afraid to look
stupid. It would make me feel too weak. He might
take advantage of my vulnerability, criticize me,
see me as needy, and push me away. Then I would
feel even worse. At that time I happened to watch

a movie: Sliding Doors (starring Gweneth Paltrow). Somehow it stuck with me that Helen, the main character displays a combination of strength and vulnerability when she meets James again on the street and expresses her interest in him even though she is not sure whether he is still interested in her. James responds with emotional openness too and they develop a close relationship from this point on. When I watched the movie I noticed that Helen didn't look weak at all. In fact, she seemed kind of courageous and strong allowing herself to be so open and emotionally vulnerable. I can see myself as Helen. I realized that what Helen can do, I could do too. I was very excited about this and I told my boyfriend about it when he came back. This film taught me how I could experience more emotional closeness if I allowed myself to be vulnerable with him. At times of emotional stress I'm usually not in touch with my strength and courage or the means to access them. But discussing my reaction to this movie scene with him, it sank in that I already carried these qualities inside me."

Alice from San Francisco, CA in 12/01/02

"I was grieving the impending end of my
marriage. I was in therapy. My husband and I had
had a big fight which I told my therapist about. I
felt he was oppressing me again. For a long time
he had been my main purpose in life. Now it was
clear the marriage was over. I had tried for a long
time to make it work. During the session I cried a
lot. I felt good. I told my therapist, "I believe that
something good will come out of this but I can't be
sure". My therapist told me that many movies
have been made that begin in despair and end in
triumph. If I could identify with characters, who
are trapped in their circumstances, and share
their disappointments as well as their unsteady
steps toward liberation, I could start finding
reason for optimism in my own situation. My
therapist said it could help me gain the courage to
do what is necessary to change my situation. She
encouraged me to let a film inspire me to learn
how to survive my loss without succumbing to it,
possibly coming out of it transformed. She
suggested several movies and asked me to choose
a film that had touched me when I had seen it
before. She said it wasn't crucial that the plot

match my situation exactly as long as a character was going through some kind of transformation. I chose the Alan Alda film, "The Four Seasons." After discussing it with my therapist, I started to enjoy my newly gained freedom after her separation. I discovered new strength and compassion. I got in touch with my autonomy and a new purpose.

Furthermore, moving to stories/testimonies from people that watched movies without conscience awareness. I conducted a public survey online, asking three question on the power of cinema. First question I asked was, Do you believe cinema has the power to change a life? Getting 15 responses that answered with a yes, and zero nos. Second question was, Thinking back, what was the one movie that brought change to your life? 13 responded with a variety of different movies. Like: 10 Things I Hate About You, Amazing Grace, About Time, Patch Adams, Back to the future, God's Not Dead, sixth sense, Passion of the Christ. Courageous, Grace unplugged, God's not dead, I Am Not Scared (Italian book and film originally titled "Io Non Ho Paura", Avatar, A SPACE

ODYSSEY, City Clickers and recently Eat, Pray, Love. Lastly, Braveheart. Now, the last question I asked for them to please share your story of how this movie has changed your life as they didn't give their name so I will keep them as anonymous to protect their identity.   So, here is there response from 15 people:

From anonymous responder #1 in an unknown location, on 7/21/2015

"It changed my life because I learned that I dont have to follow cliches in high school. I was like Cat and just did my own thing. She was a strong person who didnt date boys for reasons I respected. She was mature and told off all the stupid boys lol."

From anonymous responder #2 in an unknown location, on 7/21/2015

"I must be willing to give my whole life to the task the Lord has given me."

From anonymous responder #3 in an unknown

location, on 7/20/2015

"One of my favorite quotes from this movie pretty much sums it up. "I just try to live each day ... as if it were the final day of my full, extraordinary life." The main character goes though a lot of pain during this movie, but in the end he decides his life is extraordinary. This movie made me think of every day life differently. Am I making the most of every moment I'm given?"

From anonymous responder #4 in an unknown location, on 7/20/2015

"I recognized through Patch Adams that there are real people in the world who are willing to risk making themselves look foolish both with their ideas and their personality/presentation if it means bringing joy and hope to someone else and help them walk through suffering. While I wouldn't say it has dramatically altered the course of my life, whenever I think about Patch Adams (both the movie and the person) I am inspired to be that kind of a person myself. I know I can bring joy, laughter, and hope to others through my actions and entertainment abilities and this reignites that certainty when I begin to sink back into the mundane and self-focused rhythm of life."

From anonymous responder #5 in an unknown location, on 7/20/2015

"When I was a kid, I believed in time travel. Everything was possible. My mind was opened to movie magic."

From anonymous responder #6 in an unknown location, on 7/20/2015

"I was going through depression and had suicidal thoughts. I saw the scene where the atheist professor got hit by a car but didn't die instantly. a Pastor was there to to ask him to accept Christ and go to heaven before he died the pastor said, "you could've been killed instantly, but God gave you a few more minutes. Every breath we are given is His grace." It helped me chase away my demons and become thankful for every breath instead of bitter and hopeless for it."

From anonymous responder #7 in an unknown location, on 7/20/2015

"In the movie while the kid was talking to bruce willis,he said "some people are dead and don't even know it"that quote got stuck in my head and as I internalize my life I realize that I was spiritual dead I was not living my full potention and realize i needed someone greater than me to accomplish that,it wasn't until a few months later I began making changes and my life has never been the same,now I'm not just existing, I'm living With purpose."

From anonymous responder #8 in an unknown location, on 7/20/2015

"They each had moments that made me reflect on my personal walk Christ."

From anonymous responder #9 in an unknown location, on 7/20/2015

"The movie and book was just told from a perspective of a child. It was so innocent and the cinematography was phenomenal. Made me remember that as a child when your parents make bad decisions you are a victim. That as a child you have more of a conscious of right and wrong. That you should continue listening to that as you become an adult. That even as a "natural" acting child, God can use you by just being you. You can be a light and even a "human" guardian angel. Even the simplest things are in His great plan."

From anonymous responder #10 in an unknown location, on 7/20/2015

"God spoke to me while watching Avatar in the theater. Avatar had these plants that were like sea anemones (trumpets). The plants closed up if you touched them. God told me my spirit was like the flowers and that i was living with my spirit closed off from Him. That began a journey of asking the Lord to help me open my spirit to him."

From anonymous responder #11 in an unknown location, on 7/20/2015

"I saw it when I was six years old, in a movie theater, a big movie palace in my home town. I remember my parents got dressed up to take me to it. The movie was huge and I didn't understand it, but all I knew was I was watching a movie in outer space, and to this day it feels to me like that movie was shot on location. It filled me with wonder and an awe for what cinema could be, and I'm now pleased to make my living writing science fiction movies."

From anonymous responder #12 in an unknown location, on 7/20/2015

"City Slickers affected me: The reason City Slickers effected me is because there is a scene in which Jack Ponce (who played Curly) turns to Billy Crystal's character while they are riding and says something to the effect of: Curly: "You want to know what the secret to life is? It's this" (he holds up a finger) Billy's char: "It's your finger?!" Curly: "No, you idiot. It's one thing." Billy's char: "Well, what's the 'one thing'?" Curly: "That's for you to decide." I saw the film when I was only a couple of months away from leaving home and starting adulthood. As I stood at the abyss of becoming (more) independent, I had a thought

that both terrorized and invigorated me: I had a
choice. I could decide who the woman was that I
wanted to be, and figure out for myself what my
"one thing" would become for the rest of my life. I
remember being almost obsessed with that
thought. One thing. What would that be for me? I
had not thought about that film or that encounter
until my film & theology class five years ago when
this assignment was given. It was one of the most
interesting questions anyone has asked me. I am
now taking a PhD level course with the same
professor (but I am taking it as a master's
student) and he is delving even deeper into this
topic. I was curious enough to want to ask some of
my more reflective friends what their
experience(s) have been. It is fascinating to me,
because, over the course of our discussions, this
professor (& many other writers) believe that
there are deeper, more profound spiritual
encounters happening with people through media
and the arts than ever happens inside the church.
This is of great interest because these "divine
encounters", if you will, cannot be forced or
artificially constructed. They simply happen

when God / Spirit / Other reaches out to us."

From anonymous responder #13 in an unknown location, on 7/20/2015

"I couldn't breath, with crying, at the end of the film, because I saw William Wallace's completely selfless passion to fight for his country and to die for it. His character made me realize that I too wanted to be committed enough to what was most important to me, to be willing to die for it. That night, after the film, I decided that my commitment to follow Jesus is what I was passionate about and would die for! It changed me and made me a better person and a better Christian - forever!"

From anonymous responder #14 in an unknown location, on 7/22/2015

Responder #15, Kat Kohler from California

"The movie 'Passion', gave me a greater understanding of the suffering of Christ & His sacrifice for me. Very life altering, to truly receive such an overwhelming gift!"

From anonymous responder #15, in an unknown location

"Well, I'll share a story here. God woke me up with three words in the wee hours this very day, which reminded me of Book of Eli and, how memorizing scripture might someday be the only way we can share God's truth with others. I journal about it at 2:45AM, and then immediately was led to Psalm 119...specifically verse 11...and beyond. I don't own that movie, but I'd like to. It was a very pivotal cinematic production that even still has me questioning what's really important. Denzel is the bombdotcom."

INT. REDISCOVERED THROUGH CINEMA - DAY

Through all of this: the history of cinema; knowledge about the spirit, mind and body transformations; an experimentation demonstration of media analysis and a favorite actor with cinema therapy can be used for self-help to obtain healing and growth. Now, let's see what was rediscovered through cinema.

First, looking back on my cinema therapy sessions, and how they have brought transformation in me, for the reason to be a product of my own products that I want to help people with. While in order to be a success with clients you have to make yourself a success as your own client. Particularly, "In order to be a success with clients you have to make yourself a success as your own client." Says author and writer, Jake Jorgovan. As writer and author, Carol Tuttle said on her blog for mental and spiritual. "Be your own client first. If I'm going to help clients, I need to be my own client first. That means practicing what I teach and applying these tools to my own life."

Concerning the great debate over media effects, a professor of psychology, author and licensed clinical psychologist by the name of Skip Dine Young said. "Effects researchers feel confident in their advice because they believe the evidence is overwhelming that the media does indeed affect individuals and society: This [overview] is based on the assumption that the mass media for [italics in original] have effects ... it is that mass communication is an agent or catalyst to a variety of shifts and changes in people and institutions. The research results reveal a dominant and consistent pattern in favor of the notion that exposure to violent media imagined [italics in original] increase the risk of aggressive behavior. Insights about the impact of cinema from outside the social sciences are sometimes dismissed as anecdotal" (145 & 147).

INT. CINEMEDUCATION - DAY

On the other hand, Skip Dine Young does say.
"Movies can also be used as educational tools in
applied arts like medicine. Like, Cinemeducation
describes the use of commercial films in medical
education by demonstrating situations and
raising questions about a variety of medical
concerns. As films is utilized for its vividness, but
it also encourages identification, decreasing the
stigma of mental illness among medical students
and increasing empathy for patients" (156-157).

INT. CINEMA PARENTING - DAY

So how can cinema therapy be used in this generation's relationship with movies, to help transform our culture through social media? In the book, 'Psychology at the movies.' Author, Skip Dine Young, a Professor of Psychology at Hanover College in Indiana and licensed clinical psychologist. "Cinema therapy is the use of movies as tools in psychotherapy. Since movies allow viewers to make metaphorical connections between the content of the film and the real world, a skilled therapist can help clients make these connections to solve problems and facilitate therapeutic progress" (157). One can use movies as a means of helping clients understand troubling thought patterns (cognitive – behavioral therapy). Another might use movies to facilitate their clients understanding of their values and aspirations (humanistic therapy). Yet another therapist could use film to assist clients' in understanding their inner conflicts (psychodynamic therapy).

For example, Matt Cohen, with MTV Insight. They

conducted research to understand this
generation's unique relationship with movies, and
this is only part of what they wrote. "For a
generation that defines themselves by the content
they consume, "Like", or share, movies offer
Millennials a common language through which
they express their own experiences. Whether it's
posting a quote from The Notebook on Facebook
as a coded signal to their friends that they're
having relationship problems or sharing
movie-inspired GIFs from the blog
#whatshouldwecallme to express how they feel
about an everyday situation, Millennials are
drawing upon a vast pool of movie knowledge to
better articulate their own experiences. For an
example, Jacqui, 24, explains "For our
generation, the culture of movies goes beyond the
screen. It becomes a part of your life and a way
you identify yourself." The more I realize it, the
more I am aware of how actors have a platform
that they can use to be a movie father to a
fatherless generation and choose certain films
that would help their millennial mentee see a new
perspective from how an everyday situation is

scene.

In fact, Roman 4:17 confirms this when God told
Abraham, "I have made you the father of many
nations." So, one of the ways that we can see this
in modern times is through the movie fathers that
celebrity actors seem to be to this fatherless
generation, its brilliant. In fact, in the book,
'Cinema-parenting: Using movies to teach life's
most important lessons' by Gary Solomon with a
MPH, M.S.W. and Ph.D., wrote. "For some years, I
had used movies to help adults deal with
emotional trials brought by divorce,
abandonment, alcoholism, drug abuse and
unhealthy family dynamics. It occurred to me
that I could expand my research on the
effectiveness of "cinema therapy" to include
children. Movies often give a clearer picture of
problems and their solutions than do books on
therapy. Issues are portrayed both visually and
verbally, giving people the opportunity to identify
with the characters and their problems. As a
picture is worth a thousand words, then a motion
picture must be worth trillions. That, in a
nutshell, is the wisdom

behind cinema-parenting."

Moreover, cinema-parenting: "is based on the belief that movies made for the big screen and television can help individuals deal with personal problems and issues that are causing them emotional pain. Applied to children, it becomes a flexible tool to assist parent-child communication, social skill-building and education." While Gary Solomon with a MPH, M.S.W., and Ph.D. said. "I identified and categorized movies that dealt with specific problems, analyzed them for their therapeutic value and presented them in a manner that was easy for people to understand. When I used this approach, individuals I worked with grew, both emotionally and spiritually."

INT. MOVIE FATHERS & MOTHERS - DAY

With this, actors/actresses are seen as fathers/mothers of many nations as acting is more than just entertaining and education, while it can be cinema parenting. For instance, the actor is the cinema parent, the movie theater is the classroom (troublemakers back row/nerds front row), and the movie is the curriculum with themes that address issues and combines with a message to teach life's most important lessons.

As actors can keep this in mind when selecting roles for movies, scanning the script for themes that address issues and information provided to confirm that the movie meets their audience's needs to teach through the character's life to give an alternative perspective, help realize a wrong behavior, bring healing, growth and cause a change for the better. Thus, the stage is meant for the audience rather than for the actor as it's more about what the audience can get from it, not the actor.

To demonstrate how acting can be used to

transform a life, Actor, Edward G. Robinson explains. "An audience identifies with the actors of flesh and blood and heartbeat, as no reader or beholder can identify with even the most artful paragraphs in books or the most inspiring paintings. There, says the watcher, but for some small difference in time or costume or inflections or gait, go I. . . . And so, the actor becomes a catalyst; he brings to bright ignition that sparks in every human being that longs for the miracle of transformation."

Similarly, Leonardo DiCaprio once said. "I've been placed here to be a vessel for acting... that's why I'm really taking any part, regardless of how complicated it's going to be."

Likewise, there is a scripture, in 2 Corinthians 4:7 that confirms this. "But we have this treasure in clay vessels that the Excellency of the virtue may be of God, and not of us."

So, we identify with a person for what they have been through as they become a source of inspiration to help encourage us through whatever we're going through, so whether an audience knows or doesn't know of an actor's testimony there's something about them that will draw an audience in and connect with them for the reason of being able to relate to them. For an example, Eric K. Watts argues that "in terms of both class and race, 8 Mile portrays Rabbit as an 'oppressed minority.' Watts identifies the film's message, as while it may be 'easier' for white rappers to have commercial success, it is very difficult for them to get respect. On 'White America' (2002), Eminem rhymes: */Kids flipped when they knew I was produced by Dre, that's all it took, and they were instantly hooked right in, and they connected with me to because I looked like them. /*Eminem attributes his hip-hop credibility to Dre's sponsorship, and his commercial appeal to his white identity" (Hess 126). Through this we can see how one man can impact nation into following him, as he had millions of people bleaching their hair blonde and wearing white T-shirts while this can also show the power of influence.

Furthermore, we can see, this generation of

Millennials are finding actors that have shared experience from their life story that they can identify with and making them like their movie mentors to help them get through their own experiences as well as everyday situations. Thus, leaving me with this question, knowing or not knowing it. Could Eminem have created a mentor to mentee relationship with his audience from the screen in the Hip Hop world where he didn't fit in at and allowed other outcast to feel like they shared in the same experience? If you read between the lines, we can see this with the actor Johnny Depp as I believe there is a reason why "he chooses character roles as "iconic loners" and gives grace to them to make them turn out a success in the film at the box office." This can be seen from Wikipedia on Johnny Depp, as it says. "Depp has generally chosen roles, which he found interesting, rather than those he thought would succeed at the box office. Critics have often described Depp's characters as "iconic loners." Depp has referred to some of his less-successful films as "studio-defined failures" and "box office poison", and that he thought the studios neither understood the films nor did a good job of marketing them." Through this one can see that Johnny Depp turns the characters that people would see as failures into successes, as this is a brilliant way to choose roles.

Giving these facts, with my findings and reflections from movies in my own past experiences that there is truth in what Gary Solomon aka: The Movie Doctor says. "Most of the lessons I learned about life I learned through the movies." Yet, an audience member who wants to find healing and growth can do this by looking for character strengths to build from a favorite actor in movies. Ryan Niemiec with a PsyD, education director of the VIA Institute and Danny Wedding with a PhD and MPH. Said "It's about spotting these strengths in yourself and in others. It's about learning to use these strengths in a more balanced way to elicit greater well-being, deeper engagement with life, and better relationships. Movies are one way – and a good way – to get there.

INT. MOVIE CHARACTERS- DAY

Whereas, Nobel Laureate and physicist Sir William Bragg stated: "the important thing in science is not so much to obtain new facts as to discover new ways of thinking about them." (x). With this, new ways to approach the movies: First, find a movie with themes pertaining to the character trait you want to work on. Second, identify the problem. And third, bring the solution. For instance, the character strengths and virtues that you would look for in characters are: wisdom and knowledge (cognitive strength), courage (emotional strengths), humility (interpersonal strengths), Justice (civil strengths), Temperance (protective strengths), and Transcendence (spiritual strengths of meaning). Moreover, Ryan Niemiec with a PsyD, education director of the VIA Institute and Danny Wedding with a PhD and MPH informs. "This VIA Classification offers a common language for discussing what is best in human beings. It provides a framework for us to discuss these positive personality characteristics that are universal to the human experience. We discuss movies that portray characters who develop and maintain these character strengths and who use these strengths to overcome obstacles and adversity. In effect, when we watch a film for character strengths, we benefit from the character experiences of how the character copes with adversity by means of strengths use. Furthermore, in the VIA classification where the character strengths are shown as a pathway to well-being – namely positive emotions, engagement, meaning, positive relationships and achievement. The second image, courtesy of the VIA Institute, is a circumplex model displaying each character strength on two continual – strengths of the mind or heart and strengths that are more strongly intrapersonal or interpersonal."

To demonstrate, some objectives one can practice watching films for strengths-spotting to help more easily recognize character strengths and to inspire towards self-improvement. While Ryan Niemiec and Danny Wedding advices. "Positive psychology at the movies can be a catalyst to validate, analyze, and advance the concepts of the positive psychology movies, as it's a powerful effect of evaluation and admiration, and the process of strengths-spotting. As we view new movies in a fresh way, a way that opens up new avenues of flourishing and how to live a good life."

Therefore, in the book, 'Positive Psychology at the Movies' Ryan Niemiec and Danny Wedding both mention. "The description of positive psychology as the study of positive subjective experiences (positive emotions), positive traits (character strengths), and positive institutions. From a clinical standpoint, it is not only about fixing what is broken; it is about nurturing what is best. Simultaneously, character strengths are stable, universal personality traits that manifest through thinking (cognition), feeling (affect), willing (conation or volition), and action (behavior)" (7).

Thus, one thing that I discovered in this paper is that when you pursue change in your character, change in your behavior will follow as movies are like a mirror that lets us identify with a change that we would like to make from a character and correct our self. For instance, in the book, 'Positive Psychology at the Movies' Ryan Niemiec and Danny Wedding advise. "The medium of film, more than any other art form, is able to portray the subtleties of the human mind – thoughts, emotions, instincts, and motives – and the mind's impact on behavior. This makes positive psychology movies a natural vehicle for examining character strengths and the ways in which they are developed and maintained. Character strengths are connected with an individual's sense of self as well as with his or her behavior" (13).

In particular, every movie I watched and monologue that I read had a gift for me that added to my learning, enriched my understanding of the human nature, and fulfilled by deep desire to be of help to others as this allowed for me to walk in their shoes. With this, sparked God's commission to Oral Roberts which was to "

Raise up your students to hear my voice to go where my light is dim, where my voice is heard small and my healing power is not known. Even to the uttermost bounds of the earth their work will exceed yours and in this I am well pleased."

So, how can I interpret that into cinema therapy and use it to bring God's healing power to the uttermost bounds of the entertainment world? Social Worker, meaning "work carried out by trained personnel with the aim of alleviating the conditions of those in need of help or welfare" as many have incorporated movies into their work and this makes it so fascinating to me.

While my research on cinema therapy for this senior paper, I had a shift in my career dreams. As I no longer want to be an actor with a spotlight, but be a social worker that uses the tools of acting and cinema therapy from behind the scenes.

INT. OUTRO - DAY

In conclusion, "the protagonist of every story is the hero of a journey, even if the path leads only in his own mind or into the realm of relationships. As the hero's journey is not an invention, but an observation. It is recognition of a beautiful design, a set of principles that govern the conduct of life and the world of storytelling the way physics and chemistry govern the physical world." Says Christopher Volger. With this, I realize that I must be a product of my own products that I want to help people with. "In order to be a success with clients you have to make yourself a success as your own client." Says author and writer, Jake Jorgovan. "Be your own client first. If I'm going to help clients, I need to be my own client first. That means practicing what I teach and applying these tools to my own life." Said the writer and author, Carol Tuttle on her blog for mental and spiritual.

Summarizing my research, on how movies can change lives. Bernie Wooder, author of the book titled, 'Movie Therapy: How it changes lives' said. "Movies are the most powerful creative art form that exists today, watched and understood by everyone. It makes sense to harness this power and use it as an aid to relieve suffering." In fact, he adds. "But movies you know have got an amazing way of detecting those moments. They speak to us. Every single one of you has sat in a movie house and watched some moment of your life healed, or addressed, or touched. Something that you thought that only you knew." This is the healing power of movies, as they allow for us to drop our defenses and trust them to go in to those dark places in our life that no person is allowed access to-to shine a light of consciousness on for healing. While Skip Dine Young, Author, professor of psychology and a licensed clinical psychologist said. "Research on uses and gratifications is a social science approach to studying how the media fulfills the needs and desires of its audience. Such researchers believe that viewers have a basic system of motivations, emotions, and cognitions, and that media provides an avenue to meeting these motivations" (159). With this, the movies not only have answers to all our problems, but also had the power of inspiring and guiding us to take action and improve our lives.

One observation, that I may include with this, my passion for cinema with my burden for the oppressed (especially celebrities) has been rediscovered as I can use cinema for self-help and selflessness to move towards an abundant life of recovery. As, I have discovered a new career endeavor to pursue and that being social work. While Social workers go into isolation to form solutions to the problems of people, using science with creativity in their practice, and sometimes remaining nameless without a face all to take the burden off the oppressed as they turn around their situations for the good. Through this paper I have seen how social workers can interpret cinema therapy into their work, and it becomes a tools in the hands of these people who are the real superheroes. Another observation that I remember from a book that I read for this paper was a true story in a film titled, 'Lorenzo's Oil (1992). About a boy who develops a disease so rare that nobody is working on a cure, so his father decides to learn all about it and tack the problem himself.

Moreover, "Despite research dead-ends, the horror of watching their son's health decline, and being surrounded by skeptics, they persist until they finally hit upon a therapy involving adding a certain kind of oil (actually containing two specific long chain fatty acids, isolated from rapeseed oil and olive oil) to their son's diet. They contact over 100 firms around the world until they found an elderly British chemist working for Croda international who is willing to take on the challenge of distilling the proper formula. The oil, erucic acid, proves successful in normalizing the accumulations of the very long chain fatty acids in the brain that had been causing their son's steady decline, thereby halting the progression of the disease. There is still a great deal of neurological damage remaining, which could not be reversed unless new treatments could be found to regenerate the myelin sheath (a lipid insulator) around the nerves. The father is seen taking on the new challenge of organizing biomedical efforts to heal myelin damage in patients. Finally, Lorenzo, at the age of 14, shows definite improvement (swallowing for himself and

answering "yes" or "no" questions by blinking)
but more medical research is still needed.
Ultimately it is revealed that Lorenzo has also
regained his sight and is learning to use a
computer."

Briefly, this is an example of how an American's
family story for discovering an invention to cure
their son's oppressive disease can be shared in a
movie to inspire others to hope for their own
situations. As, I now see cinema in a new light not
for what it is, but for what all it can do to
transform a life.

Ending on a strong statement, if there is one most
important thing I can take away from this overall
paper that means the world to me. It would be the
fact that not only can cinema be used to
transform a life to bring healing and growth, but
also movies can provide a screenmentor, father,
brother and even son to troubled-some adults or
"at-risk" youth who gets labeled as a
troublemaker. With a favorite actor/actress to
help them rewrite their story, giving them hope
for an alternative ending and set them off into the

right direction for a bright future.

One last thought, and if there is one thing I noticed through this whole research is that God-The Holy Spirit was my comforter as before I would watch a movie I would say a prayer of comfort and he would use all the cinematic elements in the movie with the actor to give me what I needed. So, I wasn't really going to people for comfort, healing and growth. But rather I was going to God, and giving His something to work with to bring all those things.

BIBLIOGRAPHY

Boggs, Joseph M., and Dennis W. Petrie. *The Art of Watching Films*. 8th ed. New York: McGraw-Hill Higher Education, 2012. 1- 528. Web. 10 Apr. 2015.

Tryon, Chuck. *On-Demand Culture: Digital Delivery and the Future of Movies*. New Brunswick, NJ, USA: Rutgers University Press, 2013. ProQuest ebrary. Web. 8 April 2015. http://site.ebrary.com/lib/oru/detail.action?docID=10698341

Keathley, Christian. *Cinephilia and History, or the Wind in the Trees*. Bloomington, IN, USA: Indiana University Press, 2005. ProQuest ebrary. Web. 8 April 2015. http://site.ebrary.com/lib/oru/detail.action?docID=10137809

Sitney, P A. *Eyes Upside Down: Visionary Filmmakers and the Heritage of Emerson*. Oxford: Oxford University Press, 2008. Print.

Hess, Mickey. *Is Hip Hop Dead?: The Past,*

Present, and Future of America's Most Wanted Music. Westport: Praeger Publishers, 2007. 126. Web. 10 Apr. 2015.

Cohen, Matt. "*Millennials at the Movies: How Social Media has transformed this generation's relationship with Movies*." MTV insights. MTV, 10 Apr. 2015. Web. 9 Apr. 2015.

Fontana, Tony. *Will Smith Biography*. IMBd, n.d. Web. 2 May 2015. <http://www.imdb.com/name/nm0000226/bio?ref_=nm_ov_bio_sm>.

Wolz, Birgit. *Cinematherapy.com*. Ed. Robert Arnow. N.p., 2002-2015. Web. 11 Apr. 2015. <http://www.cinematherapy.com/>.

Regalado, Michelle. *The 10 Greatest Johnny Depp Movies of All Time*. The Movie Cheat Sheet, 24 Mar. 2015. Web. 2 May 2015. <http://www.cheatsheet.com/entertainment/johnny-depp-10-roles-that-made-him-a-film-icon.html/?a=viewall>.

Tasty Cinematography in Charlie and the

Chocolate Factory. creative planet network, 14 Feb. 2012. Web. 2 May 2015. <http://www.creativeplanetnetwork.com/news/news-articles/tasty-cinematography-charlie-and-chocolate-factory/415161>.

Giles, Jeff. "WILL SMITH'S 10 BEST MOVIES: WE COUNT DOWN THE BEST-REVIEWED WORK OF THE FOCUS STAR." *Film Critic*. N.p.: Rotten Tomatoes, 2015. N. pag. Web. 2 May 2015. <http://www.rottentomatoes.com/m/focus_2014/news/1925214/will_smiths_10_best_movies/>.

Fontana, Tony. *Will Smith Biography*. IMBd, n.d. Web. 2 May 2015. <http://www.imdb.com/name/nm0000226/bio?ref_=nm_ov_bio_sm>.

WEEKLY PRAYER FOCUS. Ed. Veronica Garcia. Hollywood Prayer Network, 22 Apr. 2015. Web. 2 May 2015. <http://hollywoodprayernetwork.org/prayer/weekly-prayer-focus/>.

Burton, M.S. *James Cromwell Biography*. IMDb, n.d. Web. 6 May 2015.

<http://www.imdb.com/name/nm0000342/bio>.

Keegan, Rebecca W. "The Legend of Will Smith:
How one man built a global movie-magnet
machine." *Times* 29 Nov. 2007: n/a+. Web. 2 May
2015.
<http://content.time.com/time/magazine/article/
0,9171,1689234,00.html>.

Boal, Augusto, writ. *Augusto Boal in Belfast*. Dir.
Augusto Boal. 2011. Northern Visions NvTv,
2009. Web. 2 May 2015. <
http://archive.northernvisions.org/tag/augusto-b
oal/>.

Gardner, Lyn, and Dee Cannon. *Character
building and what makes a truly great actor*.
theguardian, 9 May 2009. Web. 6 May 2015.
<http://www.theguardian.com/stage/2009/may/0
9/character-building-great-actor>.

Culp, Even. "Dr. Culp's Critique Questions." ORU.
Tulsa. 29 Apr. 2014. Web. 10 June 2015.

"Movie Timeline." Ask the Editors. Infoplease. ©
2000-2015 Sandbox Networks, Inc., publishing

as Infoplease. 01 Aug.
2015 <http://www.infoplease.com/ipea/A015021
0.html>.

Dirks, Tim. "Filmsite.org: Film History by Decade -
100 Years of Movies." Greatest Films (or
Filmsite), <http://www.filmsite.org/filmh.html>
Owned by AMC Networks, LLC. 2015. 1 Aug
2015.

McGinn, Colin. The Power of Movies: How Screen
and Mind Interact. New York: Pantheon Books,
2005. Print.

Young, Skip D. Psychology at the Movies.
Chichester, West Sussex: Wiley-Blackwell, 2012.
Internet resource.

Niemiec, Ryan M, and Danny Wedding. Positive
Psychology at the Movies: Using Films to Build
Character Strengths and Well-Being. , 2014.
Print.

Wedding, Danny, M Boyd, and Ryan M. Niemiec.
Movies and Mental Illness: Using Films to
Understand Psychopathology. Cambridge, MA:

Hogrefe, 2010. Print.

Botto, Juan D., narr. The Story of Film: An Odyssey. Dir. Mark Cousins. Hopscotch Films, 2011. Web. 28 Oct. 2015. <http://www.channel4.com/programmes/the-story-of-film-an-odyssey>.

Sim, Young S. "The Theory & practice of Cinematherapy." s translated manuscript on PDF file. Ed. Young S. Sim. press clippings, n.d. Web. 5 Nov. 2015. <http://www.cinematherapy.com/pressclippings/Yong-Seop-Sim.pdf>.

9 781534 653870